the Glénans
SAILING
manual

THE

GLÉNANS

SAILING MANUAL

by

Philippe Harlé

John de Graff, Inc.

Tuckahoe, New York

first published in French under the title of
cours du navigation des Glénans
(volume I)
by Éditions du Compas 1961
copyright © 1961
by Centre Nautique des Glénans
this translation copyright © 1963
by Adlard Coles Limited

the centre nautique des Glénans
commissioned the writing of this book by
Philippe Harlé
with the collaboration of
Claude Rougevin-Baville
illustrations and layout by
Jean-Paul Delhumeau
a team of other instructors and
Armelle Jobelin
have assisted with details

First U.S.A. Edition
published by John de Graff, Inc. 1965
34 Oak Avenue, Tuckahoe, N.Y. 10707

Revised U.S.A. Edition, 1967
Reprinted 1969
Library of Congress Catalog Card Number 65-21841
SBN 8286-0009-0

the Glénans
SAILING
manual

CONTENTS

publisher's note

Ten miles south of the old fishing port of Concarneau on the indented coast of Brittany lie the Iles des Glénans, forming a breakwater against the southwesterly gales blowing across the broad Atlantic. The group consists of seven major islands (if an island under a mile long qualifies as 'major') and a multitude of islets, shoals, reefs and rocks, covering in all an area of some thirty square miles.

It was on the uninhabited Ile du Loch in the Iles des Glénans that Monsieur Philippe Viannay and his associates founded the Sailing School, the Centre Nautique des Glénans, in 1947. It was something more than a Sailing School, for the founders had been members of the French Resistance and their idea was to help the young ex-members of the Resistance and their contemporaries to bridge the gap between the years of uncertainty, frustration and danger and the years of peace which were to follow. It was a move back to nature and the sea and reality, to help them find their feet. I have the impression that in this Sailing School there was, and still remains, a kind of reaction from overcivilisation and the desire to return to simple things.

The founders are dedicated men and women, and the pupils are expected to play a full part in the running and communal service of the establishment. Even a foreigner like myself can see that there is an *esprit de corps*, and what I could call a Glénans tradition. The School is spartan. It provides a roof under which to sleep and eat; for the rest it is sailing and seamanship, hard work and a full day. Beginners start in dinghies, sailing between the islands under careful observation from the lookout in the tall tower at Fort Cigogne. After experience in small boats they go on to learn navigation and more advanced seamanship in the cruising yachts with black hulls and yellow stripe, which are based on Concarneau and are a familiar sight on all parts of the coast of Brittany, and also as far afield as the south coast of England. What may be called the flagship of the training yachts is the heavy displacement old cutter *Sereine*. We know her well, having raced against her so often in the long-distance races and shared with her many strange anchorages such as in the Ile de Sein.

Undoubtedly the Centre provided something that was wanted. From small beginnings the School on the Ile du Loch grew rapidly and one by one schools were founded in the neighbouring islands at Ile de Penfret (1949), Ile de Drenec (1952), and the most interesting of all in the old fort at Ile de Cigogne (1957), where the quarters of the former garrison are now shared between the pupils of the Centre and the local fishermen. It was in these quarters, in 1961, over a dinner of soup and freshly caught crabs that my wife and I discussed with Monsieur Viannay and Monsieur Harlé the *Glénans Sailing Manual,* which had recently been published in French. As a publisher myself the book seemed to me to be unique. I knew nothing in English quite like it, covering, as it does, everything that the beginner wants to know in practice and much of the theory of sailing also, together with a great number of original drawings to clarify the text. I knew that the Centre Nautique des Glénans had become the largest school of sailing in Europe, and that the author and the instructors who had prepared the book were writing from the experience gained over the years of training of thousands of sailing pupils of many nationalities, which gave them a specialised knowledge and understanding of the difficulties of beginners. All the more so because the wind, tides, currents and the configuration of the islands combine to provide particularly varied sailing conditions.

The type of dinghy referred to in the book is the Vaurien, one of the most popular of the French dinghies, designed by Monsieur Herbulot and more or less born in the Glénans Islands. At first sight it might seem better to depict a British or American dinghy, but the theory and practice of dinghy sailing remains the same, whatever the type of dinghy, and the Vaurien may be taken as typical of many types available in Great Britain and America. Everything said of the Vaurien can equally be said of the 12-ft National for example, although the Vaurien is a better boat for a beginner to start in.

There are many books on sailing, but I think the *Manual* has the merits of being entirely original and comprehensive.

ADLARD COLES

introduction to U.S.A. edition

There are some areas of human knowledge that may be learned fully and finally; for instance, the multiplication tables or the letters of the alphabet.

Sailing a boat is *not* one of these areas.

One can reach the first plateau of sailing knowledge in a single afternoon. That is, the beginner may learn how to attach the sails to the spars, attach the lines which control the sails to the boat and even how to perform the basic maneuvers which permit a sailboat to move from point to point as the helmsman desires, regardless of the direction of the wind.

However, this is a far cry from fully and finally learning what there is to learn about sailing a boat. Nobody has and probably no one ever will.

A sailboat is a complex and fascinating vehicle. In spite of the fact that man has used the wind to help propel his vessels on the water for perhaps 10,000 years, less is scientifically known about sailboats than airplanes.

This is partly due to the fact that hydrodynamic and aerodynamic forces are acting simultaneously but differently on a sailboat, while the airplane designer has only the actions of the air to concern him (which is a complicated enough problem).

In any event, the sailor, be he an afternoon "gunkholer", an expert around-the-buoys or offshore racing skipper, or perhaps master of a cruising boat (and some are all of these), never finishes learning to sail.

As a cutting tool moves back and forth across a hardened steel plate, biting a little deeper each time, the sailor learns a little more about his boat, the wind and the sea each time he sails.

Monsieur Philippe Harle's *Glenans Sailing Manual* is the only "learning to sail" text we've seen in this office which acknowledges this and is written and presented in such a way that the reader can, like the cutting tool, pass over and over the material in it, getting a little more each time.

I do not wish to imply that either learning to sail or M. Harle's book is formidably complex. Nothing could be further from the facts. It's only that learning about sailboats is a study of surprising depth and that this book is capable of leading the reader a long way into it as the reader gains experience.

As the publishers of a magazine for sailors, we are acutely aware of the surge of newcomers to the sport and of their difficulties in finding adequate instruction in it. Many have no access whatever to sail training facilities within practical distance from their homes. In England and continental Europe, there have been many commercial sailing schools available for some years. There, the beginner may learn quickly and properly the fundamentals of boat handling and safety which are absolutely essential for the new owner to enjoy his boat—and avoid the sometimes frightening, frustrating, or just embarrassing *gaffes* inevitably committed by the inexperienced skipper.

However, enlightened sailboat dealers, builders, the U.S. Power Squadron, the Red Cross, the American Youth Hostels and an as yet small but very good group of commercially operated sailing schools are beginning to make this important primary teaching available to newcomers to this greatest of sports. This is one of the essential developments which must become common to all areas of the United States before the sport may begin to reach maturity.

We believe M. Harle's first-rate book will prove a welcome contribution to this movement in the United States and we welcome its publication here.

KNOWLES L. PITTMAN
ONE-DESIGN YACHTSMAN

introduction

This book has been written primarily with the needs of the beginner in sailing in mind; it has many aims, not too obviously connected, but in fact, basically bound up with one another:

● to give the beginner his elementary grounding, and to equip him with a rudimentary vocabulary of sailor's language, before he starts, and during the course of, his practical training;

● to give the instructor a scheme of studies, and to amplify this theoretical understanding of how a boat sails. This should enable him to give clearer explanations to his pupils about the way they should manage their boats and a better understanding of their mistakes.

With these ends in view, we have tried to explain why and how a boat moves, in language simple enough for a beginner's needs, but advanced enough for the more experienced sailer who feels a legitimate wish to understand better what is going on.

Furthermore, a wide knowledge of the problems of the beginner sailing alone, and of the self-taught sailor, has opened our eyes to the fact that a boat is more easily acquired than the knowledge of how she sails. The book has been written primarily for the pupils at the Centre Nautique des Glénans (the Sailing School), but boats and the sea are international and we expect therefore that it will appeal to a wider sailing public, and we have avoided purely local problems as far as possible.

The first chapter takes a quick and complete look at certain essential problems in order to introduce and familiarise the problems to come.

Three chapters follow, to explain the manner in which we deal with the four essentials which enable a boat to sail: buoyancy, stability, propulsion and control. These chapters will certainly be the hardest to digest. The beginner, having grasped the first chapter with some ease, will obviously be unable to get the full benefit of these later ones until he has had plenty of first-hand experience of the elements, with the tiller and sheets in his hands. On the other hand, the pleasure sailor who has already acquired a certain experience, will, we hope, take a lively interest in these chapters from the outset, and they should put his ideas into a certain order, where they have so far been a little vague.

After the first, more theoretical part, we come to the practical aspects of the matter; the management of a boat, handling under sail, safety, and technical matters. But, as differences of some importance now begin to appear, as between various types of boat, we here confine ourselves to the smaller craft.

The chapters dealing with boat handling and management do not comprise a collection of immutable and unarguable regulations; we have rather gone out of our way to make them a series of exercises in thinking out various practical problems. We have refrained from laying down the law, as our aim is to bring out the reader's critical powers, and to give him material for thought, rather than to claim to *teach him everything*.

As regards the question of safety, we have tried to cultivate a frame of mind in the prospective crew; experience has taught us that a seamanlike approach and a sense of the fitness of things are of far greater importance than any physical equipment the boat may carry; the importance of the latter however, has, not been overlooked.

Finally, the technical data are designed to form a link between, on the one hand, book knowledge of an abstract type, and, on the other hand, boats—concrete, material objects that demand knowledge and care.

The work is not, of course, meant for rapid reading, and you will certainly not get through it in a week; still less can you master it without combining practical sailing with your reading. To some, the plan of the book will appear questionable, as it deals, for example, with the theme of going about in five or six different places. We would rather have it this way; it combines progressive teaching with a better understanding of the problems. Where the complexity of the subject has forced us to put forward ideas understandable only by those with a modicum of scientific training, such ideas appear in an appendix to the chapter in question. It will not break the sequence of instruction if you skip these appendices.

You may be surprised by the strictness with which we have adhered to our scheme of presentation. Each page of text is faced by a page of drawings, which complete rather than illustrate it. Some ideas are quite clearly not capable of being conveyed entirely by the printed word, and to that extent the drawings interrupt the reading matter; it is therefore to be hoped that they will lead the reader on to deeper thought. The object will have been fully attained if you are led to illustrate your own ideas with thumbnail sketches, or even to 'doodle' them, when the various cases arise. We have, in fact, gone out of our way to avoid dogmatism, and the book *must* be read in a critical spirit; no idea we put forward is meant to be sheltered from criticism and contradiction. We simply hope that we have given the beginner, the racing helmsman, the pleasure sailor, and the instructor, material for an understanding of the essentials, and for making their own fresh discoveries on a sound basis.

PHILIPPE HARLÉ

the boat | 1

general

The components of any sailing craft can be classified under three headings:

> *the hull*, the actual body of the boat;
>
> *the rigging*, the sails and the gear which supports them;
>
> *the steering* gear.

Any sailing craft can be dissected on these lines. Each of the three groups has a rôle entirely separate from either of the others, and our intention is to analyse under these three headings the various factors which govern the speed and course of a sailing craft.

We will now explain as simply as possible the functions of the three components.

the hull

This is the essential part of a boat regardless of the purpose for which it has been designed. The yacht club pontoon, a fishing craft, a folding canoe, or a cruising yacht all have one thing in common—a hull.

The primary purpose of the hull is—to float. This term it is unnecessary to define; it is self-evident. Everyone has had occasion at times to put something in the water, and to decide, either 'It floats' or, 'It does not float'.

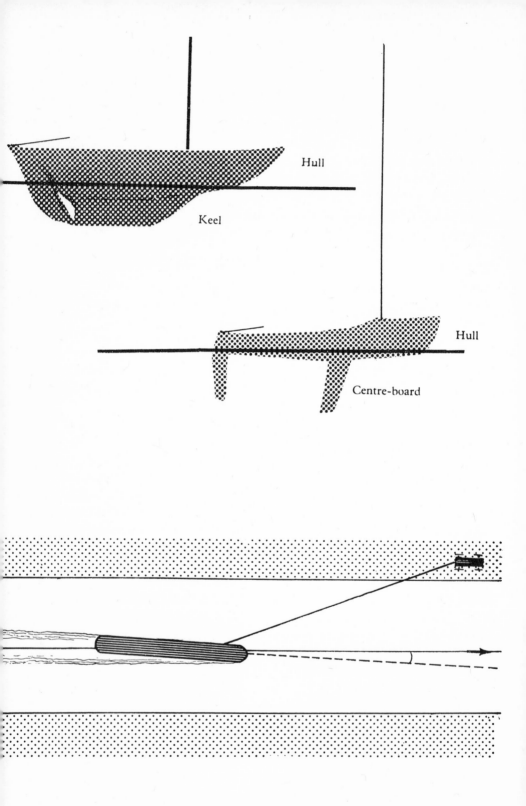

In order to float, the hull must be lighter than water. Originally a solid object made from a material lighter than water, it is now a highly elaborate affair: a water-tight shell, sometimes built from materials in themselves heavier than water. The water-tightness of such hulls has been a matter for concern over the centuries, and it was only thanks to the bailer that primitive craft kept above water—the utensil used for removing the water from the bottom of the hull and throwing it back in the sea. Even today, a completely water-tight hull is a rarity; pumps or bailers are an essential aboard every type of vessel, and it is a never-ending concern of the crew to be aware of what water has come in, and to limit what is allowed to remain.

As boats are normally intended to move on the surface of the water, the aim has been, by trial and experiment down the centuries, to find an easily moving hull form. The trend has been towards a lengthened, symmetrical shape, with a front end different from the back. It is now pretty evident that a boat moves more easily in the fore-and-aft direction than in any other, but it seems not to have been always so evident. It was presumably the difficulty of managing a boat capable of motion in any direction that prompted the design of a fixed 'front end', and so set up a fixed direction, in which it would be particularly easy to move the craft.

Important as it is that a boat should be able to move 'forward' readily, it is often equally necessary—and particularly with a craft that is to sail— that it should not be able to move sideways too easily. To this end, there is generally, under the hull, an attachment, either fixed—a *keel*, or retractable —*a drop keel*, or *centreboard*. This attachment is in shape fairly flat and thin, on the lines of an aircraft's tail-fin, and is normally on the centre line of the boat. Put under a hull, already by virtue of its shape moving more easily in a fore-and-aft direction than sideways, the keel (or centreboard) still further increases the relative ease of fore-and-aft movement, and, in short, a hull designed to sail has the following basic property:

> Under the influence of any force, it always moves in a direction nearer to its fore-and-aft line than to the direction of that force.

The simplest example of this is given by a barge travelling along a canal, towed by a tractor on the tow-path: it does not move in the direction in which the tow-rope pulls it, and does not, moreover, follow its own centre line; it travels in a direction not very far from that line. The angle between the centre line and the line along which it travels is the *angle of drift*.

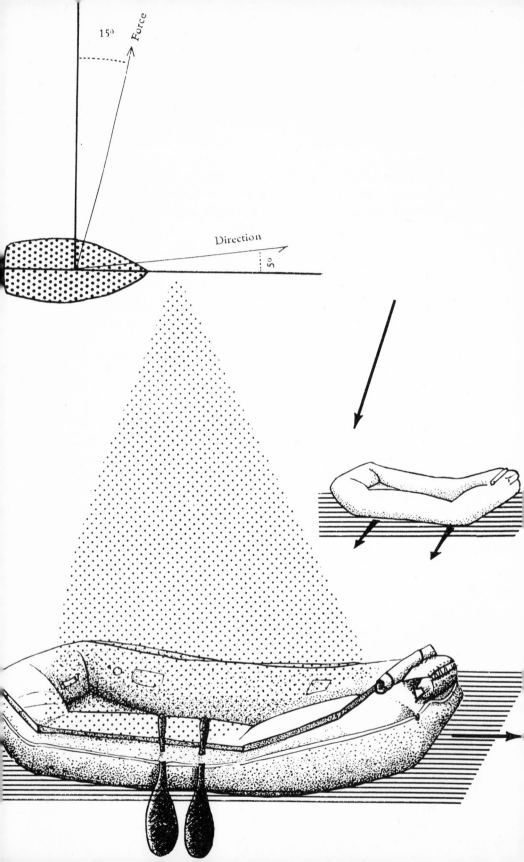

15° Force

Direction 5°

A hull can be sailed properly, when it moves forward with a small angle of drift, even when the tractive force is acting almost at right-angles to the boat. For a well-designed sailing craft, the order of magnitude might be: angle of drift 5°, when the force is acting at 15° ahead of the right-angle to the boat's centre line.

If you find it hard to agree that a vessel can so move in a direction other than that in which it is being impelled by an external force, try watching the behaviour of a paddle, which you are trying to move through the water. You will agree:

> that it moves through the water more easily in a direction parallel to the blade than at right-angles to it;

> that a force applied to the blade in any direction whatever tends still to move it in the same direction.

Failing a paddle, you can experiment with an ordinary board in a bath-tub.

The behaviour of a boat under sail is exactly the same as that of our paddle; provided that the force of the wind is directed, not exactly at right-angles to the hull, but appreciably towards its front end, the craft will move forward. The comparison, moreover, is not an entirely artificial one; inflatable rafts, designed to sail, use paddles as drop keels. Such 'pneumatic hulls', free to move in any direction, cannot be made to sail. Fitted with a pair of simple paddles, fixed vertically on one side, as in the drawing, they will move with ease only in one direction; and it is owing to this simple fact that they can be sailed.

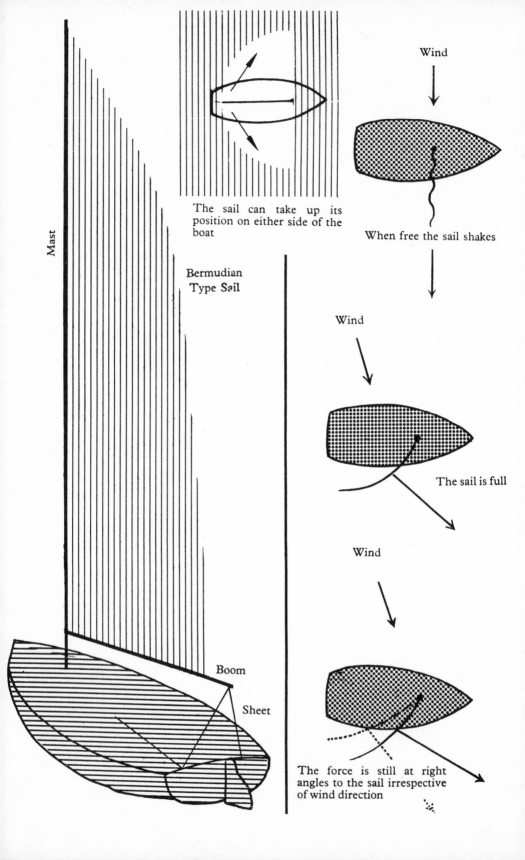

Mast

The sail can take up its position on either side of the boat

Bermudian Type Sail

Boom

Sheet

Wind

When free the sail shakes

Wind

The sail is full

Wind

The force is still at right angles to the sail irrespective of wind direction

the rigging

Under this heading we will look into the sails, how they are supported, presented to the wind, kept in shape, and controlled to the best advantage. The rig is the boat's engine. As is often the case with apparently very simple things, a boat's rig is full of hidden subtleties.

We will confine ourselves at this point to a superficial glance; enough, however, to give a good idea of how a boat works.

One of the most simple and effective of rigs consists of a single sail of the 'Marconi' type, more commonly called a Bermudian sail, though not quite the same as the original sail of Bermuda. In this rig the sail is stretched between two *spars* (long pieces of wood): the mast vertical, and the *boom* horizontal. The combination of boom and sail can pivot round the mast like a door on its hinges, and the *sheet*, a system of ropes fixed to the free end of the boom, allows its direction to be under control.

Left to itself, the sail will line up with the wind direction like a weather-vane, and *slat*; that is to say, shake like a piece of washing on the line, or a flag. In such conditions, the wind only exercises a slight force on the sail.

If, on the other hand, we pull the sheet in far enough to prevent the sail from lining up with the direction of the wind, it will cease to shiver, and blows out; it is then said to be *full*, and the wind exerts quite a considerable force. This is the force we use to propel a boat. Whatever may be the direction from which the wind is blowing, the force acts approximately at right-angles to the sail as soon as it stops slatting.

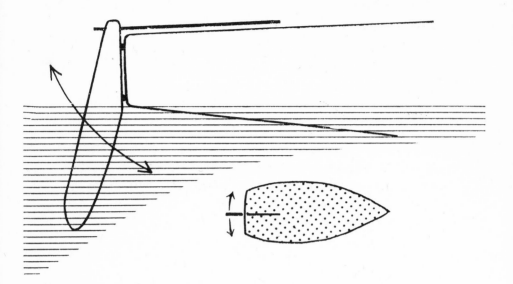

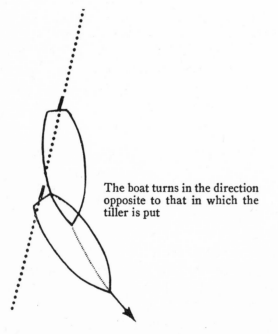

The boat turns in the direction opposite to that in which the tiller is put

the steering gear

As well as being a good thing for a boat to be able with ease to move ahead, it is necessary to be able to steer it. That is the purpose of the steering gear or *helm*. In its simplest form, it comprises:

- the *rudder*, a shaped plank dipping into the water, and fixed to the stern of the boat by a system of hinges, which allow it to pivot round a more or less vertical axis;

- the *tiller*, coming to the helmsman's hand, and attached firmly to the rudder, allows the latter's direction to be controlled and the pressure of the water on it to be felt.

The tiller acts as a transmitter, which allows the helmsman to pass his steering orders to the boat, and as a receiver which passes him information on how the boat is behaving. This second rôle of the tiller, which is always overlooked by the beginner, is not the least important one. You must therefore get used, from the very beginning, to holding the tiller lightly, in order that you may feel fully the reactions and tendencies of the boat; reactions and tendencies which are often very delicate indeed.

The action of the rudder is easy enough to understand; it behaves like the paddle blade we mentioned above; that is to say, it tries always to move through the water with one of its sharp edges leading. If, therefore, we put the tiller to the right, the rudder, tending by its action on the water to establish a flow parallel to its blade, will move the back or *stern* of the boat to the right; the boat's front, or *bow*, being moved to the left thereby, the whole boat will turn to the left. Thus, the boat turns to the side opposite to that to which you put the tiller.

It is rather confusing at first to see the boat going off thus in the opposite direction to that in which you move the tiller, but you very soon get used to it, and end up by not 'remembering' which way to put the tiller to go right or left; it has become a reflex action. We shall, too, soon see that the terms left and right, or

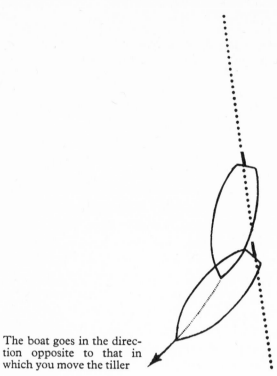

The boat goes in the direction opposite to that in
which you move the tiller

If going astern, the bow turns *towards*
the side to which you put the tiller

port and *starboard,* are not much used to describe the operation of the tiller, the helmsman being guided more by the direction of the wind. We shall also see that the helmsman has several quite efficient means of steering his craft, apart from the normal steering gear; so much so that an experienced helmsman can do without his helm altogether.

Finally, we cannot make the following point clear too soon: the explanation we gave above of the helm's action assumed the boat was moving in a forward direction; if the boat is motionless, the rudder has no tendency to displace the stern, and it is not the slightest good using the tiller; if, on the other hand, the boat *has sternway* the rudder moves the stern in the opposite direction to that in which you moved the tiller; the *bow* moves in the same direction as that to which you pushed the tiller. We say, therefore, that, when a boat goes *astern* (that is, reverses), you must *reverse helm,* by which we understand that the helm must be reversed as compared with what you would do if the boat was moving ahead. Should this not seem too clear, put yourself (in imagination) in a car, and note that:

> No manipulation of the steering has any turning effect on the car when it is stationary;

> if you want to turn the front of the vehicle to the right, you must turn the wheel to the right or the left, according as to whether you are going forward or reversing.

examples

To close this anatomy lesson, we cannot do better than to give illustrated examples. We give therefore in the following pages detailed drawings of two well-known little craft: the Finn and the French *Vaurien* (or 'scamp'), a popular French dinghy, which for practical purposes serves to illustrate the 12-ft National, which is of course better known in British waters. These examples are not chosen at random:

- the *Finn* is the very simplest of all sailing boats,

- the *Vaurien* is one of the most popular of small craft, principally by reason of its price being so moderate in comparison with its capabilities.

the finn

This is the boat used for the single-handed sailing contests in the Olympic Games. It is therefore found in very many countries.

It has a round-bottomed hull and the design allows for it to be made of moulded wood. It has a *deck*, in which a large hole provides for the accommodation of the helmsman—the *cockpit*. This partial decking keeps down considerably the quantity of water which would otherwise come aboard in a rough sea. The drop keel, in sheet metal, pivots on a pin, and can be brought up into the *centre-board trunk* or *case*, by means of a *tackle* (pronounced '*taykel*'). Inside the cockpit, aft of the trunk, you will see straps each side; these are for the helmsman to hook his feet under when leaning outboard in order to keep the boat upright and counteract the tendency to *heel* due to the force of wind on the sail.

The sail-plan comprises a single triangular sail; the boom is pushed into a mortise cut in the mast. As the mast is free to pivot in its *step*, the combination of sail, boom and mast is free to take up its position, under the control of the sheet. The latter takes the form of a four-part tackle, fixed at one end in the cockpit, at the other to the centre of the boom. Five light battens fit in pockets sewn to the free side of the sail, to prevent its getting too much out of shape.

Finally, the sail is held along the length of the mast and of the boom in the following manner; a *bolt-rope*, sewn to the sides of the sail, slides in grooves cut in the mast and in the boom.

The steering gear here comprises a lifting rudder; the *blade* can pivot between two cheek-pieces, which form the upper part of the rudder; a cord (not shown in the drawing) is pulled to lower it. In shallow water the cord is slacked off, and the rudder blade floats to the upper position. At the end of the tiller, and pivoting on it, is a *tiller extension*, which allows the helmsman full control of the tiller when he is sitting out.

The whole thing is, as you can see, very simple. The Finn is none the less a very fine goer; but it is built for international competition, and its construction is of such a high standard that it is not very cheap.

> Length: 14 ft 9 in
> Beam: 5 ft
> Sail area: 108 sq ft
> Weight (empty): 330 lb

the vaurien

This is the least expensive French boat that can be classed as a sports model. (Anything smaller or cheaper is hardly more than a large toy). And as, in spite of its cheapness, it has fine qualities, it is in consequence very widely used in France—10,000 craft in 1962. Although an individual design, the Vaurien may be regarded as a practical example of many types of dinghy available in America and Great Britain.

It is a hard-chine craft, made of plywood on a mould. The deck is not as large as that of the Finn, and the cockpit extends to the *transom* (the flat piece at the stern of the boat). The centre-board does not pivot, but drops vertically into a small well, like a sword in its sheath. It is called a *dagger-plate*. Under the side seat which can be seen in the drawing is a piece of expanded foam plastic, very light material, which gives reserve buoyancy in case of a capsize.

The rig here comprises two sails, the *mainsail* and the *jib*. The mast is held forward by a *forestay*, and on each side by a *shroud*. Between mast and shrouds, half-way up, the *spreaders* brace the shrouds, to limit the side-play of the mast. There is a universal joint at the boom called the *gooseneck*, which allows the boom end, and therefore the sail, to swing to the left or right of the mast. The main sheet runs as follows; it is fixed to the transom on the right, goes to a block on the end of the boom, thence to a block on the left of the transom, and so to the helmsman's hand.

The jib is fixed the length of the forestay by *hanks* which slide on it; its two remaining sides are free. It has, not one, but two sheets, one on each side of the boat, passing outside the shroud, then through an *eye* or *fairlead*, which determines the direction of the sheet's pull on the jib. Only one jib-sheet is used at a time, depending on the side from which the wind is coming; thus, in the illustration, the wind is blowing from the left, the jib is sheeted by the right-hand sheet, while the left one is slackened right off. The steering gear is here reduced to its simplest form, and calls for no remark.

The whole thing, particularly the rigging, is more complicated than is the Finn, but, as everything has been planned with a view to easy manufacture, the Vaurien costs much less than the Finn (about one-third).

Length: 13 ft 4 in
Beam: 4 ft 9 in
Sail area: 94.5 sq ft
Weight (empty): 209 lbs

what makes a boat go?

running (wind astern)

It is not hard to understand why a boat moves forward in the direction the wind is blowing. The sheet is eased, that is, slackened to such an extent that the boom and sail are no longer held close to the transom, but pivot around the mast until stopped by one of the shrouds, like a door opening before a draught. The boom and sail are now at right-angles to the *centre line* of the boat. The resulting force of the wind on the sail is now directed towards the bow of the boat, which accordingly goes forward, with no tendency to drift sideways. When the wind is thus coming from astern, you have the only case in which you can truly say that the wind is 'pushing the boat'.

wind abeam

Things are not going to be so simple, if we turn, for example, to the left until the boat has the *wind abeam* or is *reaching*, that is to say, pointing at right-angles to the wind direction. The boat barely moves forward, as the wind no longer has a great effect on the sail, which starts to '*shake*'. But if we now *sheet it home* a little, that is to say, if by means of the sheet we hold the boom rather more towards

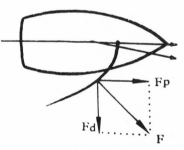

the centre line of the boat, the sail will stop shaking, and the force of the wind will now be perceptible—directed, as we have said before, at right-angles to the sail. We have seen that a sailing boat's hull has the very valuable property of moving practically straight ahead when a sideways force is exerted on it; that is what happens now: the boat moves ahead, practically along its own axis. We say 'practically', because, in fact, the boat goes ahead with a certain angle of drift, or *leeway*. It is exaggerated in the drawing; with the wind abeam, the leeway is hardly perceptible.

A more exact description would be that the Force F exercised by the wind on the sail can be split up into Fp, the propelling component, parallel to the centre line, and Fd, the drift component, acting at right-angles to it. The resistance to movement of the craft being less in a fore-and-aft than in a sideways direction, the propelling component will drive the boat forwards more effectively than will the leeway component make it drift. The resultant of the two components will lie close to the centre line of the boat.

close-hauled

If we next try to keep the boat sailing at an angle of 50° or 60° from the wind direction, the sail must be sheeted in more if it is not to shake. Consequently, the force of the wind on the sail will be exerted more across the boat, which will continue to go ahead, but with a larger angle of drift, now quite perceptible.

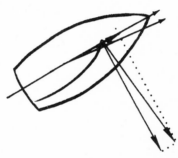

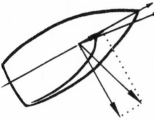

If we try to *point* even *higher*, that is, to sail in a a direction still closer to the wind, the sail will have to be sheeted still closer than before to stop it shaking. The wind force will then be very close to a direction across the boat, and, in spite of all its will to go ahead, the yacht will do so with difficulty, and the leeway will be great. To revert to the terms we used before, the propelling component Fp will decrease in proportion as one 'pinches' the wind still more. The sheet has to be hauled in tighter, and the drift component Fd continues to increase. In other words, the closer you try to point, the slower the boat goes, and the more leeway you get. Eventually, you reach a position when pointing closer to the wind will give no further improvement, the leeway being so much increased.

Thus, for instance, if you try to get 5° closer to the wind, the leeway angle will increase by 6° or 7°.

When a boat is sailing as close to the wind as it is advantageous to get, it is said to be *close-hauled*.

head to wind

Finally, if we put the boat's head straight in the direction from which the wind is blowing, the sail, however hard sheeted in, still shakes; the boat is no longer propelled forward, but is braked, stops, and then starts to go astern. The boat will behave in much the same way on all headings between 'close-hauled' and 'head-to-wind'; there is therefore a 'forbidden zone', in which the boat will refuse to go ahead; it stretches, fan-shaped, from the 'head-to wind' direction to 'close-hauled' on either side. If the helmsman tries to steer into this zone, he rapidly loses speed, and drifts so much that he will get out of the zone as soon as he can. If he really wants to get to a point in the 'forbidden zone', he will have to resort to a new technique—*tacking*; that is to say, sailing in zigzags.

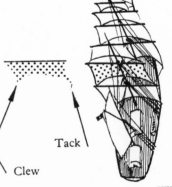

Clew

Tack

Wind

nautical vocabulary

We are now going to define the meanings of a certain number of sailing terms. These definitions are quite essential, and the reader should have no hesitation in referring back to them in the case of any doubt in the future. The great thing in appreciating marine language is, to grasp the principle that in a sailing craft everything is referred to the wind—bearings, orders, one's own reflexes, and one's observations.

port and starboard

These terms mean respectively left and right, as seen by an observer aboard a boat looking forward. They are used to indicate objects on board, or other objects in relation to the boat.[1]

tacks

This word is used to indicate the side from which the wind strikes the boat. You say that a boat is 'on the starboard tack' when it is getting the wind from starboard; the origin of the expression is as follows: the name 'tack' is given to the lower corner of the side on which the sail is taking the wind (the tack of a Bermudian sail is the corner at which the boom joins the mast). In the days of square sail, it was the port or starboard corner at the bottom of the sail which became the tack, according to the side from which the wind came. Thus, if the wind came from starboard, the bottom starboard corner was the tack, and the ship was said to be on the starboard tack.

[1] In English practice, in a powered craft, the orders may be given, 'port' or 'starboard', meaning that the ship's head is to be put accordingly; but in most other languages 'red' and 'green' are taking their place with the same significance. 'Port' and 'starboard' as helm orders used to refer to the tiller—which usually in a steamer did not exist—and meant the opposite of what they do today, which caused much misunderstanding.

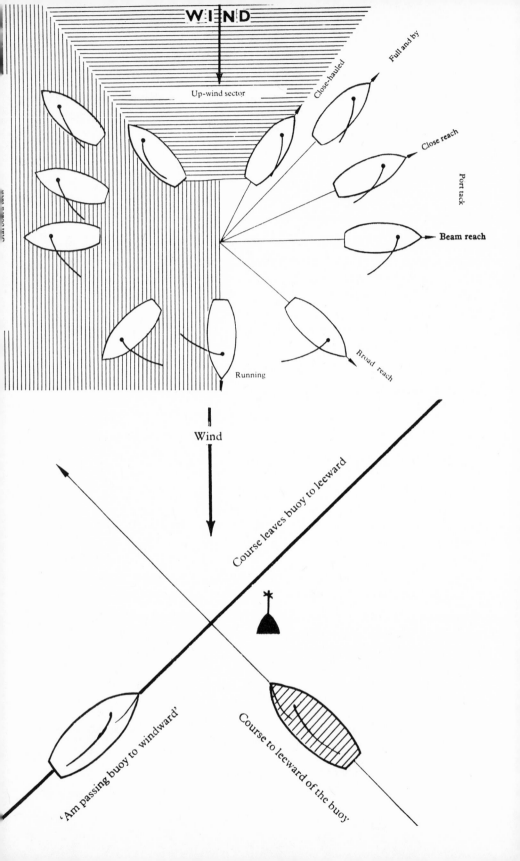

points of sailing

A *point of sailing* indicates the direction of a boat's head relative *to the wind*. The different cases we considered above to explain how a boat sails corresponded to the different points of sailing—*running, reaching* and *close-hauled*.

The main points of sailing are:

> *on the wind:* close-hauled, close-reach, full-and-by,
> *off the wind:* beam reach, broad reach, running free.

But often you have to use more elaborate expressions to define a point of sailing exactly; for instance "close-hauled" includes *pinching* as close to the wind as it is possible to get at the expense of considerable loss of speed through the water, sailing *hard on the wind* which is eating up to windward as close as is consistent with speed, or sailing *full and by* which implies sailing not quite so close to the wind as the boat can point but at considerable gain of speed through the water.

Of course, a boat can be on a given point of sailing on either tack. To describe exactly the conditions in which it is sailing, you must indicate the point of sailing *and* the tack.

windward—leeward

These expressions indicate the position of something relative to another object. The thing to *windward* is met by the wind before that to leeward. In a boat, for instance, unless the wind is dead ahead or astern, you will always distinguish the windward side from the lee one; everything thrown overboard to windward tends to blow back aboard; everything thrown to leeward goes clear. Ignorance of this principle has made landsmen the heroes of funny stories before now.

These words are often used to denote the position of a sea-mark. For instance, *coming out of Southampton Water into the Solent with a westerly wind, you have Fawley Refinery to windward, as more than one sense will tell you; while the coast stretching down to Lee-on-Solent and Portsmouth will be on your lee side.*

The respective positions of two things can often be denoted in two ways; thus, a helmsman passing a buoy can say—'I am passing to windward of the buoy'; or, equally well—'I am leaving the buoy to leeward'.

These words are pronounced 'wind'ard' and 'loo'ard'.

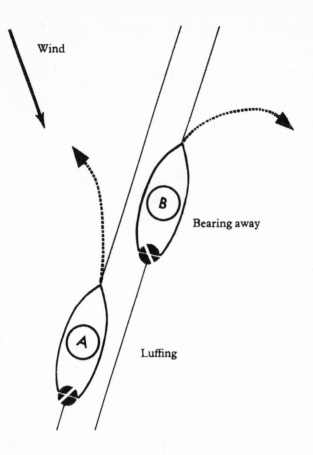

Wind

B

Bearing away

A

Luffing

Luff, the verb, means to turn into the wind as above.

Luff, the noun, means the leading edge of the sail.

luffing—paying off, bearing away

These words indicate a change of direction of the boat's head in relation to the wind. If, when moving in a given direction, a boat turns nearer to the wind, it is said to *luff*. If it changes course away from the wind, to bring the wind more astern, it is said to *bear away*—or to *pay off*. So, for instance, to avoid a looming obstacle, a boat might:

luff up to pass to windward of the obstacle, *or*

bear away to pass to leeward.

Given that, to change a boat's heading, you put the tiller to the opposite side from that in which you want to go, you must

to luff, put the *tiller down*—to leeward;

to bear away, put *the tiller up*—to windward.

We have already mentioned that the words 'left' and 'right' are not used to describe changes of heading. In point of fact, everything aboard a sailing craft is so subordinated to the direction of the wind, and of course to the tack on which the boat is sailing, that all your reflexes and language refer unconsciously to the terms luffing or paying off, windward or leeward. We will now mention one or two facts which even more detract from the usefulness of 'left' and 'right', and also will emphasize the difference between 'windward' and 'leeward':

● The boat *heels*, that is, leans over, under wind pressure, the windward side of the boat is therefore higher than the lee side; everything to windward has a tendency to slide down to leeward including the crew, who have to hang on hard when the heeling is great. On occasion in a small boat the crew can avoid a capsize only by getting their weight as far to windward as it will go. Finally, it is the fact of the boat's heeling that makes the helmsman sit to windward, facing to leeward. To luff, he pushes the tiller away from him, to bear away, pulls it towards him.

● Wind, spray and rain—they all come from windward. A change of weather is heralded by a change in the look of sea and sky to windward. In all weather matters that affect the helmsman, the future is to windward, the past to leeward.

● As the boat has a natural and obstinate tendency to luff, luffing is letting it go its natural way, bearing away is forcing the craft against its will; and, as the helmsman is sitting to windward, luffing is letting the tiller go off by itself, bearing off means pulling it consciously towards him.

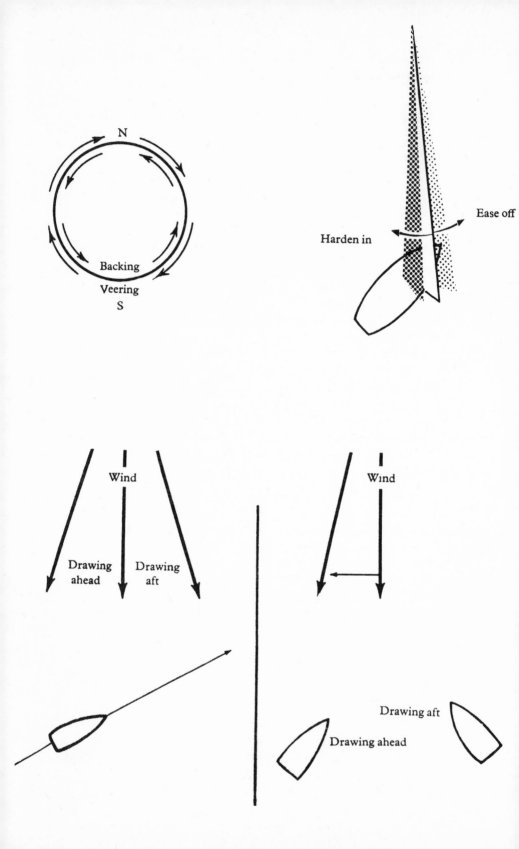

● Finally, the movements of the sails vary; luffing requires sheeting in, bearing away allows them to be slackened off.

hardening in sheets—easing (or veering) sheets

These terms refer to the direction of sails in relation to the boat; *sheeting in* a sail, by *hardening in* the sheet, brings it in towards the centre line of the craft; *easing off* a sheet, or *veering* it, consists in letting it out to some extent, so that the sail will be nearer at right-angles to the centre line. Note that *to check* a sheet has the special meaning to ease or slack it off slowly.

drawing (or hauling) ahead— drawing (or veering) aft

These expressions refer to a change of wind, as experienced by the boat and its occupants. It is, however, usual English practice to refer to changes of wind by reference to the points of the compass; it is said to *back* when it goes anti-clockwise, say from north through west to south, and to *veer* when this is reversed, and the wind goes clockwise, from, say, south through west to north. The custom in many other countries is to refer the wind direction entirely to the boat, and describe it as *drawing ahead* or *drawing aft*; the difficulty is, in this case, that a knowledge of the heading at the time of the speaker's craft is necessary, if the change of wind is to be properly understood.

sailing free

A boat is sailing free when she is sailing on any point other than close-hauled. That is to say, when she is sailing so that she is free to point closer or further off the wind.

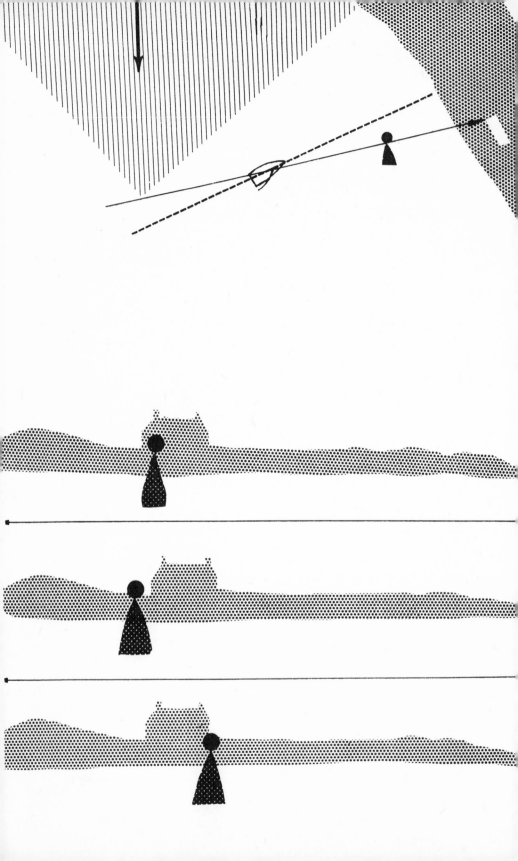

getting from one point to another

From any particular point, it is quite easy for a boat to get to any other point, so long as it is situated outside the 'forbidden zone' that we defined earlier, when speaking of 'head to wind'.

It will suffice if the helmsman lines up the *stemhead* with the point he wants to get to, that is to say, aims the front of the boat at it. But there is always some small correction to be made, owing to the *leeway* which is almost always present to some degree. It is therefore necessary to line up the stemhead a little to windward of the objective.

It is not too easy to decide how much leeway to allow for; it can soon be found if there is a background to the desired point of aim.

> If, in fact, the allowance is correct, and you are moving on the straight line to the point, the latter will be seen to be stationary in relation to the background.

> If the mark appears to be moving steadily to windward along the background, you have not allowed enough for leeway, and must luff a little.

> If the mark seems to move to leeward, you have allowed too much and must bear away somewhat.

But this all supposes that the water, the aiming-point and the background are all stationary with relation to one another; more plainly, that there is no current (in which case the water would be in movement with reference both to the mark and the background). Should there be a current, the direction and magnitude of your

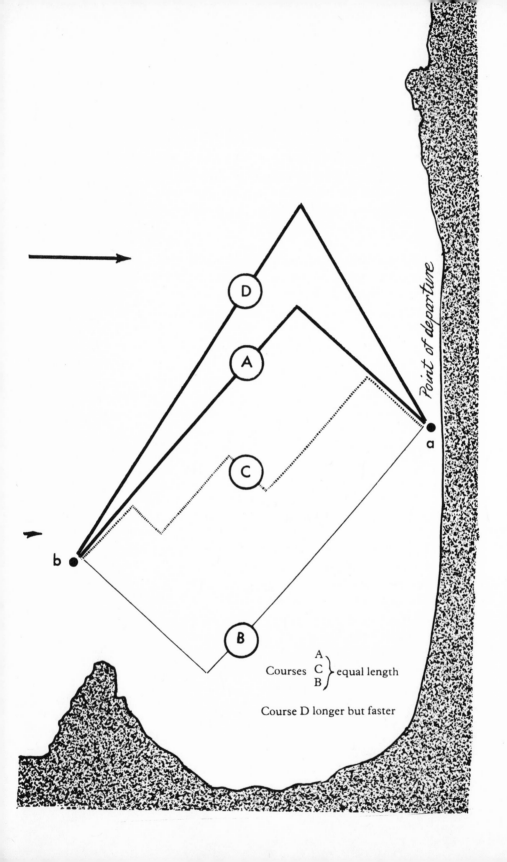

Point of departure

a

b

D

A

C

B

Courses
A
C } equal length
B

Course D longer but faster

correction may have to be modified. This we mention just in passing; it is a little apart from the present subject-matter.

If we are now trying to reach a point in the 'forbidden zone', we have to revert to the technique we have spoken of—*tacking*, or *making boards* (or tacks). Here is the process: the boat starts, for instance, close-hauled on the port tack, gets to the point where it can reach the mark close-hauled on the starboard tack; we say the mark has been reached in two boards (or tacks), one on the port tack, one on the starboard.

It would obviously have been possible to start on the starboard tack and finished on the port, or again to have made a number of short boards close-hauled. All these courses, A, B and C on the drawing, are of equal length, and will take roughly the same time to follow.

But it would have been equally possible to start full-and-by on the port tack, not close-hauled, and so continue till the mark could be attained full-and-by on the starboard tack. This course is obviously longer than the preceding ones, but, as the boat sails faster when a little off the wind than when close-hauled, the distance *may* be made in less time. Actually, of course, there is an infinite number of possible routes to a point in the forbidden zone, some being shorter but covered more slowly, others longer but faster. The difficulty in making a mark to windward lies in deciding what route to follow to get there in the shortest time.

It is not easy to pick the best course; much depends on the boat, the state of the sea, the strength and reliability of the wind, and the skill of the helmsman. The decision calls for a lot of experience. The only general advice to be given is: it is better to sail a bit too full than too close; for when you are pointing too close to the wind the boat slows up a good deal, and the leeway increases, often unnoticed by the helmsman. Sailing moderately full, you are at least sure of good speed and only moderate leeway.

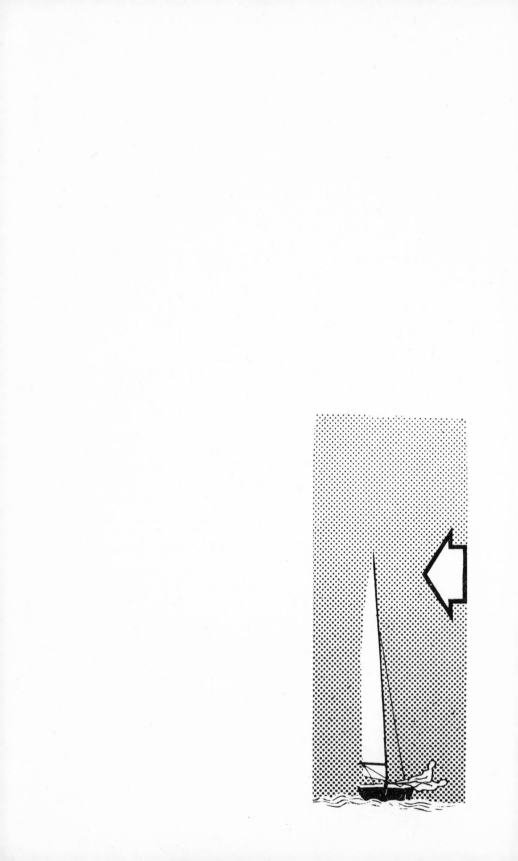

behaviour of a boat on the different points of sailing

The point of sailing on which a journey must be made depends on the points of departure and destination; the fastest way from one to the other, apart from tacking, and certain very particular cases, is the straight line. We will now deal with means of getting the best out of your boat on the different points of sailing.

trimming the sails

The most important point is the trim of the sails; are you to sheet in, or let the sails run free? Generally speaking, the best point at which to sheet the sails is that at which they are just about to start shaking. For the best trim, then, veer the sheets until the sails begin to shake, then draw them in just enough to stop the shaking.

If the craft is running free, and the sail is sheeted in rather too much, you will get a sort of shivering; the sail is being taken aback by wind which is finding its way behind it. This, of course, calls for the easing of the sheets, not for harder sheets.

control of heeling

Generally, a boat is designed to go best when floating upright in the water, and goes less well when heeled. It is a further drawback of an undue heeling angle that the boat creates more disturbance in the water, and gives a quite illusory impression of moving faster. In a small boat, the crew must get its weight outboard, so as to keep the boat heeling as little as possible, that is to say, the higher the force of the wind, the farther to windward must the weight be. In the case of the crew being unable, even when *sitting out* (that is to say, with feet under the toe-straps, and bodies as far outboard as they will go), to keep the boat upright, it is well worth while to ease a little sheet, even to the point of allowing the sail to 'lift' and shake slightly; the boat will generally go faster like this.

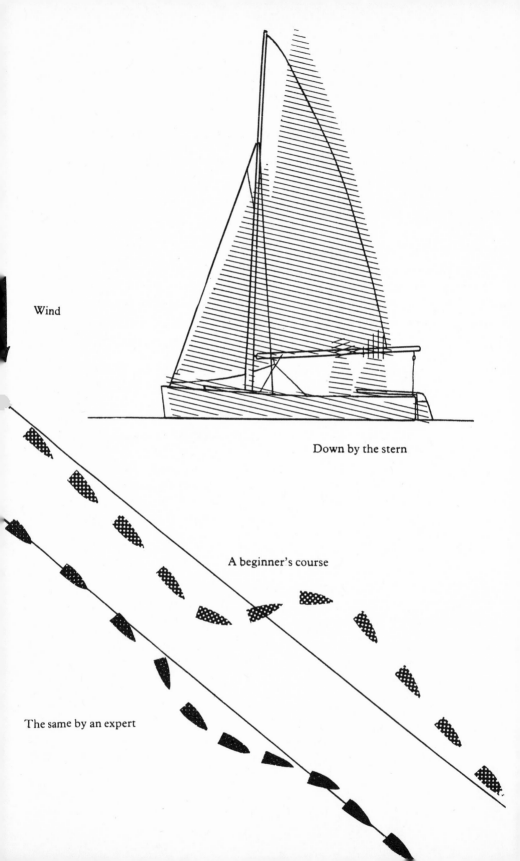

Wind

Down by the stern

A beginner's course

The same by an expert

control of fore-and-aft trim

It is equally necessary to think about the position of the crew from the fore-and-aft aspect, for the longitudinal angle of the boat—its *trim*—has a big influence on the speed and handiness of the craft. Generally, beginners have a tendency to trim too deep by the stern.

As a rough guide, a boat is down by the stern when the transom begins to bury itself in the water and drag along a great turbulence of water with it.

centre-board adjustment

When close-hauled, the movable centre-board, when fitted, must be fully down, for it is when close-hauled that there is most tendency to leeway. As soon as you come appreciably off the wind, you can raise the centre-board bit by bit, and when the wind is fully astern, the board will no longer affect the propulsion of the boat. But even in this latter case, the boat will answer the helm the better for having a little of the board down.

In any case, it is better to have a trifle too much than not enough board down.

at the tiller

On every point of sailing except close-hauled, even when full and by, it pays the helmsman to steer as straight as he can, with no more *yawing* than can be helped; every movement of the tiller, as well as correcting the course, applies a brake. Unavoidable yaws must be corrected gently, especially when the wind is light. It should, too, be borne in mind that yaws are more easily dealt with if taken at the earliest stage, the moment they start to be apparent. Particular care is needed in this regard with a heavier craft; bringing the boat back too sharply to its course risks falling into the opposite error. For instance, if, in correcting a yaw to the right, you come back abruptly on to course, the boat from its own inertia will try to go on to the left of the course. This is why you will always see beginners zigzagging.

On the other hand, if you want to get to a point straight up-wind, and consequently have to tack, it is a good thing rather to feel your way, to get the best compromise between:

> *pinching the wind,* shortening one's course at the expense of speed,

> *letting draw* too much, and increasing the speed at the expense of increasing the distance to be covered unduly.

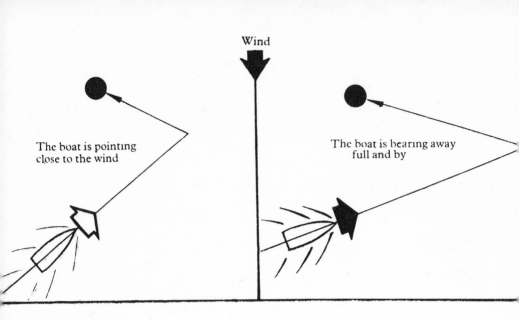

Wind

The boat is pointing
close to the wind

The boat is bearing away
full and by

The transgressor is liable
to loss of speed owing to
sail shaking

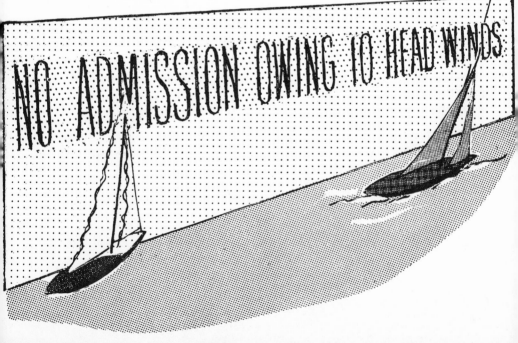

NO ADMISSION OWING TO HEAD WINDS

For instance, the helmsman, seeing the boat going well, tries to point a little closer. Then he runs the risk of imperceptibly slowing up, and having to 'let draw' again to regain speed. And this the more so, as all slowing up, by tending to increase leeway, makes sailing the boat more difficult, leads to still more slowing up, and so on. You will therefore find it almost impossible to pick your course once and for all and maintain it without any yawing at all.

the special case of a boat when tacking

What principles, then, do apply for getting as well to windward as possible? The sails must never be eased out enough to shake. In a fairly strong wind a hard pull on the sheets is called for, while if the wind is unduly strong you may have to let the sails off a trifle to limit the heeling angle.

You must always keep up speed, and, for that purpose, must bear away the moment the boat shows signs of slowing.

But, providing these two conditions are fulfilled, you must constantly feel your way, seeing if the boat won't go a little closer. At any moment the wind may have gone round a bit aft, allowing a closer course; or the helmsman may have borne away bit by bit unconsciously; he must therefore always be luffing up a little to make sure he is really close-hauled, but obviously stop luffing as soon as the first lift appears, and bear away again, in order not to lose speed.

When close-hauled, imagine yourself as walking along the length of a wall, which separates you from the forbidden 'head-to-wind' zone. You must constantly check that you are not straying away from the wall, but must now and again edge in and feel for the wall, that is to say, ensure that, at the smallest luff, the sails begin to lift.

It is, then, evident that *eating up to windward* calls for considerable experience. Racing is a fine way of getting such experience, because the helmsman can compare the performance of himself—and of his boat—with that of others whose methods of sailing differ from his own. During a race, it is always on the up-wind that you see the gaps opening up between the old hands and the beginners. On the other hand, the gaps are least noticeable on the down-wind legs.

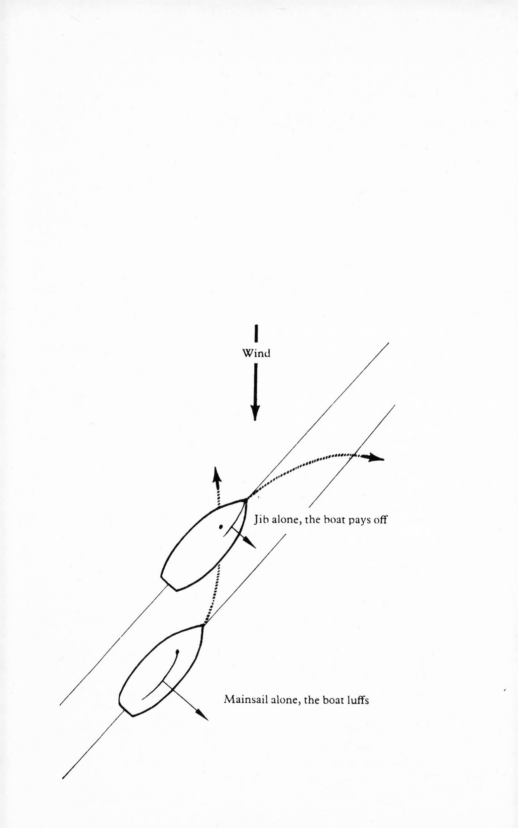

Wind

Jib alone, the boat pays off

Mainsail alone, the boat luffs

elementary boat-handling

Having dealt with the behaviour of a boat on the various points of sailing, we shall now describe the means by which you pass from one point of sailing to another, with or without change of tack. First, though, a paragraph to explain:

the directive action of the sails

When a boat's rig comprises more than one sail, each has, by virtue of its position, a certain influence on the boat's manoeuvring. We will confine ourselves to considering the case of a boat rigged as a *sloop*, carrying mainsail and jib.

As the jib is set forward, the effort exerted on it by the wind, more exactly its leeway component,[1] tends to make the boat bear away. This shows itself while the jib remains sheeted, the craft has a pronounced tendency to pay off down wind.

On the other hand, the mainsail, set alone, tends to bring the boat up into the wind.

Generally speaking, the rigging is so organized that—so long as both sails are correctly sheeted—the boat will have a tendency to move ahead close-hauled in a straight line, without luffing or paying off (actually it is most desirable that she should have a slight tendency to luff). But it is often possible, if you juggle a bit with the trim of the sheets, to give a boat an artificial tendency to luff or to pay off, an effect often used to help carry out some evolution. To this end, you must remember that you induce:

- a luff when you harden in the mainsail and ease the jib,

- bearing away when you ease the mainsail and harden in the jib.

[1]The propulsive component takes no part in the tendency to pay off, as it does in the tendency to luff.

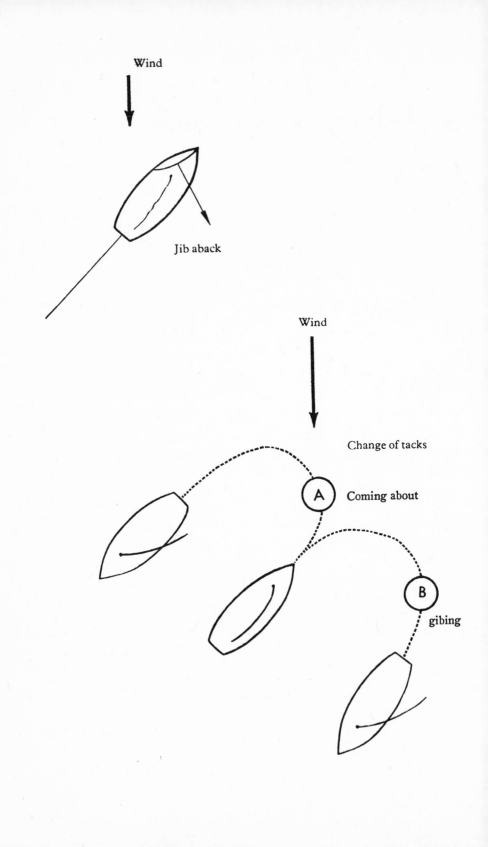

Wind

Jib aback

Wind

Change of tacks

A Coming about

B gibing

Finally, the jib can produce very strong reactions, especially in certain cases. If the boat is lying head to wind, sheeting home the jib to one side or the other will tend to pay the head off on one tack or the other.

Suppose that the jib is thus sheeted on the opposite side to normal (with its convex side more or less on the boat's centre line)—it has no forward propulsive effect (rather the reverse), and it is said to be *aback*.

Now let us come to changes of heading, and first to:

changes of heading on the same tack

Take the case where you want to change from close-hauled on the port tack to running on the port tack or vice versa. You must either bear away in the first case or luff in the second.

To *bear away,* or pay off from the wind, the helmsman puts his tiller to windward. At the same time he lets his sheets out to suit the new point of sailing.

It is best to slack off the mainsail first, which makes the evolution easier, as the boat then has a tendency to bear away by itself. Besides, it is of value to slack off the sheets a little faster than strictly necessary, and let the sails shake somewhat; it is always dangerous to have the sheets hardened in more than necessary, for this makes the boat heel more.

To *luff,* the helmsman puts the tiller *to leeward*; at the same time he sheets in his sails so that they will be properly trimmed on the new point of sailing. It is again advantageous not to haul in too fast on the main sheet; there is the risk of the boat luffing up too abruptly for one thing; for another, it is, as mentioned above, always dangerous to have the sails sheeted in harder than necessary.

A luff is normally easier than bearing away, as a boat has a normal tendency to luff, particularly when it is heeled. If you find any difficulty in luffing, hauling in the mainsheet more quickly will always help.

change of tacks

A boat sailing on the port tack (for instance on a broad reach), and wishing to return to its point of departure, can change its heading in two ways:

- starting with a luff, and going through the head-to-wind position;

- starting by bearing away, and going through the stern-to-wind position.

Wind

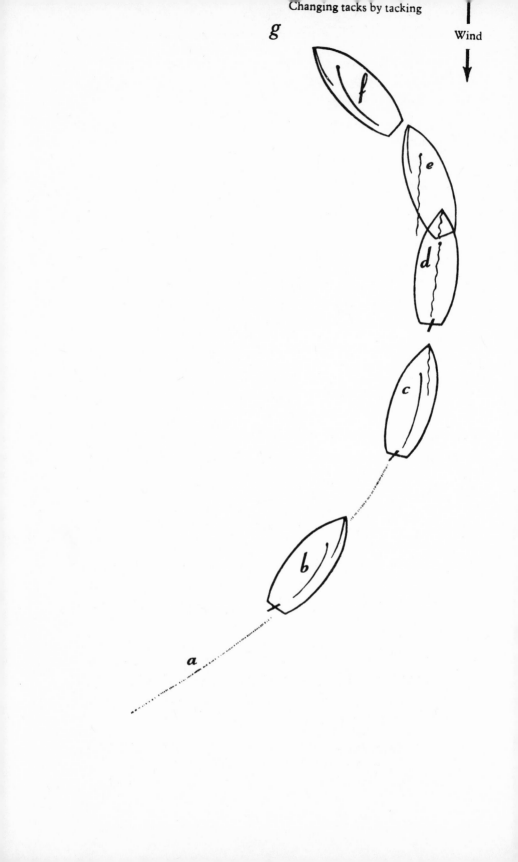

In either case it is a change of tack; one is said to have *gone about*, or *tacked*, in the first case; *gybed*, in the second.

Each time a boat has to alter course involving a change of tack, the helmsman has a choice of two methods:

> luffing, going through the wind, and bearing away on to the new tack,

> bearing away, putting the wind on the stern, and luffing up on the new tack;

each of these methods has its advantages and its drawbacks.

tacking

Here is the way to do it:

A Luff gently until close-hauled; don't forget to sheet in the sails bit by bit, and so as not to cut down your speed.

B Put the helm down firmly, so that the boat comes head to wind.

C As soon as the jib starts to shake, let go its sheet.

D The boat comes head to wind; let it come through the *wind's eye*, or pass the head-to-wind position.

E The boat, still carrying way, starts to pay off on the new tack; pay off a bit of main sheet, so as not to stop it.

F As soon as the boat has borne away enough for the sails to draw, sheet them home again (the jib now being sheeted on the side opposite to where it was at the start of the evolution).

G Bear away as required on to the new point of sailing, and sheet accordingly.

remarks

During stages C, D, E the boat is not being propelled. On the contrary, the sails are holding it back. It is therefore essential that the boat should have had at the start (B) enough speed to go through the following stages by its own momentum (*way* is the word); moreover, you have to get through the 'no-drive' period as quickly as you can, or the boat will stop before it has gone through the eye of the wind.

Wind

Backing the jib makes
going about certain, at
the expense of speed

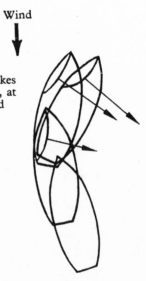

Tacking may be difficult, especially if the boat is unhandy, or if there is so much of a sea that your speed will be knocked down too soon. But it is never a dangerous manoeuvre with modern rigs (it could be so in the old days).

mishaps and how to remedy them

In itself, tacking presents no difficulty at all. But, if for one reason or another the helmsman does not succeed in going about, and *misses stays*, he may find himself in a spot if he has not got room for another try.

The reasons for missing stays are many:

- insufficient speed when you start to go about;
- the crew sheets the jib home too soon;
- too violent, or too half-hearted handling of the helm, which loses way;
- speed lost too soon, particularly through not sheeting in as you start to luff (phase A). This neglect to sheet in is a fault so common among beginners that they are more usually successful in going about from the close-hauled point than from sailing free.

These causes for failure to get about carry their own remedies to ensure success after a setback.

Nevertheless, heavy weather and an unmanageable boat can, with the most skilled crews, make going about very hard work or even impossible.

We will therefore give details of some ways of ensuring success in difficult circumstances, or of bringing the operation off when success hangs in the balance:

Back the jib; you do not let fly the jib the moment it starts to shiver— the wind takes it on the reverse side—it is taken *aback*, and thus helps the boat's head round. This is not suggested as a normal procedure, because it stops the boat and causes loss of time; but, in cases where going about is difficult, owing to a boisterous sea or an unhandy craft, or when, owing to lack of space, missing stays could well put the boat in a tricky situation, say near rocks, backing the jib is an excellent way to make certain of going about.

We have seen that one result of backing the jib is loss of speed; you must, therefore, sometimes, when reduced to doing it, do something else—

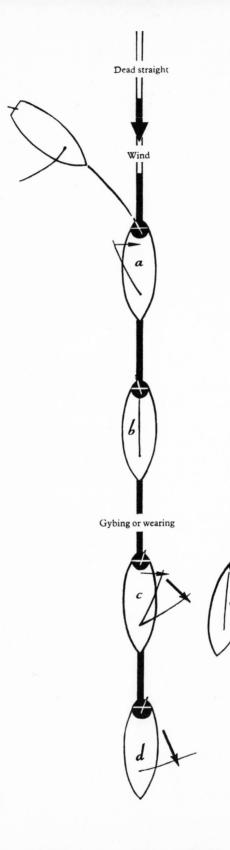

Dead straight

Wind

a

b

Gybing or wearing

c   *c'*

d

reverse helm. If the boat stops and starts to go astern, the action of the rudder will be reversed, and what you did normally to make the boat luff, helm to leeward, will now tend to pay the head off, back on to the original tack. You must therefore reverse helm the moment the boat starts to gather sternway, put the tiller the opposite way, and so finish the job. You must not be too impetuous; you must wait till the boat is going astern; that moment you will judge by the movement of the water along the hull.

By making use of these two expedients, you will never fail to go about, except in the worst of weather conditions, or with an altogether exceptionally unhandy craft.

Failure to go about comes only from underestimating the difficulty, and neglecting to take these measures: a not infrequent occurrence.

going about with the wind astern
wearing ship or gybing

This is the procedure:

A Run off till the wind is right aft, slacking the sheets right off.

B *Steering all the time so as to keep the wind exactly astern,* haul the mainsail right in, until, that is, it is as near as possible to the centre line of the boat.

C The sail will then *gybe*, that is, the wind will catch it on the reverse side, and send it flying on the other tack.

D As the sail goes over, you pay off the main sheet rapidly, slowing it progressively as it nears the end of its travel. At the same time, you must take the greatest care not to let the boat luff, which it will have a very strong tendency to do; this tendency you must counter with helm.

E Now luff steadily on to the required course, and adjust the sheets as necessary.

It is possible that the sail will not gybe of its own accord, in which case pay off *just a little* more, until the wind does catch it on the reverse side, and gybe it.

remarks

The boat is being propelled throughout. A gybe can therefore always be undertaken, which is not the case with a tack. On the other hand, there are difficulties; first, you want plenty of room, and there are two risks—an involuntary gybe, and *broaching-to*.

An involuntary gybe may be extremely violent, especially if you have borne away beyond the wind astern position, and the gybe happens before

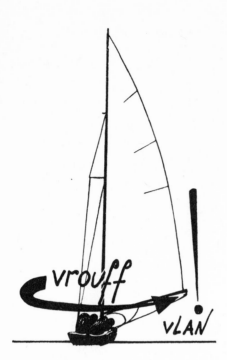

The CHINESE gybe
The only remedy is to gybe back and try again

you have the sail sheeted in. The boom swings over from one tack to the other unchecked, rather than being strictly controlled. The angle it sweeps through is a very wide one, and it attains considerable momentum, may knock an unwary crew on the head, and may carry away the shrouds it comes up against. The luff which tends to accompany a gybe can be very violent in heavy weather, and the boat may broach to; the whole thing is very dangerous, and may well end in a capsize.

To avoid these two troubles, you must

- have the wind *exactly* aft throughout the evolution. The best way to judge this is to watch the ripples on the water; they are exactly at right-angles to the wind;

- steer dead straight during phases B, C and D, except as indicated at C′ in the drawing, when you pay off that little more to start the boom on its gybe.

mishaps and what to do about them

The Chinese gybe:

if the sail manages to gybe before it is amidships, the bottom half of the sail gets across, while the upper half gets hung up by the cross-trees or by a batten catching on something, and stays on the original side. You can easily tear the sail. If this mishap befalls you, there is one thing to do, and only one— gybe back to get on the original tack. Anything else is bound to fail, and will risk tearing the sail. (*It may be noted that the term Chinese gybe is not a reflection on Oriental seamanship, which is of a very high order; the junk rig is designed to carry out a gybe in this manner without unpleasant consequences.*)

Luffing before a gybe:

at phase B, if the helmsman has not taken care to keep the wind dead aft, the boat may broach to on the original tack. The result is exactly the same as an uncontrolled luff *after* the gybe.

The involuntary gybe:

the helmsman may have negligently borne away too much, or there may be an unexpected change of wind. It is the more likely if the sheet has not been hardened in enough, and often assumes a Chinese form.

On all points of sailing with wind astern you must always have your sheets slacked well off, and must take the greatest care not to sail *by the lee*—wind more than dead aft.

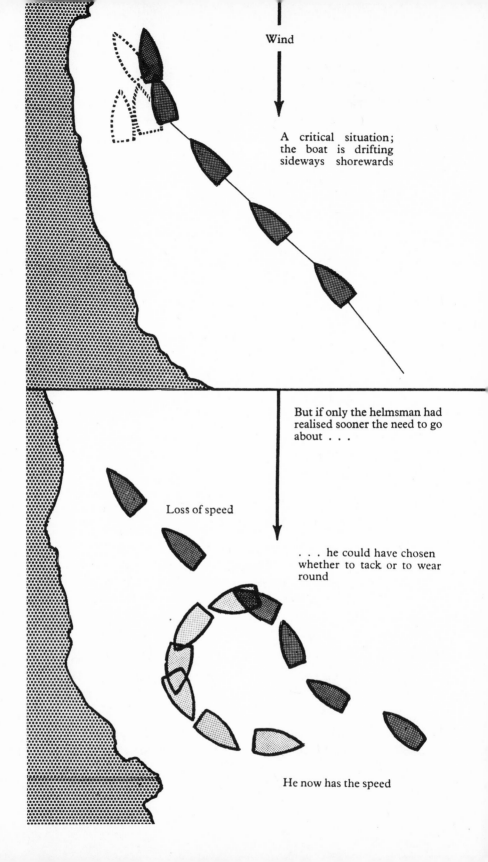

Wind

A critical situation;
the boat is drifting
sideways shorewards

But if only the helmsman had
realised sooner the need to go
about . . .

Loss of speed

. . . he could have chosen
whether to tack or to wear
round

He now has the speed

comparison of advantages and drawbacks
as between tacking and gybing

Tacking being less dangerous, it is always preferable, other things being equal, in small craft. It is therefore eminently worth while to learn how to do it properly.

Gybing can be done without inconvenience in fair weather, but should not be tried by a beginner in a fresh wind. Even more must the beginner avoid an involuntary gybe.

When *sea-room* is lacking, you must take special care not to miss stays, and so put the boat in a dangerous position. If you do so nonetheless, remember that a gybe is never so easy, and never takes so little room, as when you have just missed stays.

What we have said up to now will enable anyone who has taken it in to get along pretty well with a sailing dinghy. We have skated over some explanations, so as not to complicate this first introduction, which we have kept simple. But it does contain the essentials, for all rather specialized evolutions (coming alongside a quay, picking up a mooring, leaving from a beach) can all be quite simply deduced from what has been dealt with.

For the curious, or for the perfectionist,
we now propose to analyse the different
factors which affect a boat's sailing.

Archimedes, the celebrated Naval Architect

the hull | 2

The hull will be studied under two aspects:

> static and dynamic

static

The principle of Archimedes states the facts about how a body floats; it may be well to recall its terms:

'Every body immersed in a liquid is buoyed up by a force equal to the weight of the liquid it displaces. This thrust acts vertically upwards and is applied to the centre of gravity of the displaced volume of water.'

So far as a boat is concerned, we may interpret the first part of the principle thus: a boat afloat on water will sink to the point where it displaces a weight of water equal to its own weight. So much for the idea of buoyancy.

For a study of the trim and stability of the boat, we must look at the second part of the principle.

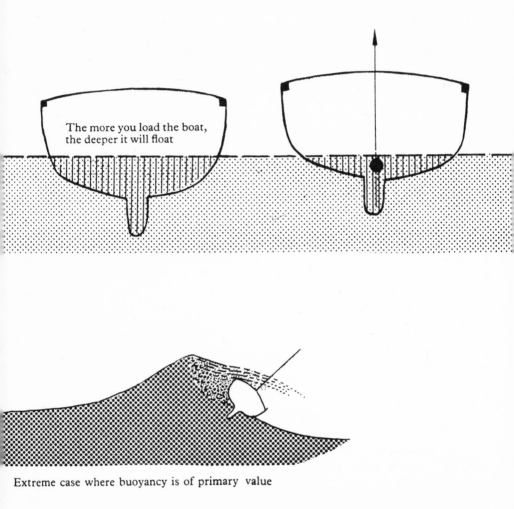

The more you load the boat,
the deeper it will float

Extreme case where buoyancy is of primary value

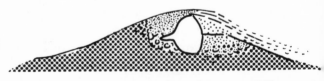

and, of course, stability too

displacement and buoyancy

The weight of a boat is described as displacement, because it indicates the amount of water the boat will displace when water-borne. The *submerged volume*, the volume of the under-water part of the boat, depends therefore on the displacement, and also on the density of the water. Thus, a boat weighing one ton, floating in water of a density 1 will find its level when the submerged volume is about 32 cubic feet.

Obviously, if one loads the boat further, its weight will increase, and it will sink deeper to increase the submerged volume, and hence the displacement.

But the shapes and volumes of the submerged parts of the craft do not by themselves determine its characteristics. The upper works, or non-submerged parts, are also of great importance. Under extreme conditions of heel they contribute their part to the buoyancy of the boat; in this sense it may be said that the upper works constitute a reserve of buoyancy.

Suppose, for instance, that the boat is accidentally put right under water for the moment; the thrust tending to bring it to the surface is derived from the total enclosed volume of the boat—the normally submerged parts plus the upper works; the boat will recover the quicker in proportion as this thrust—compared with the weight of the boat—is increased. A vessel can be put in this situation in bad weather; and a good enclosed volume is then of the greatest importance. So much so, that for a given displacement, a boat's safety will rise with the ratio:

$$\frac{\text{Total enclosed volume}}{\text{Submerged volume}}$$

This ratio, commonly known as the *buoyancy ratio*, might in a way be described as a coefficient of safety.

At the same time, you cannot compare on these lines boats which differ too greatly from one another; a large boat calls for less buoyancy than a small one.

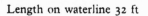

Length on waterline 32 ft

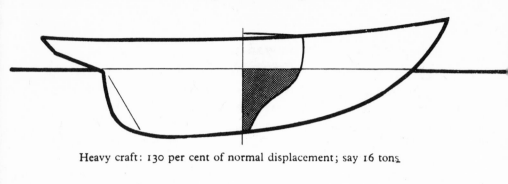

Heavy craft: 130 per cent of normal displacement; say 16 tons

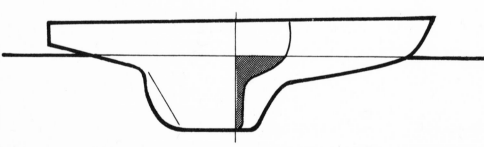

Normal: displacement; 12.5 tons

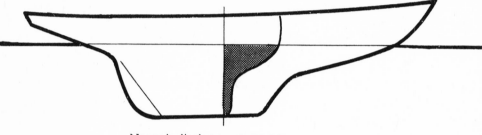

Light: 60 per cent of normal displacement; say 7.5 tons

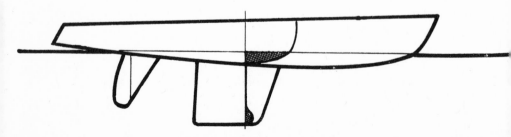

Ultra-light 40 per cent of normal displacement; say 5 tons

order of magnitude of displacement

If a given boat is enlarged, maintaining the original proportions, the under-water volume increases with the cube of the length, so will the weight if all *scantlings* are proportionately increased. Thus, if all dimensions are increased by 10%, the displacement rises by roughly 30%.

This explains why the weight of a boat, very broadly speaking (and to some degree its price) rises very much more steeply than its length.

Again, for a given length on the waterline (*LWL*), the under-water volume can be varied only within certain limits if you are not to get a completely shapeless vessel.

The following table will give an idea of the displacement/LWL ratio which conforms to accepted ideas of shapeliness for cruising craft from dinghies upwards:

LWL in ft	Displacement (tons)
12	0.75
16	1.5
18	2.5
22	4.2
25	6.25
28	7.85
30	12.25
33	16.5
36	20.5

These figures are obviously not final and unalterable, and you will find excellent craft with very different displacements for the same length. You could have a reasonable craft anywhere between 40% and 130% of the displacement indicated above for its LWL.

When a breaking wave reaches the boat, it largely depends on the amount of free-board whether or not it comes on deck; buoyancy only attains its full importance when the boat is under water.

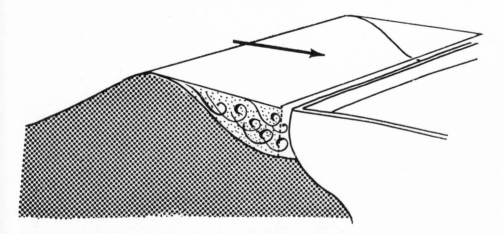

At 130% you would have a heavy, unhandy craft.

At 60%, if building on conventional lines, the designer would need to be a very clever man.

A 40% craft would be a mere feather sitting on the water, and could only be built by special techniques—moulded wood, plywoods or plastic materials.

But the vessels that win the ocean races year after year, the good—and comfortable—seaboats, the ones that everyone acclaims as such, come, with rare exceptions, within these standard displacements.

So far as concerns small dinghies designed for day sailing, or for racing in sheltered waters, ruling displacements are far less than those for cruising yachts, mainly because they are not ballasted—the crew being its own mobile ballast; besides, reduced displacement and weight are obtained at the sacrifice of comfort and habitability. This tendency leads to flat and shallow under-water lines, as beam cannot be very much reduced. Such craft call for sailing with minimum heel, but have surprisingly high speeds; they are exciting and sporting boats, rather than sea-going vessels.

the search for buoyancy, and its influence on hull shape and displacement

You cannot go on for ever adding to the upper works of a boat; the only result would be excessive *windage*; to improve the buoyancy ratio, therefore, the trend is to cut down displacement and build boats light. Contrary to widely held views, a light boat is safer than a heavy one in bad weather, so long as weight has not been saved at the expense of other qualities—stability and robust construction.

Moreover, light weight gives a boat the following qualities:

- it goes to windward better in heavy weather;

- a dry boat, as the water finds it harder to make its way over the deck;

- cheapness—less wood, less ballast, less canvas;

- better manoeuvrability.

But undue emphasis on lightness makes for a frail and expensive craft.

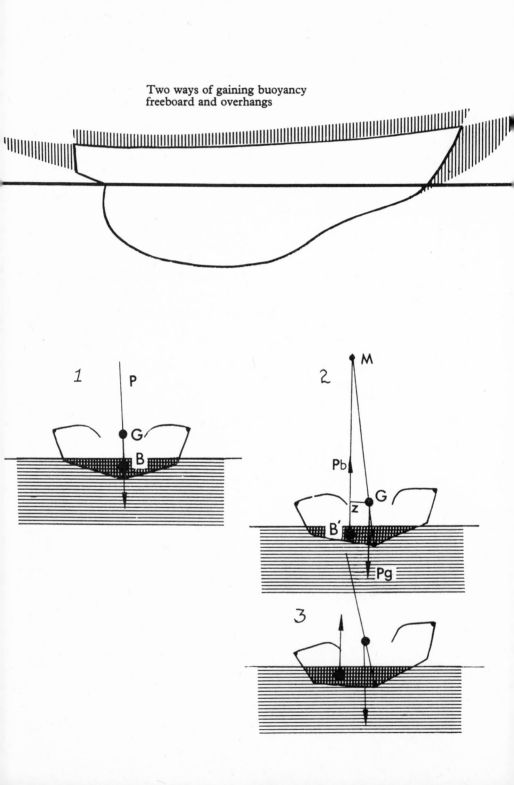

Two ways of gaining buoyancy
freeboard and overhangs

Suppose now that we have fixed the displacement of a vessel and designed its under-water lines accordingly. How does it get the necessary buoyancy?

The first thing you can juggle with is the *freeboard*, the height above water of the sides of the boat. Increasing freeboard gives increased above-water reserve buoyancy.

But, given a maximum freeboard, you can get more volume by extending the upper works beyond the LWL, fore and aft. This gives *overhangs*. Broadly speaking, besides giving additional reserve buoyancy, they have the advantage that they take the shape of natural extensions of the under-water lines, and increase the effective length of the boat when heeled.

From what has been said it follows that:

> a light boat will need no overhangs; it will also get the desired buoyancy without resource to excessive free-board.

> a heavy craft will not be able to dispense with over-hangs except at the price of excessive freeboard, or alternatively of lack of buoyancy.

trim and stability

The *trim* of a vessel is the position of rest it will assume when motionless in calm water. The *stability* is its power to return to normal trim when the latter has been disturbed from any cause, wind, sea, or otherwise. The trim of a boat is defined, and its stability explained, by the second part of Archimedes' principle: 'The thrust of the water vertically upwards bears upon the centre of gravity (CG) of the displaced water.' This CG we call the *Centre of Buoyancy (CB)*.

Take, for instance, a boat with its CB at B (see drawing), and the CG at G. This means that:

> for all the forces exercised on the hull by the water you can substitute a single force Pb applied at B and working vertically upwards.

> for all the forces exercised by gravity on the various parts of the boat (their weight) you can substitute a single force Pg applied at G and working vertically downwards—equal to the total weight of the boat.

> Moreover, Pg=Pb, for the thrust equals the weight of the boat.

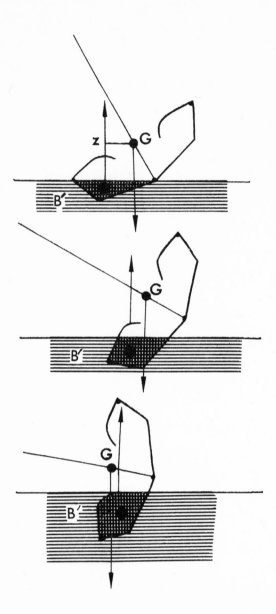

It might seem that, in the drawing 1, page 74, G being above B, the boat must capsize under the combined influence of Pg and Pb.

This is not so in fact; as soon as the boat heels, the shape of the underwater volume is altered, the centre of buoyancy moves to B', on the side to which the boat is heeled. The combined effect of Pg and Pb tend to return the craft to its initial position, which was the stable position of the craft, or its normal trim. This proves that there is nothing impossible about a boat returning to its trim even though G is above B. The sole condition for stability is: the centre of Gravity G must be below the point M, a point whose position is fixed by the intersection of a vertical line through B' (the boat being heeled) and the boat's plane of symmetry.

This point is known as the *metacentre*. Its position depends *entirely* on the shape of the boat. The more beamy the boat, the higher will be the metacentre, because the CB B' is displaced farther.

The stability, so defined in general terms, may be measured by the value of the righting couple creating by the forces Pg and Pb. The couple is defined as the product of the weight of the boat and the horizontal distance between G and B'. For a craft of given displacement, GZ will increase proportionately with GM and with the angle of heel. In the interest of stability, therefore, it is of the greatest value to increase GM, thus:

- to raise M, by adjusting the hull form,

- to lower G, by adjusting weight distribution (value of placing ballast low).

This is what sometimes causes a distinction to be drawn between 'stability of shape' and 'stability of weight'. At first sight it seems wrong that stability should result from an interrelation between shapes and weights, and one seems to have achieved nothing when one raises or lowers G and M by an equal amount.

This fallacy arises, because we have so far considered only the case of slight heeling.

This is what happens when the boat heels more:

The centre of buoyancy B' begins to move fast, the righting couple therefore increases with GZ. But after a certain angle of heel, B' hardly moves, and GZ diminishes, finally disappears. If the boat now heels a little more, the combined effect of Pg and Pc tends to capsize rather than right the craft. A given boat is therefore stable only within certain limits; up to a certain angle of heel, after which it capsizes.

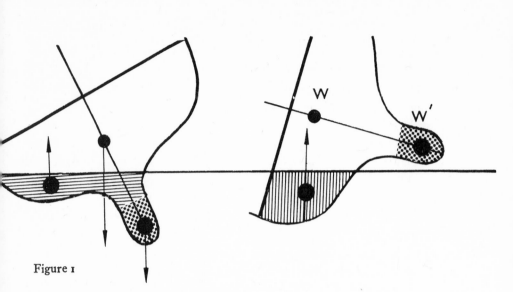

Figure 1

When the craft has got to a certain angle of heel, a weight **W′** placed low is more useful in maintaining stability than a weight **W** placed high. This is particularly true at very high angles of heel, approaching the capsize point.

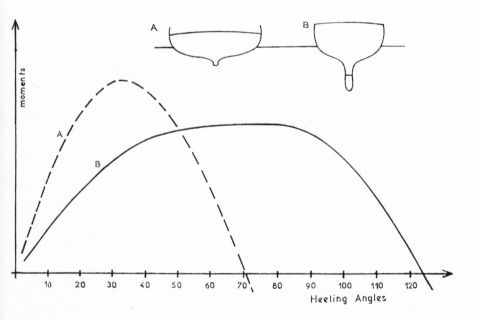

From this, we gather that the metacentric theory—as we define it above—holds good only at low angles of heel. For the higher angles, the position of the CG becomes all-important; the lower it is, the greater the heeling—before capsizing point is reached. It may therefore be said that the shape of the boat exercises its main influence on stability at low angles of heel. This is what is meant by *initial stability*

The stability at higher angles of heel is the result of the distribution of weight, and the position of the CG, and this is what is meant by *reserve stability*.

The theory of stability of shape is tied up with initial stability; that of stability of weight with reserve stability.

the curve of stability

The curve of stability, obtained by plotting the angle of heel against the moment of the righting couple, gives by itself a complete insight into a boat's stability.

The slope of the curve at the outset represents initial stability; this depends on the height of the metacentre above the CG. The summit of the curve will be at the intersection of the maximum righting couple and the heel angle at which it is attained.

Capsize angle will be indicated by the point at which the curve cuts the base line. We illustrate the trend of stability curves for two craft of very different types:

the one broad in the beam, flat and unballasted. Its righting couple rises steeply, to a fairly high maximum, but disappears at a heel angle of 70°;

the other craft is narrow-gutted, deep in the water and generously ballasted. Its righting couple rises less steeply, attains its maximum at 75° heel, and does not disappear till 125°.

the effect of bilge water

Let us suppose there is a certain quantity of water in the bilges of a boat. What keeps the boat afloat, what in fact actually counts as buoyancy volume, is the under-water volume not occupied by this liquid. At slight angles of heel, this volume will not alter greatly in shape.

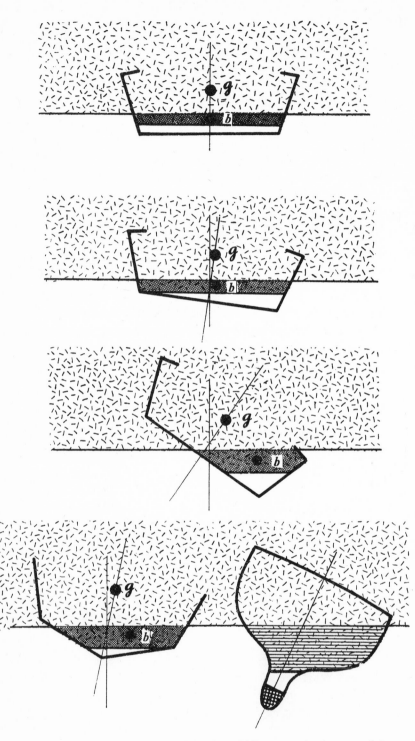

Location of bilge water in the turn of the garboard

As the centre of buoyancy will not be much displaced, the righting couple will be weakened. It might even form a capsizing couple tending to increase the heel.

The presence of bilge water, then, reduces the stability of a boat, and may even capsize it.

Fortunately, if there is not too much water, only initial stability will be upset, for, when the boat heels farther, the bilge water will remain in the chine and will keep its shape; then the real buoyant space will take on new shapes in the normal way.

That explains why a flat-bottomed craft (a 'flattie', for instance), when containing bilge water, will possibly be unstable in its normal trim, but will have two positions of stable trim—when heeled appreciably to one side or the other.

In the case of a boat with a sharp V-bottom, the bilge water will make itself felt only after a certain angle of heel has been attained for its shape will vary little with mild heel. Finally, in the case of a yacht with a marked turn in its garboard section, forming a deep central well, it will be noticeable only at very considerable angles of heel.

the value of stability

Safety demands that reserve stability should correspond to the conditions in which a craft is to sail.

For racing, or day sailing on frequented waters, it is not strictly necessary. Good initial stability will diminish capsizing risks; it is generally possible to make for home on signs of the weather worsening, and, lastly, assuming a good watch is kept ashore, a capsize is not a particularly serious matter.

On the other hand, if a longer cruise is in mind, or even if you intend to go outside the supervised area, it is essential that your craft should be able to make up for poor seamanship, and stand up to heavy squalls without capsizing. This means adequate ballasting, to maintain positive stability at angles of heel up to 90°.

Finally, if by reason of length and duration of cruises you undertake, you cannot be certain of the weather, and of reasonable seas, and if, in consequence, you must allow for the worst possible weather, you must be ready for any emergency.

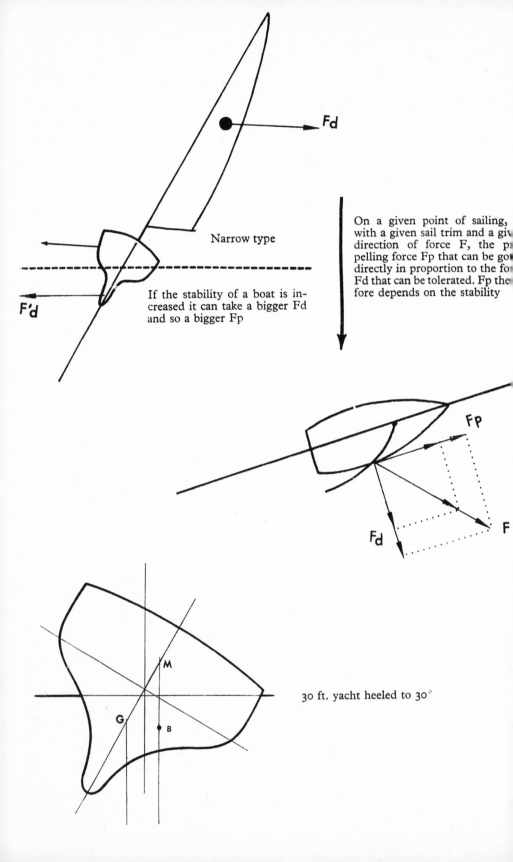

F_d

Narrow type

F'_d

If the stability of a boat is increased it can take a bigger Fd and so a bigger Fp

On a given point of sailing, with a given sail trim and a giv direction of force F, the p pelling force Fp that can be go directly in proportion to the fo Fd that can be tolerated. Fp the fore depends on the stability

F_p

F_d

F

M

G

B

30 ft. yacht heeled to 30°

In very heavy weather, therefore, a breaking sea can knock down quite a large vessel with great violence. It might seem necessary in these circumstances to have positive stability up to a heel angle of 110° or 120°.

Reserve stability may be inessential, but initial stability—any stability, in fact—is a factor making for speed. In order to sail, and in particular to make distance to windward, stability is needed to prevent too great a heel under the wind pressure on the sails.

This pressure, or rather, its leeway component, Fd, is applied fairly high up in the sail plan.[1] This leeway component is opposed by the counter-resistance F'd exerted by the water to leeward of the keel.

These two forces Fd and F'd form a couple tending to capsize the boat, but compromising by heeling it to a certain degree, opposed as it is by the righting couple induced by stability. If, to secure a good performance, you want to keep your heel within certain limits, Fd must be kept within a certain value—which depends on the stability. In other words, stability limits the amount of sail area the boat can carry.

For a given point of sailing, with a given sail trim, and with a given direction of wind force on the sails, the ratio of propelling force to leeway, Fp and Fd, is fixed. And, as Fd has its practical limitations, it follows that Fp has, too.

To sum up, the essential point is, that, for a given point of sailing, the propelling power the boat can use varies directly with its righting couple. Stability, therefore, is an essential factor of the power of the boat, especially in making to windward.

On a large craft, the designer can juggle with sections and weight distribution; the latter consists not only in cramming in as much ballast as possible, but also in keeping down top weights—decks, cabin tops, spars. The result of the calculations is that, for a racing yacht, ballast goes in up to nearly 75% of the total displacement. A good ocean racer will have 40–50%, while for a cruising yacht 30% is a fair proportion. We show, for a 30-ft. cruising yacht, the respective positions of the CB and CG.

[1] As an initial approximation, at the centre of gravity of the sail plan, or *Centre of Effort*.

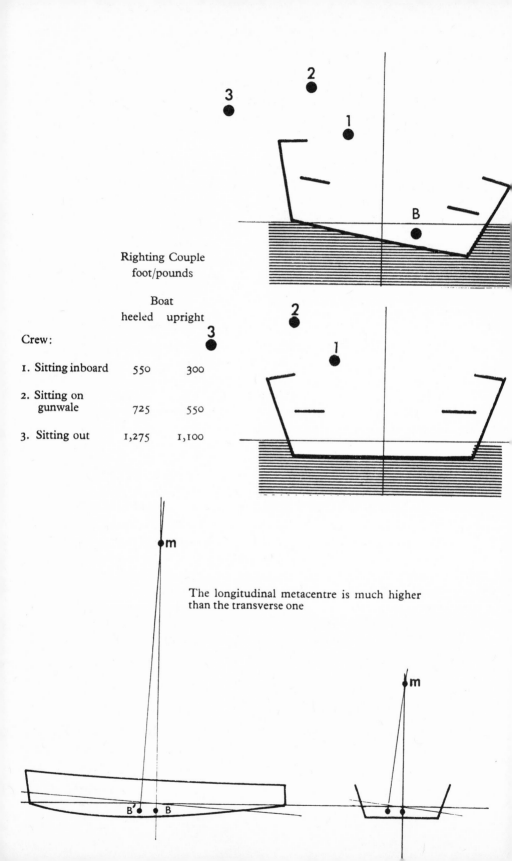

Righting Couple
foot/pounds

Crew:	Boat heeled	upright
1. Sitting inboard	550	300
2. Sitting on gunwale	725	550
3. Sitting out	1,275	1,100

The longitudinal metacentre is much higher than the transverse one

On a small craft the crew is the ballast, and you can't put the crew too low; it is, on the other hand, movable. To show how much the crew can add to the stability of a small craft, the table opposite shows the value of the lever GZ of the righting couple, for a small craft, upright and heeled to 10°, with the crew in different positions.

fore-and-aft trim and stability

We have shown how, when a boat heels, the transverse movement of the centre of buoyancy tends to right it and bring it back to its trim. Similarly, if the craft is inclined in a fore-and-aft direction, its centre of buoyancy will move longitudinally, and a couple will be formed, tending to restore the boat to the one condition in which the CG will be under what he may call the fore-and-aft, or longitudinal metacentre (the intersection point of the perpendicular from B', the centre of buoyancy of the inclined boat, with the perpendicular from B, the normal CB). Actually, the longitudinal metacentre is always higher than the transverse one, for, just as the latter depends on the beam, the height of the longitudinal metacentre depends on the length.

As a boat is normally longer than it is broad, if it has transverse stability it will have longitudinal stability also.

The question of longitudinal stability, therefore, is not of great importance. Longitudinal *trim*, however, is of the greatest importance, as a 5° error in trim, for instance, disturbs the boat's performance far more than the same angle of heel. Now, the various movable objects on board—the crew, among others—can make quite large fore-and-aft movements, and, consequently, upset the trim of the boat quite a lot. That is something you must never forget.

Aboard a dinghy, then, the crew must always take care to be in the right place. Too far aft, too far forward, the stability, the speed, and, in particular, the handiness of the boat can be cut right down. It is not too much to say, for a light centre-boarder, inches are important with regard to the crew's positions.

On a cruising boat a frequent check of the fore-and-aft trim is advisable. A good skipper will take advantage of every run ashore to get a distant view of his craft, to check her trim, and to re-stow weights when called for. So far as possible, he will take the

Not unduly exaggerated

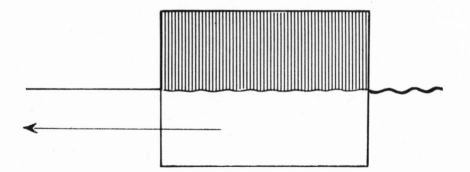

opportunity when all the crew are aboard and all is stowed ready for sea. When at sea, moreover, it is a good thing to see that the crew is not perched permanently at one end of the boat. You must in particular avoid having three-quarters of the crew in the bows when you have some specially important evolution to carry out. Stays are often missed owing to a lack of this precaution.

While speaking of the fore-and-aft distribution of weights, we should mention the great value of concentrating them amidships. Undue scattering of weight, while it may not affect the trim, will make the boat's pitching sluggish; it will apparently find it hard to get its ends clear of the seas, it will be a wet craft, and generally sail badly. Whenever re-stowing weights to correct trim, therefore, it will be found of the greatest value to shift weights from the heavy end to the middle, rather than from one end of the boat to the other.

dynamics

The various facts impeding the forward movement of the boat come under the laws of hydrodynamics, laws a good deal more complicated than the essential principle of hydrostatics, that of Archimedes.

We are going now to make a brief analysis of the different causes of this resistance.

frictional resistance

If we try to draw a thin plate of metal through the water, we find that we have to overcome a resistance due to water friction on its surface. This resistance originates mainly in the viscosity of water, but also to some degree on the condition of the surface of the plate; a clean, polished surface offers less resistance than a dirty, pitted one. This resistance increases roughly with the square of the speed through the water.

On the whole under-water surface of a boat, *wetted surface*, a similar friction occurs. The resulting resistance may be reduced by:

- reducing the wetted surface;
- cleaning and polishing it.

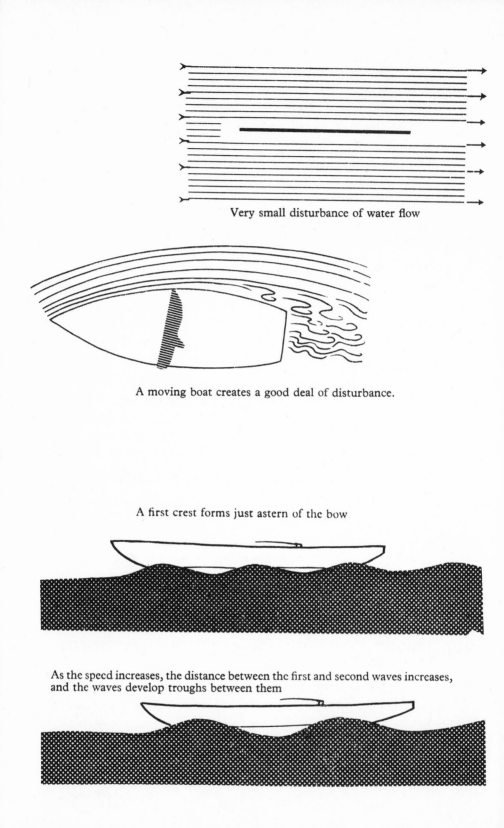

Very small disturbance of water flow

A moving boat creates a good deal of disturbance.

A first crest forms just astern of the bow

As the speed increases, the distance between the first and second waves increases, and the waves develop troughs between them

residual resistance

The plate we have just used as an example had neither thickness nor volume; it barely disturbed the water flow, unlike a boat in movement, which divides the water, with some disturbance to the smooth flow lines, and leaves the water to come together again after the boat has passed, which again causes a certain amount of turbulence in the water. The result is a resistance to forward movement, which rises more as the water is more disturbed by the passage of the boat.

Called *residual resistance*, its magnitude depends on the general shape and dimensions of the wetted surface, in particular of the largest section.

This resistance can be reduced by fining down the forms of the hull and giving the yacht the best possible lines. It has long been thought that the shapes of fishes could advantageously be imitated.

People have even gone so far into detail as to prescribe a 'cod's head and mackerel's tail'.

This theory now seems of more than doubtful value. A fish is a flexible organism, which passes its life in the one element of deep water, whilst a boat is relatively rigid, and has to cope with two elements, and with the disturbances on the zone between them—surface waves. Making these waves, if they are to be of any size, takes energy from the boat, which is not available for propulsion. This is the basic cause of residual resistance.

It will be of value to look at the means by which these waves are produced.

A first crest forms just abaft the bow. The second is produced at a distance d from the first, a distance which varies with the speed:

$$d=\left(\frac{V}{1.2}\right)^2$$

where V is in knots, d in feet.

If the speed goes up, the distance between first and second waves increases and troughs form between them; when the speed rises to a certain value, the second wave will be at the end of the waterline; this speed will be

$$Vc = 1.2\sqrt{L}$$ L being the length on waterline in feet.

If the speed now increases a little, this wave will leave the stern, and form a big trough. At the same time, resistance to movement grows enormously. In other words, beyond the critical speed Vc, quite a large increase in propulsive power will give a negligible gain in speed.

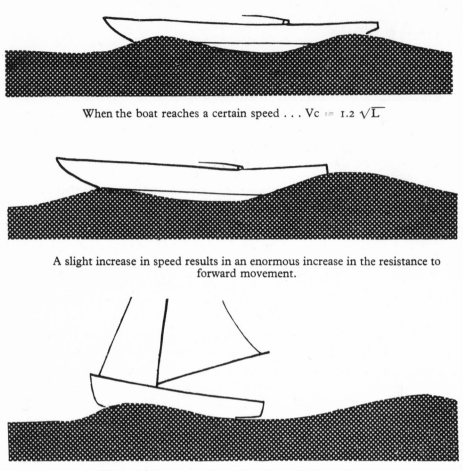

When the boat reaches a certain speed . . . $V_c = 1.2 \sqrt{L}$

A slight increase in speed results in an enormous increase in the resistance to forward movement.

When the boat goes faster than the critical speed.

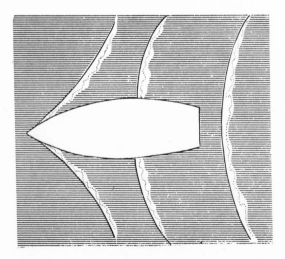

This applies to such an extent that the critical speed V_c is to all intents and purposes a speed limit, or barrier, which can only be broken with difficulty; to do so you must have either a powerful engine or a large sail area and a strong quartering breeze. A remarkable thing happens when a boat does break through the speed barrier, a thing which helps to explain the great increase in resistance to forward movement. The boat's trim changes radically.

When the boat is moving faster than its critical speed, the crest of the second wave drops astern; it follows that, with the bow riding on the crest of the first wave, the stern drops into the following trough, the craft rears up; this change of trim is enough to be quite plainly visible. The immersed surface, and consequently, the resistance to forward movement, is dramatically increased.

In certain cases you can take advantage of this change of trim. For instance, if the boat is flat bottomed it will be subject to a dynamic lift exactly the same as that given by the air to the wings of an aircraft. This lift is enough to support a light boat, which is then not floating by virtue of its displacement at all, but is literally *planing* and barely skimming over the water surface.

When this happens, resistance to forward movement is far slower in building up, and may even decrease.

In point of fact, a sailing vessel will barely exceed its critical speed unless it is capable of planing, that is to say capable of taking dynamic lift from the water, at a speed less than, or only very little above, its critical speed.

Generally speaking, it can be said that a boat is subject to a speed limit determined by its length on the waterline and given by the formula:

$$V_c = \frac{4}{3}\sqrt{L} \qquad V_c \text{ in knots, } L = \text{LWL in feet,}$$

Which gives for various craft:

14 ft International dinghy	L=14	V_c=5	knots
Itchen Ferry	L=20	V_c=6	knots
30 ft yacht	L=22	V_c=6.5	knots
36 ft craft	L=30	V_c=7.25	knots

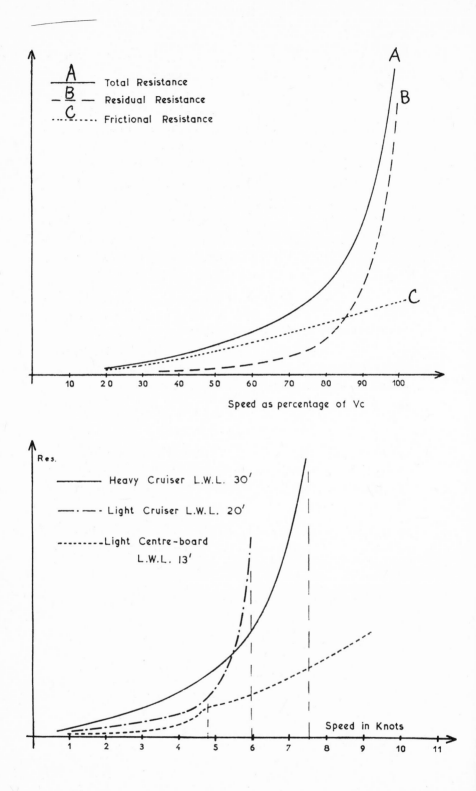

A ———— Total Resistance
B —— Residual Resistance
C ····· Frictional Resistance

Speed as percentage of Vc

Res.

———— Heavy Cruiser L.W.L. 30′

—·—· Light Cruiser L.W.L. 20′

········ Light Centre-board
L.W.L. 13′

Speed in Knots

relative importance of the different
components of resistance to forward movement

Friction resistance varies very nearly exactly with the speed.

Residual resistance goes up very slowly at first, much faster as the vessel approaches its critical speed. At low and medium speeds, therefore, frictional resistance predominates; while at speeds near the critical velocity residual resistance is most important. For a speed of 80 to 90% of the critical, both causes of resistance are of equal value. We show graphically, in terms of V, the variations of frictional resistance, of residual resistance, and of the total of these two.

influence of heel and leeway on
resistance to forward movement

Resistance to forward movement is most annoyingly increased by a marked heel, and more so by appreciable leeway. When both supervene together, as generally happens, the result is serious indeed.

According to Philip L. Rhodes, trials of a model racing craft heeled to 30° and with a leeway of 4° showed a resistance one and a half times as great as for the same model sailing upright without leeway.

D. Phillips-Birt quotes other trials. For the vessel he tested,

with no leeway, resistance went up 5% for 25° of heel;

with 25° of heel and 5° leeway, resistance rose 55%.

From this you will gather that anything which lets the heel increase, and, even more, the leeway, will tend to slow up the boat.

On the other hand, if you are sailing with leeway, anything that will reduce the leeway will reduce the resistance and put up the speed.

We shall return to this in more detail later.

influence of a dirty bottom on a craft

When a sailing craft's speed is low, by reason of being on the wind, or of the wind being light, a dirty hull will have the disastrous effect of increasing the frictional resistance, which predominates at such speeds. Everybody knows a dirty boat will not sail in light weather, but there is a tendency to forget the importance of a clean hull for beating to windward in any weather.

real speeds and bar speeds

From what we have said about the speed barrier, it is not hard to draw the conclusion that the speeds of certain craft get grossly exaggerated. Figures higher than 10% over the critical speed are exceptional—yet some skippers gaily boast of 20% and 30% or more. We unhesitatingly declare that such estimates of speed are not to be taken seriously; 'bar speeds' is a fair description of them. There are exceptions which one might be inclined to believe about centre-board craft (not that lies are not told about them, too) or extremely light cruisers; *Artica II* (LWL, 30 ft, LOA 37 ft 6 in) once covered 204 miles in the 24 hours, an average of 8.5 knots. Here we might draw attention to the fact that a counter stern increases the effective LWL of the boat, and gives a higher critical speed than would be indicated by the LWL at rest.

speed characteristics of different craft

Vaurien

A light craft, with narrow sections and little residual resistance below the critical speed, the *Vaurien*'s flat bottom and wide stern give it the power to plane. Its wetted surface is relatively large owing to the broad beam. In light airs the *Vaurien* is a trifle slower than boats of equivalent size, by reason of the large wetted surface. Nevertheless, it easily attains its critical speed by virtue of the low residual resistance.

But the critical velocity is very sharp, and in conditions approaching it a pretty large wave is set up. On a reach, if the wind speed is high enough, and the crew can hold the boat up, it planes pretty fast (at 6–8 knots). The transition from displacement sailing to planing is sudden.

Gwin Ruz, Glenans sailing craft Mk I, designer Herbulot

A light craft with a fairly extensive sailplan, it gets up to 5.5 knots easily, with little wave formation. Beyond that speed, waves form quickly, and it will not exceed 6 knots.

Sereine, a heavy displacement sloop 34 LWL, designed by Dervin

Although very heavy, and under-canvassed, she gets along very well in light airs, thanks to her relatively small wetted surface. Above 4–5 knots, wave resistance builds up, and is severe at 6.5 knots. She reaches her 7.5 knot theoretical speed limit with great difficulty.

some types seen in British waters

A light dinghy of about 13 ft on the waterline and little residual resistance below the critical speed of about $4\frac{1}{2}$ knots, the Enterprise has a fairly flat floor and wide stern, and this shape together with a fairly powerful sail plan, gives it power to plane. The wetted surface is relatively large on account of the broad beam. The Enterprise has a good performance and easily reaches its critical speed in light winds by virtue of its low residual resistance.

The change from displacement to planing is pretty sharp, and in conditions just below this speed a large wave is set up.

On the reach, if the wind is strong enough, and the crew can hold the boat level, speeds up to double the critical speed can be reached.

16-foot Wayfarer

A larger boat with general similarities to the Enterprise on an increased scale. The boat is intended for fast day cruising and occasional racing, with crews of 2/3 for the latter, and family parties of up to 6 for the former.

If the all-up weight is kept low, speeds up to 10 knots can be reached in suitable winds.

Folkboat

This is a keelboat of 25 ft overall, and with sleeping accommodation for two and sometimes more people. The LWL is about 19 ft and thus $5\frac{1}{2}$ knots is about its theoretical maximum. Due to the overhangs which enter the water more as the speed increaes, the absolute maximum speed will be about $6\frac{1}{2}$ to 7 knots.

It is a present-day trait among heavy craft to attain their speed slowly as the wind freshens. Light craft, on the other hand, want a certain amount of wind to get them moving, then get up to their limit of speed very quickly. Some are practically racehorses.

appendix
displacement buoyancy, trim and stability

displacement and trim

You must never forget that the water-lines and the indicated displacement on the plans of a boat are little more than estimates. The true displacement is not an immutable figure laid down by the designer, but the outcome of the process of building. It is, then, necessary, if a boat is to have the lines intended:

● that the designer's figures be right. Making an accurate estimate of weight is a most laborious task.

● that the builder has followed the designer's specifications precisely, so far as they concern sizes of scantlings and quality of materials.

● that the various shifting weights—stores, gear and crew are properly distributed.

When a boat is required to float exactly to a predetermined waterline, it is usual to leave some spaces among the ballast, so that they can be filled with lead to adjust the weights with precision.

In practice, and as a general rule, over-loading the stern diminishes the speed, overloading the bow reduces the stability. Nonetheless, on trials it is often found that the designer's intended trim is not the most satisfactory.

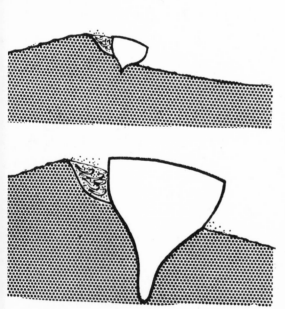

buoyancy and freeboard

Freeboard has its own importance, apart from the buoyancy it gives the vessel. When a breaking wave strikes the boat, whether or not it comes on deck depends chiefly on the freeboard; buoyancy only attains supreme importance from the safety angle when the boat is submerged.

stability from the energy point of view

The work done in heeling a boat to a given angle is represented by the area enclosed between the x-axis, the curve of stability and the line parallel to the y-axis which corresponds to the heel angle. The work done in capsizing the boat is the area between the curve and the x-axis, which it re-cuts at a point corresponding to the capsize angle. Apart from the shape of the curve, this area does represent something of importance; it gives the boat's reserve of stability, stated in terms of energy. The greater this reserve, the more difficult it will be to capsize the craft.

This leads us to another aspect of a boat's stability:

To heel a stable craft, work must be done, opposing the force of gravity acting on the centre of gravity, and the thrust of the water acting on the centre of buoyancy. A boat will be stable to the extent that energy must be expended in increasing its heel, that is to say, to such an extent that the effect of the increased heel will be to raise the CG and lower the CB—or at least to increase the distance apart of these two centres. Putting it in another way, if a boat is to have good reserve stability, it is desirable to put the centre of gravity as low as possible (ballast), and the centre of buoyancy as high as it can be got (a broad, shallow boat).

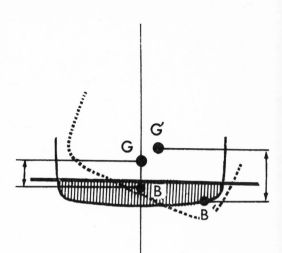

relative position of the metacentre, CG and CB

Moving the CB from B to B′ in the drawing, when the boat is slightly heeled, occurs by reason of the distortion in the shape of the under-water volume; the part of the under-water volume newly immersed takes the form of a wedge OAD, the part which has left the water that of a wedge OEF.

It is easily established:

● that the static moment of these wedges is proportional to the moment of inertia J of the *buoyancy surface*,

● that the distance BM from the CB to the metacentre is:

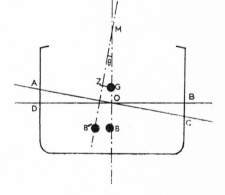

$$BM = \frac{J}{V}$$ V being the contained volume.

This distance is called BM, the metacentric radius, and it is referred to as ρ.

The displacement B to B' of the centre of buoyancy for an angle of heel θ, then, is expressed by:

$$BB' = BM \sin \theta = \rho \sin \theta$$

If, however, a is the distance BG from the centre of buoyancy to the centre of gravity, the lever, CZ, of the righting couple is expressed:

$$GZ = GM \sin \theta$$
$$GZ = (\rho - a) \sin \theta$$

It is therefore the value of $\rho - a$ that fixes the initial stability of the boat, and, hence, its behaviour at small angles of heel.

The value of $\rho - a$ varies with the type of boat; small for a liner, 2 ft 6 in for small pleasure or cargo ships; it may rise to, and even exceed, 6 ft 6 in for broad-beamed, flat craft carrying heavy cargoes low down.

rolling

When a boat has been temporarily heeled, it will right itself, but will only regain its original trim after a series of oscillations; this is rolling.

The value of the rolling period is given by the solution of the following differential equation (period of double oscillation):

$$T = 2\pi \sqrt{\frac{I}{W(\rho - a)}}$$

where W = weight of boat, I = moment of inertia of boat.

A boat will have a shorter rolling period (or quicker roll) according as its $(\rho - a)$ is higher, or its inertia lower. An easily performed experiment will prove these facts. It consists of climbing the mast of a light-displacement boat—say a ton or two; as you climb, the CG of the craft becomes higher (and $\rho - a$ diminishes), while the moment of inertia increases. The rolling of the boat gets slower and slower. But look out—if the rolling becomes really *very slow*, it is a sign that $\rho - a$ is verging on zero, and that the boat is liable to capsize; its stability is on the point of extinction.

For a given degree of rolling, therefore, the ill effects on the stomachs of the crew, on the hull and on the rigging are proportional to the rapidity of the roll. A large $\rho - a$, while having the advantage of making for a stable craft, has the drawback of making the roll far less tolerable. Furthermore, a boat with a short rolling period will be quicker to react to a wave tending to cause a roll. It follows that a craft of high initial stability rolls easily and with an uncomfortable motion. On the other hand, it must not be assumed that a boat that rolls is not stable.

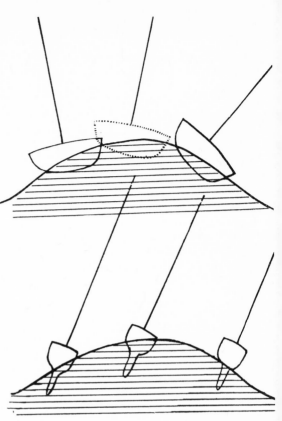

As a sailing craft needs stability to carry sail, the object will be, in order not to make the motion too exhausting, not to give it too high initial stability; reserve stability, obtained by ballasting, will be preferred. Narrow-gutted and heavily ballasted craft always sail with a heel, as they lack initial stability; but they have a very gentle roll. Broad-beamed and lightly ballasted boats, on the other hand, sail upright but have a quicker roll.

But there are factors yet to be mentioned in connection with rolling; there are various inhibiting factors, which tend to stop rolling. They have no effect during the actual movement, but after a spell of rolling they diminish the oscillations progressively, and finally neutralize them. This is known as *damping* the oscillations. Damping covers everything which tends to brake the rolling—everything, that is, tending to absorb the energy, be it friction of the water on the boat's bottom, keels, bilge keels, and so on, and most of all, resistance of the air acting on sails and rigging. It is this latter which makes a vessel under sail stop rolling faster than any other craft. Sail is an essential factor of comfort; you have only to see what a hell a boat becomes if under-canvassed, or at anchor in choppy water. Note, in passing, that on the one hand speed enhances the efficiency of keel surface as a roll absorber, and the speed of the wind, on the other hand, that of the sails in the same rôle; and that all the roll-absorbing factors we have mentioned play the same part as the shock-absorbers of a car (the latter damp the vertical oscillations after a bump).

Finally, rolling, apart from its unpleasantness, can be dangerous if its amplitude becomes large enough.

There is a risk of this happening if the seas meet the craft with a frequency akin to that of the latter's rolling period. Each wave arrives in step with the oscillation imparted to the boat by the last wave; the roll soon builds up to a very high amplitude, particularly if no stabilizing device is fitted. This is known as *rhythmic rolling*; it is rarely a real danger to small sailing craft, but it can heel a motor-boat right to its capsize angle, or at least far enough for a shift of cargo. With small motor-boats it often happens when going to windward in a choppy sea; if it starts to get serious, you must try to alter the frequency with which waves are met, either by slowing up or altering course a little.

On big ships, with a high rolling period (20 seconds or more), this phenomenon will only happen with a following sea, when the speed of the vessel diminishes the apparent period of the waves; their natural period rarely exceeds 15 seconds.

pitching

What we have said above applies, broadly speaking, to pitching as to rolling; the finer points are:

● As the longitudinal metacentre is placed higher than the transverse one, the $\rho - \alpha$ we are now considering is much larger. On the other hand, the moment of inertia has not increased correspondingly. (The moment of inertia of the rigging—among other things—does not enter into the calculation, as it does when rolling is considered).

It follows that the pitching period is shorter. As a result, except amidships, where it is not felt, pitching is more violent and trying than rolling. At the bow of a 30-ft craft the vertical acceleration forces can exceed the force of gravity; this explains why, as the bow drops, things on the foredeck come adrift; you will often see unlashed anchors 'taking off' and unsecured hatches flying open; similarly, when the bow rises, anyone crouching forward will feel himself being pinned down to the deck (often on a light and lively boat it is hardly possible to work forward except sitting or standing; you cannot remain in a squatting position).

● Sails damp pitching far less than rolling.

● On the other hand, overhanging ends to a boat are excellent pitch dampers.

Craft with no overhangs, especially if they are heavy, and the weight well spread out (which makes for a high longitudinal moment of inertia), take much longer to recover from a bout of pitching than a lighter boat, or one with good overhangs.

On old-fashioned yachts, it would seem that one of the main advantages of having the jib at the end of a long bowsprit or jib-boom was its anti-pitching effect.

It follows, of course, that pitching can be synchronous, just as can rolling. It is less dangerous, but very trying, and it reduces the speed of the boat. But it hardly ever becomes serious, except in heavy craft with no means of countering it.

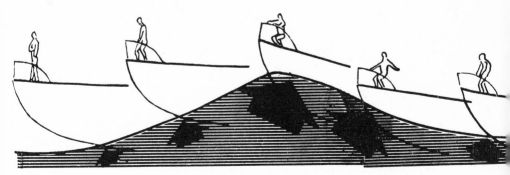

appendix
under-water resistance to forward movement

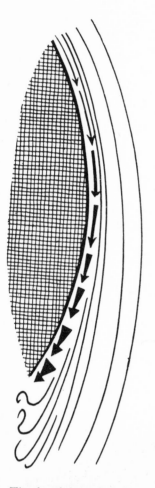

The drawing assumes the boat to be stationary in a moving current. In the border layer, the water is progressively braked.

To overcome underwater resistance to progress, a boat has to use up a certain amount of energy that has been provided by the engine or by the wind. This energy sets up two types of disturbance in the water; it will be of use to look into these; they are

● a wake;

● a wave formation.

The first is due to friction on the underwater surface; this has the effect of dragging water along in the direction of the craft's motion; a sort of current is formed astern, known as the *wake*.

Again, after the boat has passed, the water is stirred up by oscillations which appear as wave forms.

The dragging of the water after the boat is due to its viscosity; wave formation is due to the fact that water has a certain weight and a certain inertia.

frictional resistance

The water in immediate contact with the hull has no motion relative to it. It is not, therefore, strictly speaking, a question of friction between boat and water, so much as of water against water; this where the viscosity comes in. The boat tends to drag after it a layer of water called the *boundary layer*. This is the cause of frictional resistance; the boat drags after it a quantity of ever-changing water.

The boundary layer gets thicker as you move aft; the dirtier the bottom, the more quickly it thickens; a clean boat has less *drag* than a dirty one.

At a given point, this thickening depends on the distance from the bow. Baker quotes the following thicknesses:

12 in. at 125 ft from the bow.

24 in. at 450 ft from the bow.

36 in. at 700 ft from the bow.

At the stern of the small sailing boats we are dealing with the border layer will not be more than 3 in or 4 in thick.

As the water in immediate contact with the hull is not in motion, and as it is a matter of friction of water against water, there is no point in carrying on the polishing of the bottom unreasonably. It must, of course, have a properly finished surface, free of rough patches, the top coat of paint must be carefully put on, but it is pure fallacy that a mirror-like surface will help. Time spent on a super-finish by many small-boat sailors would be better devoted to training. In effect, the hull finish might be the deciding factor in a match between two evenly matched champion helmsmen; it will never let a bad helmsman beat a good one, especially on inshore waters, where fitful winds are the greatest test of a helmsman's skill.

wave resistance

There are several explanations, some more imaginative than exact, to explain wave resistance and the speed barrier.

Part of the effort made by the boat in penetrating the water comes back at the point where the second wave forms near the stern; it pushes the boat through the water somewhat in the manner that a cherry stone will fly out when pressed between finger and thumb.

Wave formations tend to disturb this compensatory effect between the energy *given out* by the boat against water pressure forward, and that *received* from the wave pressure aft. When the bow wave is so elongated that the second wave is clear astern of the boat, the latter is no longer in a position to give back any energy astern, and the result is a large increase in resistance to forward motion.

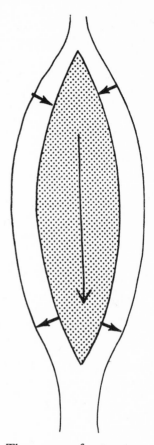

The masses of water are split by the passage of the boat, but they join up again on their own.

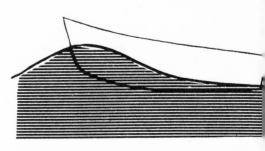

You don't get back astern all the energy you have expended forward.

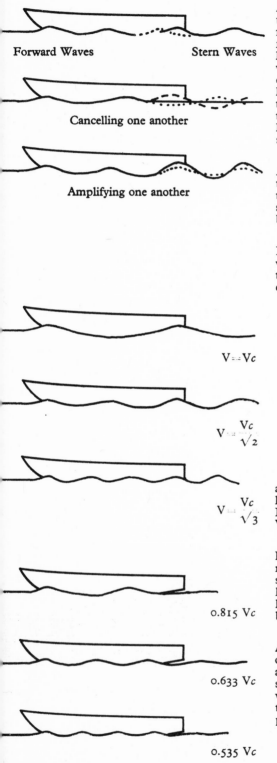

Forward Waves   Stern Waves

Cancelling one another

Amplifying one another

$V = Vc$

$V = \dfrac{Vc}{\sqrt{2}}$

$V = \dfrac{Vc}{\sqrt{3}}$

0.815 Vc

0.633 Vc

0.535 Vc

Another explanation is as follows: trains of waves form fore and aft, their first crests forming respectively at the forward and after ends of the waterline. If the crests of the one coincide with the hollows of the others, they will cancel out, and the boat will produce little disturbance; if, on the other hand, the crests of the two trains coincide, the effects accumulate, the boat makes large waves, and there is strong resistance to forward motion.

As the length of the waves depends on the speed of the boat, you will see that the resistance will increase with the speed, and the relative positions of the bow and stern waves will be vital.

In particular, the resistance will be high when the length of the wave is equal to the LWL, or to 1/2, 1/3, 1/4, etc., corresponding to speeds:

$$Vc$$

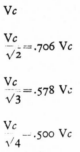

$$\frac{Vc}{\sqrt{2}} = .706 \ Vc$$

$$\frac{Vc}{\sqrt{3}} = .578 \ Vc$$

$$\frac{Vc}{\sqrt{4}} = .500 \ Vc$$

and this resistance will be low when the length of the wave is 2/3, 2/5, 2/7 of the LWL, corresponding to speeds: 0.815 Vc, 0.633 Vc, 0.535 Vc.

Residual resistance, then, varies irregularly with the speed, and is represented by a very sinuous curve, full of hollows and ridges according to the lengths of the waves produced by the boat.

Actually, these irregularities, which occur at comparatively low speeds, are usually drowned by frictional resistance. They appear only on craft with a wetted surface small in relation to the displacement (large ships), or on poorly designed vessels.

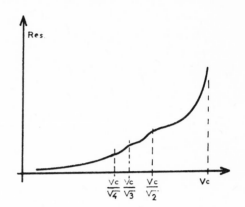

Generally, the only clear protuberance on the curve is the one representing the wave of the same length as the LWL. It is generally so well marked that it imposes an effective limit on the vessel's speed, that is, the critical speed. In practice, there is little that the crew can do to affect the residual resistance; it is the outcome of the designer's plans. It must always be remembered that the trim of a boat can sensibly influence the resistance to forward motion, and so the speed. It is therefore essential to pay great attention to keeping the boat in its best trim, generally the trim forecast by the designer.

Finally, remembering the grave effects of heeling, and of leeway, it is essential to cut them both down. You must also bear in mind that both heel and leeway make a great stir in the water round the boat, and often give an impression of speed as false as it is spectacular.

sails and keels | 3

effect of the wind on a sail

When the wind exerts a certain force on a sail, it is because the sail exerts an equal and opposite force on the masses of air in movement in its vicinity.

The force exerted by the sail on these masses of air has the effect of modifying their movement, both as regards speed and direction.

In other words, it is because the sail slows or modifies the direction of the air stream, that it obtains the pressure effects which provide the boat's propulsive power.

In practical terms, the wind is diverted by the sail, and what happens is as follows:

A mass of air, heavy, more than $2\frac{1}{2}$ lb per cubic yard, and elastic hits the sail, rebounds from it, and moves off in a different direction, exactly as a tennis ball does when it hits a racket held firmly

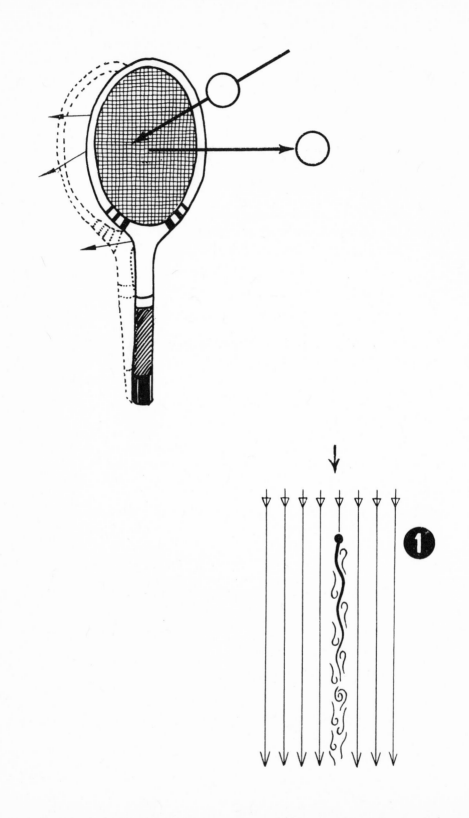

at arm's length. The forces set up in the two cases are similar, although more obvious in the second case; actually, however firmly the racket is held, it does recoil under the shock. The explanation of this is that for the brief instant when ball and racket were in contact they brought to bear on each other equal and opposite forces, the one having the effect of repelling the ball, the other making the racket recoil. The comparison is rather a clumsy one, but what you must remember is this reciprocal effort exercised on each other by two bodies coming into contact.

In fact, in the case of the sail there is no actual rebound of masses of air from a flat surface, but rather a continuous deviation of wind current from a curved plane. But all the time there is an interplay of forces between sail and air.

We should therefore know better than to study the effect of wind on sail without at the same time considering the effect of sail on wind.

Reasoning on these lines is fully justified in practice; the crew of a boat may often find it easy to follow the way the wind flows on to the sails, but it is not so easy to see the whole of the effects to which the sail is subjected.

reciprocal effects of wind on sail

Here is what happens to a sail as it is gradually sheeted in from a freely flapping position:

▮ The sail is not sheeted. It slats and causes some eddies in its immediate neighbourhood and under its lee. This indicates some slight slowing up of the wind, but has no effect on its direction.

The force exerted on the sail is slight and in the direction of the wind.

We have something similar to water friction on the bottom of the boat, and this force, though feeble, cannot be neglected, especially if the sail is flogging in a high wind. Note, too, that it is this force which puts the brake on the boat when it comes head to wind, whether for the purpose of stopping, or in course of going about.

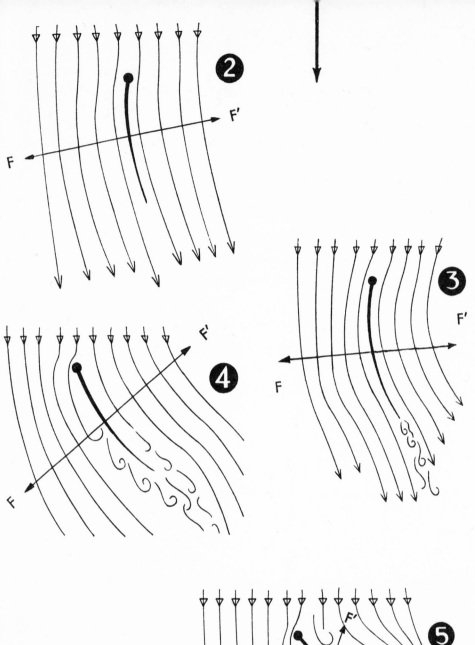
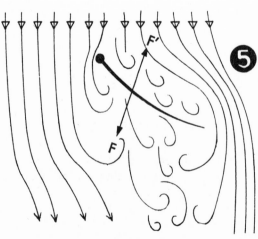

2 Trim the sail just enough to stop it shaking. Hardly any turbulence is left in the air flow, but it is noticeably diverted. A fairly strong force F is being exerted on, and normally at right-angles to, the sail. This force is equal and opposite to Force F' exerted by the sail on neighbouring air masses, which it diverts equally on both sides—to leeward as well as to windward. It should be noted that, in speaking of a force exerted normally at right-angles to the sail, it would be more correct to say, at right-angles to the *chord* of the sail's arc.

3 If we trim the sail a little closer, it will cause a more definite diversion of the wind. As this deviation of the wind calls for more force, so the counter-force exerted by the sail on the wind is greater; moreover, this force is no longer exercised at right-angles to the sail, but *ahead of that angle—towards the bow*.

4 We continue to trim in the sail; it will convey a bigger and bigger deflection to larger and larger masses of air. The power of the sail rises proportionately. The force is still exerted well ahead of the right-angle to the sail. The flow of air is still regular, but some turbulence is apparent as the air leaves the sail.

5 With further sheeting in, so long as it is done smoothly, a sudden and important change of the air flow occurs. Trying to do too much, all the sail is doing is diverting the wind under pretty bad conditions; heavy turbulence is caused, and the amount of air deflected to leeward of the sail is far less. Thus the wind flow is stopped rather than deflected, and the sail is an obstacle rather than a guide to the air flow. The power of the sail is greatly diminished, and it is exerted in an unsteady direction, well behind the right-angle to the sail.

This sudden change is obviously disastrous from the propulsion point of view. More important still, it is not enough just to ease the sheet a little to restore the correct air flow. To do that, though it would not appear so at first sight, the sheet must be eased out almost to the point where it starts to lift.

This phenomenon corresponds to what the airman calls a *stall*, the result of loss of speed. This stall is practically incurable, except by letting the sail right out.

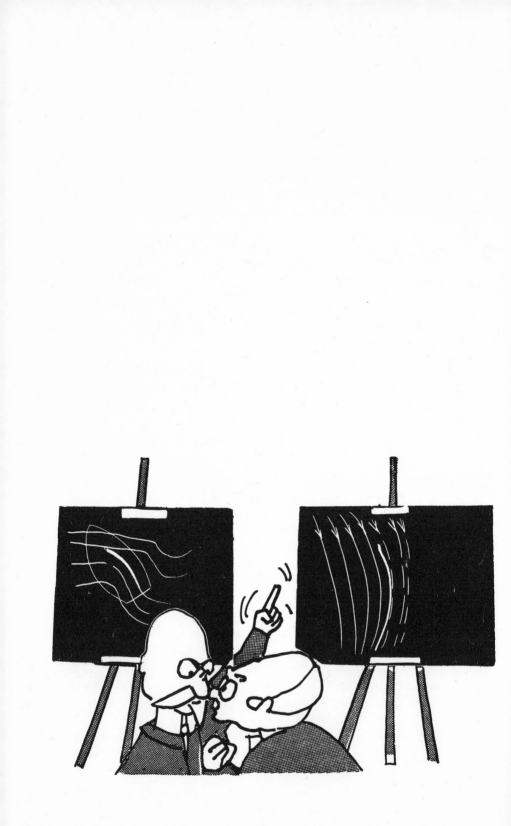

To recapitulate:

normal conditions

The air flow, gradually diverted from its normal path, brings a useful force to bear on the sail, forward of the right-angle to it.

The transformation to a state of turbulence is sudden, all too easy, and irremediable.

The power of the sail is increased as it is sheeted in, reduced as the sheet is slackened.

state of turbulence

The air flow is broken; considerable disturbances occur.

The now weak force on the sail acts to the rear of the right-angle.

This force hardly varies with further hardening of the sheet.

state of transition

The smooth air flow is abruptly destroyed when you go from one state to the other.

When excessive sheeting-in turns the normal condition to a state of turbulence, the power of the sail dies away.

from theory to practice

Controversy surrounds the aerodynamics of the sail. Plenty of authors have tackled the subject. Their conclusions have been contradictory, but they are all of value, and we have kept a large appendix for them. They have been very helpful to us in understanding and expounding our own practical experience.

The exposition above of the interacting forces between wind and sail is only an outline. It is the outcome first and foremost of personal observation; neither strict accuracy nor infallibility is claimed for it. It is none the less well worth keeping in mind, for it explains most of the observed effects, and conclusions drawn from it hold good, as indicating the right way to use the sails in practice. There are some additional phenomena, of which we are about to speak. Then we will go into some experiments we have made, which, it is hoped, will fill the gaps and complete our outline.

The power is greater at intermediate angles than at a right angle

additional phenomena

As a perfectly regular wind is uncommon, it may often happen that the inherently turbulent air flow makes even more abrupt the transition from normal to disturbed conditions and leads to a premature stall—a stall, that is, while the sail is still trimmed in a manner which would lead you to hope for normal conditions. Even if this does not happen, experience shows that a sail gets much less power from a turbulent air stream than from a steady one.

The mast imparts a good deal of disturbance to the air flow over the mainsail, with effects similar to the natural turbulence just mentioned.

The rigging (shrouds, stays, halyards) also have some drag acting in the direction of the wind, quite irrespective of the trim of the sails. It follows that the resultant force exerted by the wind on the whole boat—sail area *plus everything else* above water—which is what we have to count on for propulsion, does not necessarily act in the same direction as the force on the sail *alone*. The difference is generally of no help to the boat's sailing powers. The fact that such parasite forces exist, independent of the trim of the sails, may lessen the effect of re-trimming the sail, in the case of a stall.

The movements of the craft, rolling and pitching, disturb the sails and rigging and keep altering the relative wind on the sail.

experiments

It is possible to try for yourself the variations in the force exerted on a sail, and in its trim, by holding a sheet of plywood in a fairly strong wind.

You will soon appreciate that the force exerted by the wind on this material is practically at right-angles to it, grows if you increase the angle of incidence between the plywood and the wind, reaches its maximum, still at a fairly small angle, then drops abruptly (a stall), and hardly alters any more if you increase the angle with the wind.

Observe that, in the latter phase (of disturbed air flow), the force brought to bear is very unsteady, and that the three-ply shakes quite a bit. Exactly similar instability is observed in a sail at the smaller angles of incidence if the wind is fluky in direction. Finally, you will have certain difficulties, due to the fact that the resultant point at which the airstream acts on the sheet of plywood varies according to the angle of incidence; for medium angles—but *before the stall*—will be about one-third the length of the sheet from the windward edge.

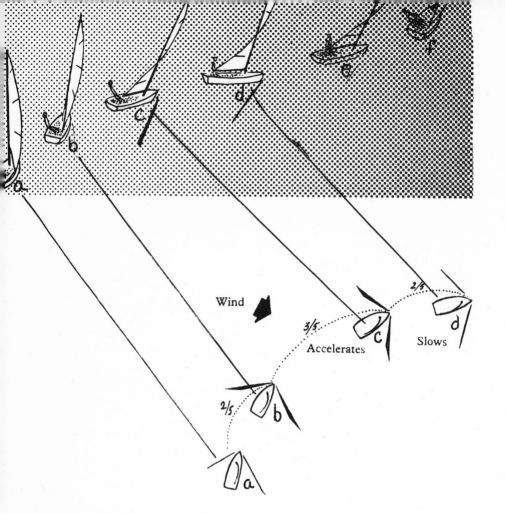

Wind

3/5

Accelerates

Slows

2/5

2/5

Old-time rigs, with their compli-
cations, gave an enormous wind
resistance.

With all sail furled, very great
windage remains.

With a boat, you can make a still more revealing experiment, given a moderate, quite steady wind and calm sea. Starting off full-and-by, with the sails just not lifting, pay off steadily without touching the sheets. The sails take more and more wind, the boat steadily accelerates and starts to heel—because the power produced by the wind is increasing—then suddenly comes upright and slows up, and the sails go limp; we have passed into a state of turbulence. If we want to get back to a proper air flow over the sail, which in this case, will be indicated by an increased heeling angle, we must luff up, nearly to the full-and-by point of sailing. This shows clearly how sudden the change of conditions is, and that it can only be remedied by either easing the sheets or by luffing generously.

Sometimes, too, the following happens; a boat with a generous sail area, close-hauled with a light breeze, towards daybreak—the time when the air flow is smoothest and the helmsman least alert—begins to go sluggish as though lacking wind. The skipper comes on deck, sees the wind has drawn aft, and eases out a little sheet; the heel at once increases, and the boat moves faster. The only explanation is, that with the sails sheeted in too hard, the airflow had become disturbed, unnoticed by the helmsman. The increased heel proves the increased power got from the wind when sheets are eased and the air flow is smoothed out. But this is a rare experience; a prerequisite for a clear demonstration is that the wind must be *extremely* steady.

practical conclusions

windage

It is of the greatest value to reduce the top-hamper of a craft, that is, everything offering a passive resistance to the wind, ruinous to the boat's sailing powers with a wind anywhere forward of the beam. Everything above water is top-hamper—the upperworks, cabin top, crew's bodies, and every item of rigging that is not sail. Obviously, a number of these things are too valuable to do away with altogether. But every one of them must be cut down to size—to the minimum compatible with the use to be made of the craft, and with its seaworthiness. Everything that cannot be scrapped must be studied from the viewpoint of shape and size, to the end that it may offer minimum wind resistance. It may be noted in passing, that it was their enormous top-hamper and windage which prevented the sailing ships of the old days from showing to advantage when on the wind.

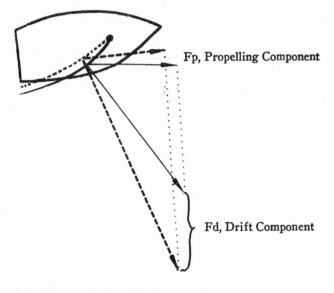

Fp, Propelling Component

Fd, Drift Component

Sheeting a sail home further than
necessary raises the pressure exerted on the sail, but lessens the
propelling component.

jib and mainsail

For a given sail area, a jib will pull better than a mainsail, because the mast does not interfere with the air stream reaching it.

handling of sheets, close-hauled and full-and-by

Although the wind pressure on a sail increases as it is sheeted home (at least when not sheeted in unduly hard), it seems that there is nothing to be gained, when the wind is forward of the beam, by sheeting in a sail beyond the point at which slatting stops. Actually, further hardening in of the sheet will increase the thrust on the sail, certainly resulting in an increase in leeway, but not necessarily in the propulsion component, for the direction of the thrust will have changed. It is impossible to lay down a general rule on this matter; experience alone will tell the best trim of a sail for a given point of sailing and wind force. But one can say that, with a steady wind, and provided one is not sailing too close, the best thing to do is to sheet in just short of the point where the sail starts to lift, taking the greatest care not to stall the sail. But in every other case, particularly when hard on the wind, or if the air flow is disturbed, it is most doubtful whether there is anything to be gained by harder sheeting. Nevertheless, except to prevent excessive heel, or in certain cases of choppy seas or very light breezes, there is no point in letting the sail shake or lift freely. It should once more be made clear that we speak of a sail 'lifting' when it is flapping along its leading edge, or *luff*. If the trailing edge, or *leech*, is shaking, that is evidence that the wind is leaving the sail in a state of turbulence, and there is no harm done if the fluttering is not excessive—it is, rather, a good thing.

handling the sheets when sailing off the wind

Between a beam and a stern wind things are different altogether, and we have little influence on matters. In point of fact, if the wind is abaft the beam, the sail will not lift, even if the sail and boom are allowed to run off right up against the shrouds. The distortion of the sail which results disrupts the wind flow to some degree, which helps turbulence to set in, and, if the wind is not too far abaft the beam, it will often help to sheet in somewhat. If you go further off the wind, the sail must be out as far as possible, and again the flow may become turbulent, without the helmsman knowing. In such conditions, it pays to luff almost up to lifting point now and again, to re-establish the air flow. And, finally, when the wind is almost astern, nothing can prevent turbulence, which explains a boat's relatively poor performance on this point of sailing.

If the sails ares correctly sheeted . . .

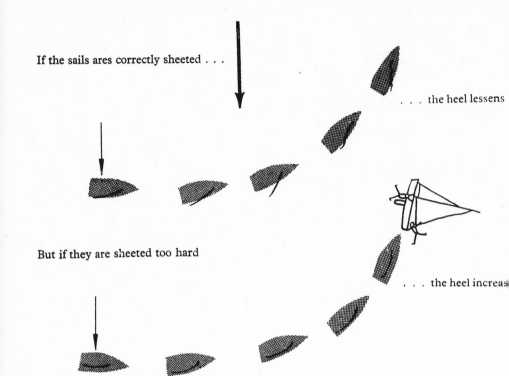

. . . the heel lessens

But if they are sheeted too hard

. . . the heel increases

danger of over-hardening sheets

We should like here to explain what we have already said twice over—that overtight sheets are a danger. When sails are properly trimmed, if you luff, the heel tends to lessen, since the angle of incidence of the wind on the sail lessens, and the thrust is reduced in proportion. This reaction of the boat you very soon get accustomed to. Suppose now you are reaching, with the sheet still hard in. The air flow is turbulent, and there is little power in the sail. If you now luff, a time will come when the air flow smooths out, and the heel will increase abruptly, for the pressure on the sail has risen drastically. This often happens to beginners, who are often so taken by surprise that they capsize—and the worst of it all is that they rarely understand why.

manipulation of sheets when under way

We also said above that you can help a boat to luff or to pay off by juggling with the mainsail- and jib-sheets. This is based on the fact that wind pressure on a sail is increased when it is sheeted in and reduced as the sheet is eased off. Now this holds good only so long as the sail is in an undisturbed air stream; it may well be that if your air stream is turbulent the result may be quite different from what you expect. For instance, on a beam wind, if the jib is suddenly sheeted in very hard, the air flow will go turbulent, and there is every chance the boat will try to luff, whereas, had the jib been hardened only moderately, the tendency would have been to pay off. Here we have something well worth bearing in mind, when you try to assist an evolution by sail handling; handling sheets will only give results *if they are properly trimmed in the first place*. Otherwise the result will be in doubt, and the reaction of the boat may well be the exact opposite to that intended.

sails—full or flat?

Thinking of the deflection of the wind stream leads to the question of whether a sail should be flat, or have generous belly, or bag? With a full, heavily cambered sail, you will get more power, because it deflects air more than a flat sail. On the other hand, it will need sheeting a little harder if it is not to lift. Lifting does not really stop completely until the wind is almost at a tangent to the sail's leading edge, or luff. Therefore, you can sail closer to the wind with a flat sail.

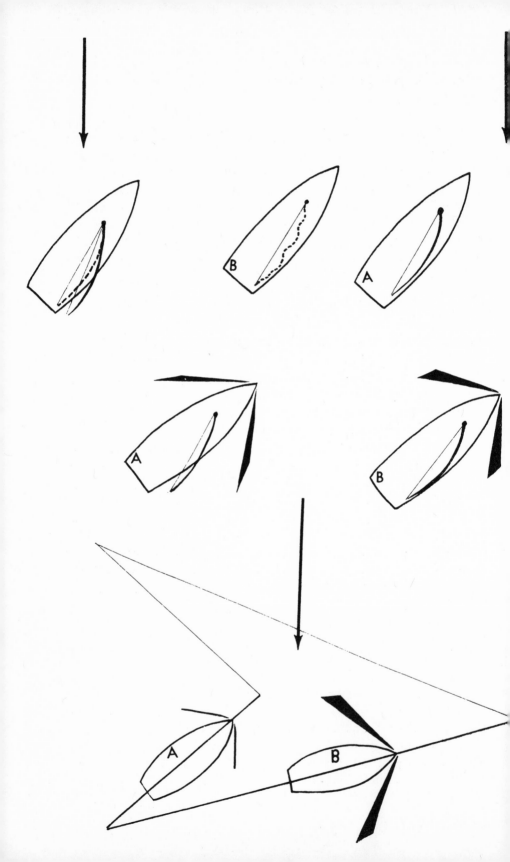

Putting it in another way, if we have two identical boats, A and B, one with a flat sail and the other with a sail with plenty of fullness in it, they will behave quite differently.

If A goes as close to the wind as possible, B will not be able to follow suit, for, even sheeted flat in amidships, the sail will still lift.

When B is sailing close-hauled, A will be able to keep the same course, but will not go so fast, for B will have a more powerful sail.

In a moderate wind, when both are doing their best to get to windward, the odds will be about even; A will be going more slowly on a shorter course, B travelling faster, but going a longer way round. On other points of sailing, reaching or running, B will have a little more speed.

It would seem, then, that in a race with a reasonable wind, with a course including some beating and some off-wind sailing, the boat B will automatically win. It is by no means a certainty; the power to hold a better wind may give boat A a very definite tactical advantage in some circumstances. It might be said that, in moderate weather you can sail as well with any degree of fullness in your sail (barring extremes, of course). The important thing is, to adapt your sailing to the cut of your sail. With a full-bellied sail you should avoid sailing too close; with a flat one you should keep close to the wind.

In a stronger wind, the mass of air passing the sail is so large that a small deflection will generate a very large force; great flow in a sail is then useless, and the flat sail is of the greatest value, as it need not be sheeted in so hard, thus obtaining a high driving force with the smallest possible amount of leeway.

On the other hand, in a light breeze, the mass of air will be small, and must be sharply deflected to get enough force. A deep-bellied sail is therefore of great value in these circumstances, in which, in any case, you will not be able to sail very close to the wind; if too close-hauled, your propulsive component will be too low.

We shall see that a boat's crew can, to a large extent, adjust the flow of a sail. Each outing will call for a different setting.

It should be flat for fresh winds or much windward work.

It should have lots of belly for light winds, or if off-wind sailing is the order of the day.

Wind

A   D   E

d

Luff

Leech

The depression on the lee side has two or three times the value of the weather-side positive pressure.

The pressure and depression are both higher along the leading edge (luff) than along the trailing edge (leech), especially when sailing close to the wind.

Whenever sailing conditions change, these adjustments should be made. Having done this, your racing tactics should conform to the shape of your sail.

> full, it will give you more speed off the wind, and better acceleration as you bear away.

> flat, you will be able to point closer to the wind.

the distribution of forces on a sail

So far, we have studied the effect of wind on a sail as a whole, irrespective of local variations, at different parts of the sail. Several authors, notably Manfred Curry, have gone into this question, and from their studies can be drawn profitable conclusions, which would have been hard to arrive at by plain observation.

Experiments have consisted of measurements of wind pressure on each part of a sail, both on the windward and leeward sides. Essentially, results were as follows:

> the wind causes a positive pressure over almost the whole of the windward side of the sail;

> there is a negative pressure over almost the whole of the lee surface;

> the depression on the lee side has two or three times the value of the weather-side positive pressure;

> the pressure and depression are both higher along the leading edge (luff) than along the trailing edge (leech), especially when sailing close to the wind.

The main conclusion to be drawn, surprising at first sight, is that most work is done by the lee side of the sail. Of the total thrust generated by the sail, the sum of the pressures on the two sides, two-thirds or three-quarters comes from the lee side. This indicates that the sail deflects the masses of air passing to leeward more efficiently than those passing to windward. More attention must therefore be paid to avoiding disturbing the air flow to leeward than to windward. For example, a crew member standing near the sail will harm the air flow far less if he is to windward than if he stands to leeward.

Again, a sail will generate far more pressure close to the mast (or, in the case of a jib, the forestay); the greatest attention must then be paid to such areas. In fact, a sail lifting near its luff is a much more serious affair than a little light flapping near the leech.

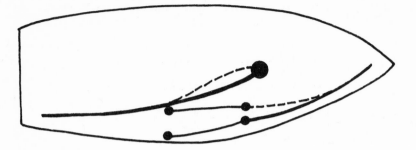

Foresail sheeted in, too near to centre line of boat

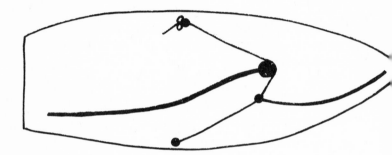

Windward sheet fouled

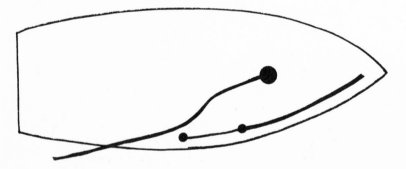

Mainsail not sheeted hard enough

interaction between sails

When several sails are close neighbours, it is impossible to assess what happens to the one without taking the others into account.

We must consider the cases of boats carrying several sails, and also craft sailing in company, or on converging courses.

case of a boat with several sails

We will think only of the case where a jib is used with a mainsail, much the commonest combination today.

A jib is a sail with its *tack* made fast on the centre line of the boat, forward of the mast. Thanks to its position, the air streams on which the jib has acted pass to leeward of the mainsail. Now, we have seen that most of the work is done on this lee side of the mainsail. It is then easy to see that the jib may have a great effect on the working of the mainsail, for good or ill, according as to how the wind leaves the jib. It is a controversial question, so we will first look at some undeniable facts, then at certain arguable points.

1. The action of the jib on the mainsail is of no benefit if it is set up so as to pour wind into the mainsail so as to blanket the luff, or leading edge, causing lifting of that part of the sail. This may occur:

> if the *jibsheet fairlead* (the eye through which the jib-sheet is led, and which determines the direction of its pull on the jib), is too far in towards the centre line of the boat;
>
> if the mainsail is sheeted out farther than the jib;
>
> if the windward jib-sheet is fouled and not free to run.
>
> In all these cases it follows that the jib—at least in part—destroys the low-pressure area, normally found under the lee of the mainsail, and so reduces the effect of the wind on it.

To avoid these evils, it will be found useful:

> to put the jib-sheet lead away from the centre line of the boat; this must not be exaggerated. It would be impossible to sheet the jib in hard enough when on the wind, if the fairlead was too far out;

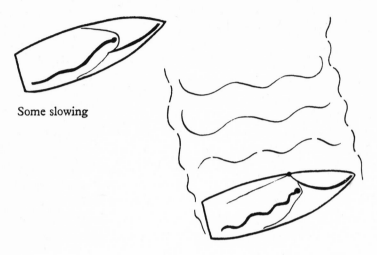

Some slowing

Boat stopped, drifting sideways fast

to sheet the mainsail and jib in conjunction with one another; that is, so as to ensure the jib does not interfere with the wind of the mainsail;

to ensure always that the weather jib-sheet (the one not in use) runs completely clear, and exerts no pull on the sail. The farther the *clew* of the jib (the corner to which the sheets are attached) is out from the centre line of the boat, the less the windward sheet will tend to clear itself.

This harmful influence of a jib-sheet which is hooked up to windward is so pronounced that it may be used with advantage to slow up the boat—when on the wind—without dropping the mainsail, or letting it flap. Such braking effect can be controlled:

by pulling the jib clew well to windward, which brings the boat to a dead stop;

pulling the jib-sheet lightly to windward will result in some slowing;

while one may ring the changes on all intermediate positions.

2. It is, on the other hand, much more doubtful whether the jib can affect the mainsail beneficially. Some authorities, Manfred Curry for one, account for such an effect by the fact that the air stream passing between jib and mainsail—owing to the restricted passage between the two—undergoes a considerable speeding up, and this increases the negative pressure to leeward of the mainsail. This may be so to some degree; but it is a highly arguable point, and we will come back to it in the appendix to this chapter.

interaction between two or more boats

A sailing craft sets up certain disturbances in the wind, which can have an influence on another boat under sail in its vicinity. For instance, if two boats are converging on opposite tacks, the one passing to leeward of the other will experience a brief but abrupt shift of wind. It is well to know about this, to avoid unpleasant surprises, and such faults as passing *too* close under the lee of another craft will cause a sudden loss of wind. The boat will come upright, with the possible result of entangling the two masts together, a pretty common accident—and a very unpleasant one.

It will generally be when racing that a number of boats will be sailing close together, and it is then that a knowledge of the tactics of taking another boat's wind will prove of value.

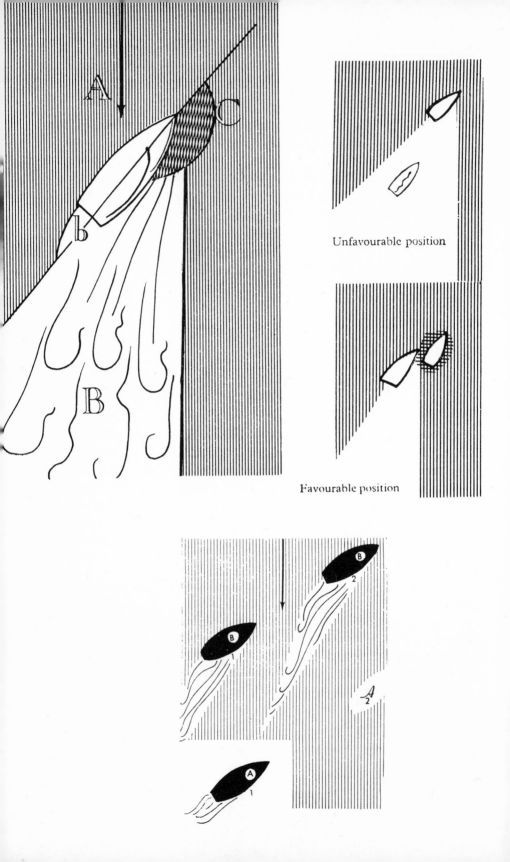

Unfavourable position

Favourable position

Let us, then, take a look at what is going on around a boat sailing to windward.

A. To windward and forward of the boat, to all intents and pur-purposes, no disturbance exists.

B. To leeward, between the wind direction and the wake of the craft, there is a great deal of disturbance; a boat which comes into that area, while making good the same course, will find that the wind is weaker, is much disturbed, and has also drawn badly ahead of it. This effect reaches out for the equivalent of several mast lengths in a very pronounced manner, and will still be felt quite a lot farther away. This zone has a small extension at b in the drawing, a little to windward of the wake, and close to the stern.

C. Just ahead and to leeward another boat will find the wind draws aft, and will benefit still more by reason of the fact that the first boat will find itself in a position rather like b in the drawing. This is what racing enthusiasts call the 'safe leeward position'. In practice it is a great deal easier to describe it on paper than to get yourself into it—as Ted Wells says of it—'There are so many *ifs* and *buts* . . .' In particular, the two boats must get very close to one another, and the one that is to benefit from the safe leeward position must not yield an inch of ground, under the penalty of seeing himself, so far from benefitting, actually losing his wind.

What you must realize is that you will always do badly in the lee, or astern, of another craft; in particular, if you have to follow another boat closely, you must be a bit to windward of its wake—a yard is plenty.

Finally, we must explain that a boat A (lower drawing) sailing just to leeward of boat B does not really lose a clear wind. The wind it is receiving at 2 passed B-2 when the windward boat was still at B-1, so is not disturbed. The time the wind takes to get from B-2 to A-2 is the time the windward boat took to get from B-1 to B-2, and for the lee boat to get from A-1 to A-2.

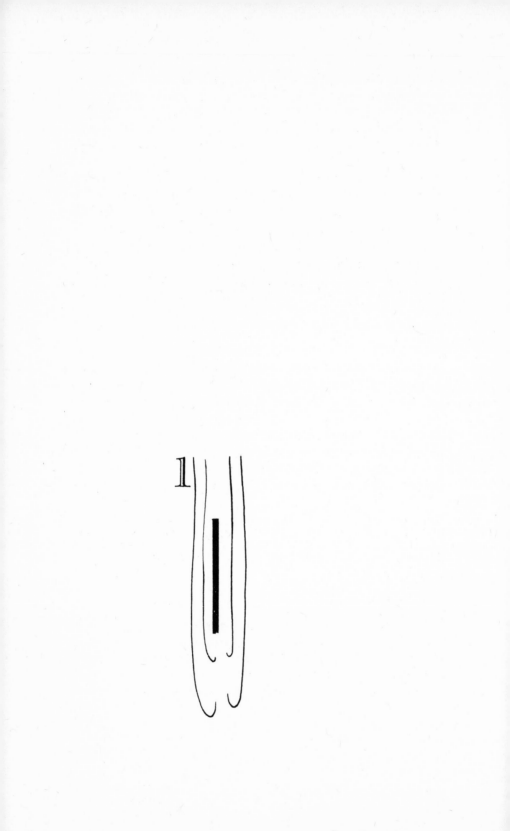

effect of water on the keel

The keel of the boat being part of the hull, we should perhaps have studied its action in the last chapter; but the things that happen, on and near it, are so similar to what happens to a sail that this seemed the better place for it.

Before going on, let it be clear that we call the *keel* any comparatively flat, thin object, put under the hull to minimize sideways drift. That was how it was defined in the early pages of this book. All that we say in this chapter about the keel applies equally to a centre-board or dagger-plate if fitted.

Strictly speaking, the word 'keel' refers to part of the hull structure, which does not necessarily protrude below the ship's bottom, as, for instance, on most steamers. Finally, some sailing craft have neither fixed nor drop keel in our sense of the word, but get along more or less with the hull shape as their only anti-leeway device.

The work of the keel may be considered as displacing the masses of water which pass under the boat, and generating by reaction a transverse force opposing the *leeway component* of the force exerted on the sails by the wind.

It is therefore possible to consider the case as similar to that of a sail, always supposing that you are dealing with a stationary boat in a moving current, and not a boat in motion through a stationary body of water. It comes to exactly the same thing, so long as you are only thinking of the water/keel reaction.

The only difficulty will arise from the fact that the water current has a direction and speed equal and opposite to that of the boat, *and so variable.* We must therefore take account of the effect on the keel when speed and direction of the water vary.

interaction between keel and water

Let us look at the disturbances caused by the keel to the flow of water, and at the same time at the force exerted by the water on the keel.

When the water flows along the line of the keel it behaves exactly as does the air stream flowing along an unsheeted sail. It is not deviated, but lightly braked by friction; any force it exerts on the keel is in the direction of the current flow.

This is the case of a boat with forward motion and no leeway, Figure 1.

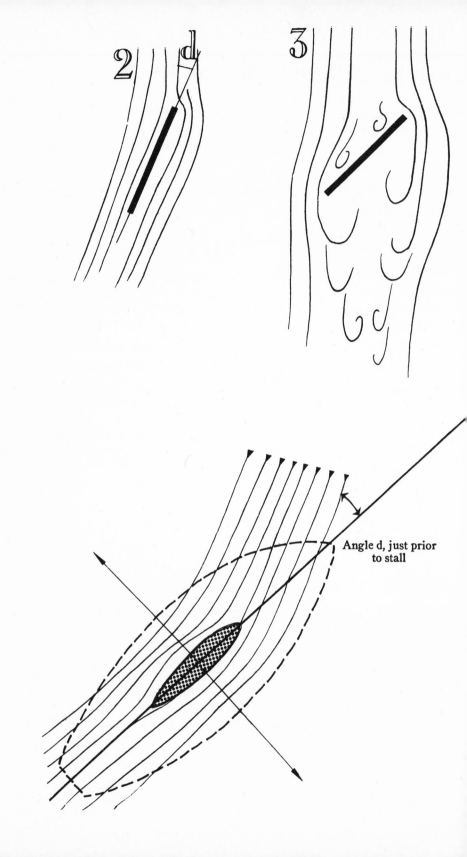

Angle d, just prior
to stall

When the water strikes the keel at an angle of incidence d, everything happens in the same way as when air meets a lightly sheeted sail; the water current is diverted, and a fairly strong force is set up at right-angles to the keel. This force is equal and opposite to that exercised by the keel on the neighbouring masses of water which it is deviating.

This corresponds to a boat moving forward with leeway angle d, Figure 2, page 136.

If the angle of incidence of the water with the keel rises, when it reaches a certain value a sudden change occurs in the flow conditions: there is no longer an orderly deflection of the water, but a severe formation of eddies. This 'stall' is accompanied by a great reduction in the force exerted on the keel. This phenomenon— exactly like that produced by a stall on the sail—is irreversible, in the sense that you have to bring down the angle of incidence of the water on the keel to a very large extent before the flow can reestablish itself. See Figure 3, page 136.

All effects produced on a keel are much more clean-cut than those on a sail, mainly because the keel is a rigid unyielding object—as opposed to a sail—and because water is less liable to disturbance than is air. It is possible therefore to give a much clearer picture of what happens:

● The force exerted by the keel is proportional:

> to its surface area;

> to the angle of incidence of the water (provided the stalling angle is not reached);

> to the square of the speed of the water;

> it will double if the speed increases 40%.

● The value of the stalling angle will rise with a thicker keel, and drop in proportion to its *aspect ratio* (the ratio between its fore-and-aft breadth).

This angle of stall will generally run from about 12° for a long drop keel to, say 20° for a thick fixed keel. For very thick sections it may go up to, and beyond, 30°.

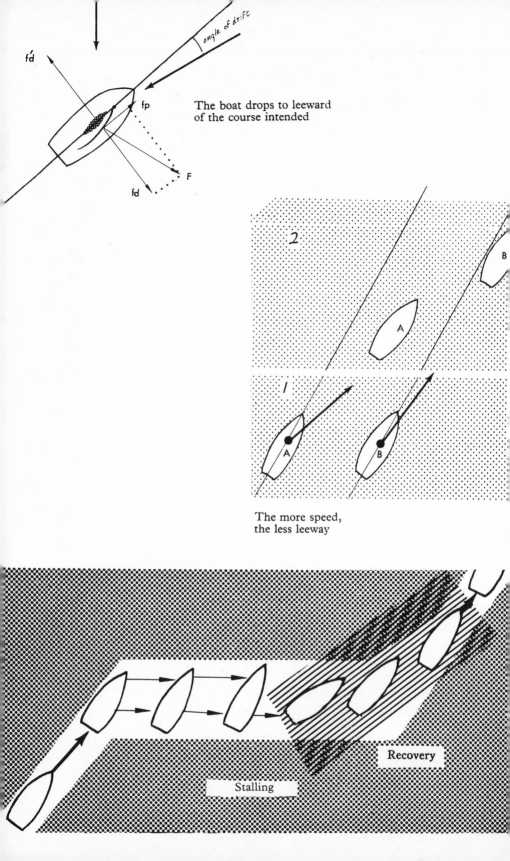

angle of drift

fd́

fp

fd

F

The boat drops to leeward
of the course intended

2

B

A

1

A

B

The more speed,
the less leeway

Recovery

Stalling

the keel as an inhibitor of leeway

Take the case of a boat sailing close-hauled. The wind exerts a force f on its sails, which can be broken down into:

a propulsive component, fp;

a drift, or leeway component, fd.

Under the effect of this force f the boat will move forward—as we have already seen—at a certain angle of drift, or leeway. Water then meeting the keel at a given angle of incidence, equal to the leeway, will exert on it a force $f'd$ at right-angles to the boat's centre line, in the windward direction, opposing the drift component fd.

Suppose for the moment that the boat maintains a constant speed. It will sail with leeway such that $f'd$ is equal to fd. In fact, if $f'd$ were less than fd, their resultant would be on the lee side, which would increase the leeway, which would rise until $f'd$—increased proportionately—was equal to fd.

On the other hand, if $f'd$ were higher than fd, the leeway would fall off.

It is therefore fair to say that the boat will find its own angle of drift, by arriving at a precise compromise between $f'd$ and fd.

Suppose now the boat's speed increases, force $f'd$ will rise, and the leeway will lessen. Conversely, a drop in speed will cause the leeway to rise.

It may then be said that, if a boat is acted on by a given wind, and its head kept on a given bearing, it will automatically keep a steady amount of leeway as a function of its speed, because it will establish a transverse force balancing the drift component imposed by the wind on the sails; the higher the speed, the less the leeway.

Under all normal sailing conditions, this balance will be achieved without the drift angle reaching stalling-point. But, if the boat slows up excessively, for any reason, the drift angle may rise to that critical point. In this event, there will be a stall, force $f'd$ will drop steeply, and the angle of drift will rise considerably, possibly going quite suddenly well above the stalling angle. The only way to get back to a tolerable amount of leeway is to bear away and let fly the sheets, so as to diminish the drift component in the wind force on the sails.

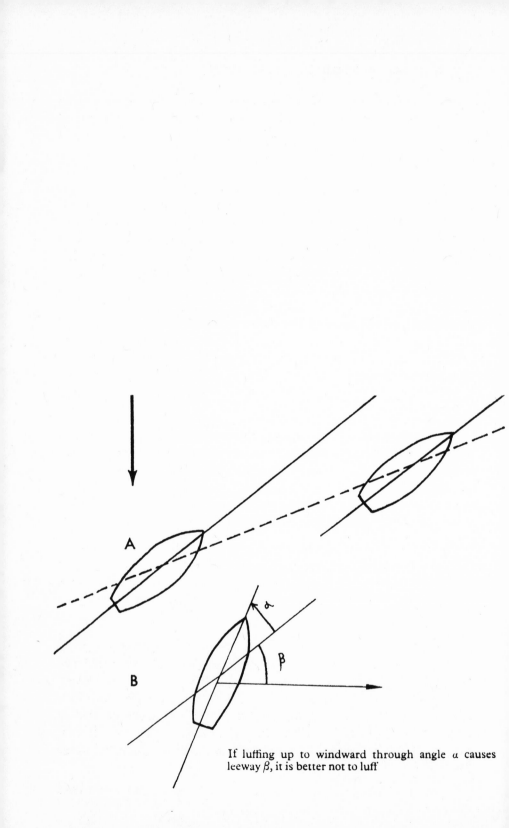

If luffing up to windward through angle α causes leeway β, it is better not to luff

note

Bear in mind once more, that this phenomenon is exactly similar to what the airman and glider pilot call a stall or loss of speed. It is possible to compare a glider with a boat; the keel with the wing:

f corresponds to the force of gravity,

the angle of drift is the angle of incidence of the air stream on a wing.

If the speed of the glider drops, the angle of incidence must increase to keep the lift equal to the weight of the machine. There will be a stall if, as the speed is lost, the angle of incidence reaches its critical value. In which case, the glider loses its lift.

practical conclusions

magnitude of drift angle, or leeway, in relation to points of sailing

The angle of drift is the higher as the course is nearer the wind; as the boat points closer to the wind, the propelling component decreases and the leeway one increases. The speed of the boat therefore drops, and, with the increase in the leeward component, the leeway rises. If you bear off, the propelling component rises fast, while the drift component reduces. The boat will therefore go faster with less leeway—with still less leeway inasmuch as the force exerted on the keel by the water varies with the *square of the speed*. You will see that a small rise in speed means quite a large reduction of leeway.

To sum up, owing to what we have said:

● One rarely benefits by pointing as close to the wind as the boat will go: the increased leeway largely nullifies any gain from pointing better;

● as soon as you are slightly off the wind, the leeway drops to a very small angle. On a good ocean racer, for instance, if you are farther off the wind than full-and-by, the leeway may be disregarded. With a dinghy, the centre-board may be partly raised with a beam wind, and practically raised altogether when on a broad reach or a dead run. It is never a good thing to raise it completely; the boat steers badly, and slides about. When a boat slides or yaws, it develops leeway, which increases the resistance to forward movement (under-water resistance, heeling influence and leeway), which is like putting on the brakes.

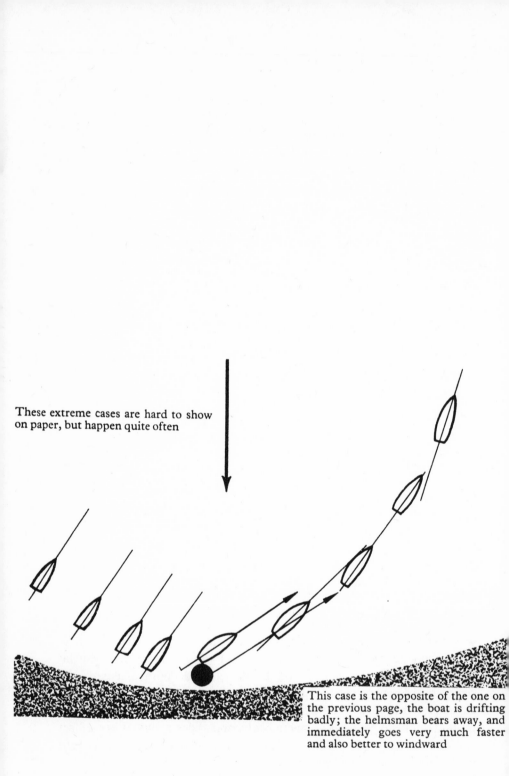

These extreme cases are hard to show
on paper, but happen quite often

This case is the opposite of the one on
the previous page, the boat is drifting
badly; the helmsman bears away, and
immediately goes very much faster
and also better to windward

behaviour of the boat when on the wind

Remember what we said in the chapter on the hull, under the heading 'dynamics':

- Resistance to forward movement rises if the angle of drift increases, and if the speed of the boat increases;

  similarly, it drops if the leeway and speed diminish.

Think now of a boat close-hauled, with a steady wind, and on a constant course, and suppose that, temporarily and for some accidental cause, it is slowed up a little, its resistance to forward movement will tend:

  to increase, because the drift angle will rise at once;

  to diminish, because the speed has itself diminished.

One cancels out the other, and the total resistance will hardly vary; the balance between propulsive and braking forces will barely change. This means that, when the temporary check has passed, there will not be much acceleration, or tendency to return to the original speed.

Similarly, when a temporary increase of speed occurs, there will be tendency to maintain the increased speed.

From this we may conclude, that an expert helmsman, who knows how to get the maximum advantage from every chance to gain speed, will get along *when close-hauled* very much faster than an inexperienced man, who will, because he lacks experience, allow successive checks to accumulate; while, off the wind, quite ill-matched helmsmen will return much the same speeds.

In practice, it is quite common for a really good helmsman to travel twice the speed of a beginner when close-hauled.

the stall

For a given speed, the angle of leeway corresponds to the drift component of the wind force on the boat, and there will be a stall when this component reaches the point where the boat is at the critical drift angle. In other words, if you don't want to stall your keel, don't let the leeway rise above a certain degree, which depends on the speed; the higher the speed on the boat, the more leeway can be tolerated.

Because the centre-board is partly raised this boat is bearing away a little to compensate

This boat is trying to point high, but is drifting away from the intended course

As a general rule the anti-drift surfaces of a boat are arranged to be proportional to the sail area, so that the boat will tolerate sails sheeted hard-in even at quite low speeds. But, if the speed is really low, the centre-board will tend to stall if the sheets are hauled tight. You must therefore take care that, when some particular manoeuvre has brought your speed right down, you ease sheets slightly to gain speed and avoid a stall. This is especially important after a difficult tack.

In the case of a boat sailing with centre-board half or right up, you cannot sheet in hard, even at quite high speeds, without stalling. It is impossible to sail close to the wind, and only by bearing off to full-and-by will you be able to hold your speed and you must ease sheets to suit. This is a thing you must remember when lack of water will not let you drop your centre-board fully—crossing shoals, leaving a beach, and so on. It must be borne in mind, however, that in these circumstances a boat will sail:

- either with a tolerably high drift angle ($5°$ to $10°$), if there is enough speed for the amount of centre-board showing to balance the drift force,

- or with very high angle of drift ($25°$ or more) if the speed is so low that a stall does occur.

In any case it will never sail with an amount of leeway midway between these two (of the order of $15°$), because a stall and the recovery from it are both marked by a sudden change in the angle of drift of the boat. This is specially noticeable when several craft are leaving a lee shore in the hands of helmsmen of different capacities.

appendix on sails and keels

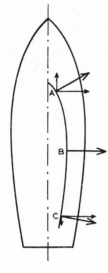

General note on cut and trim of sails

Take the case of a boat with a full-cut sail, properly sheeted, and let us see step by step what goes on.

Force is exerted at one particular point, or, to be more exact, over a small area round that point, the result of the positive and negative pressures on, respectively, the windward and lee surfaces of the sail. The force therefore acts on the sail at right-angles to the surface at the point in question. The force acting on a small area around point A, near the luff, is divided into:

● a useful propelling component;

● an unwanted leeway component.

At a point B where the sail is parallel to the centre-line of the boat, the basic force is working athwartships; it can have no propelling element, and is of no value.

At point C, where the leech of the sail is beginning to close in towards the centreline, the force breaks down into:

● a useless thwartships component,

● and a positively harmful braking element.

Generally speaking, every portion of the sail which is divergent to the centre line of the boat does its bit towards propulsion.

Every portion which *is* parallel to the centre line is useless, and even slightly harmful; for the leeward component indirectly brakes the boat by increasing the resistance to forward motion.

Finally, any part of the sail which tends to expel the air stream off it to windward of the centre line is positively harmful.

From this it will be gathered that a sail must always be set in such a manner that its leech does not curve back towards the centre line of the boat.

146

If we now take once more a sail (1), identical to the above example, we must:

● either ease the sheet to position (2); but then we shall not get so close to the wind; a wind will be necessary, farther aft, to keep it from lifting;

● or flatten the sail and sheet farther outboard, so that we can keep as close to the wind as with (1).

We may note in passing that if we cut sail (1) off short at point X we should have as much useful force as with sail (3)—for it would cause equal deflection of the wind—in fact, we would even have more usful force, for, the sail area being less, there would be less frictional loss.

A sail may curve to windward on the leech in this unfortunate manner, either because it is cut with too much flow; or because it has a fault such as a pocket or girt near the leech.

In the first case, if it is a mainsail, it can be improved by flattening it by cutting some of the round off the luff or the foot; or, if it is a jib, by shifting the sheet fairlead outboard.

In the second case, it is a fault of the sailmaker's; perhaps the leech was made too short; or there is a persistent girt which has arisen over a period of time, caused possibly by fatigue of the material. If it is a mainsail, longer battens could put matters more or less right. If it is a jib, it is a disaster; it will deflect wind on to the lee side of the mainsail, and there is practically nothing to be done, short of remaking the sail. You could fit battens, but these will soon break, by thrashing against the mast when going about.

If, on the other hand, the leech is not taut enough, it will flap even when the sail is sheeted home. This in itself is no serious matter, but in extreme cases this flapping may shake the whole sail, spoil its set, make the right sheet adjustment hard to find, and disturb the crew's concentration by its noise.

The happy medium is hard for the sailmaker to find. A good way of getting it for a jib is to cut the leech concave, and to stiffen it when necessary with a line running in the tabling. Certain ocean-racing skippers attach great importance to this, and adjust this leech-line constantly.

To take up again the question of useful and valueless parts of the sail, we might think of its action as taking the wind gently from the direction in which it comes, bend it easily, and expel it out along the centre line of the boat; to catch the wind, use it, and let it go.

Certain authors hold that a boat is driven by *jet reaction*, a jet of air being thrown out astern.

This expression is correct, in the sense that there is a jet effect on the sails, just as there is on the blades of a turbine.

But the comparison with a jet aircraft is exaggerated; the latter *injects* energy into an airstream to increase its speed; a sail has no energy to add to the flow of air.

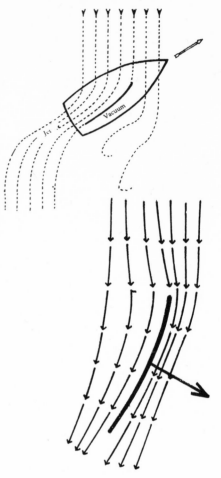

A controversy arose in the columns of the magazine *Yachting* around the years '50 or '52 between two American authorities on this question.

H. F. Whiton says: 'Reaction propulsion, or jet propulsion, does exist; air reaching the sail is compressed and accelerated, forming a jet which drives the boat.' The work done by the sail is therefore mainly done by the windward face; in our view the fact that air is at the same time compressed and accelerated is a definite contradiction of the most elementary laws of the mechanics of fluids.

H. P. Grant says: 'The above outline is false. The air is *slowed* and its pressure increased on the windward side of the sail. It is accelerated, and its pressure diminished, on the lee side.

'Experiment proves that the air is more accelerated to leeward than slowed to windward, hence it is a fact that the lee side of the sail does most of the work.'

To our ideas, this second hypothesis conforms at once to experience, and to, the laws of fluid mechanics. It does not however, rule out all discussion on jet propulsion; it depends what you mean by jet propulsion.

In fact, reaction, deflection, pressure, suction—they are not contradictory theories, but represent different aspects of a single group of related phenomena.

The same object looks different, seen through the microscope, with the naked eye, or at a distance through binoculars.

We have used the term 'deflection' because it seems to us the handiest, and because it allows for consideration of the various conditions of air flow, which is so essential and so often neglected.

Manfred Curry, author of *Sail Aerodynamics and the Art of Winning Races*, has been the master mind behind many racing men since 1930.

His work, a little out of date by modern standards, is not to be recommended indiscriminately to beginners. On the other hand, it is a mine of information to those experienced enough not to be too fascinated by a wealth of material details, and by the thousand and one experiments he describes.

A fascinating part of the book is the description of wind-tunnel experiments with model sails. For example, let us examine two graphs, plotting the forces exerted on sails with different angles of incidence of the wind.

The wind is blowing along the axis OX on the sail whose chord meets this axis at an angle θ. The force exerted OF is represented by point F, on the arm of the angle θ. The experiment was repeated for various sail angles and a curve was obtained, graduated in degrees.

The curves given are for a gaff mainsail, A, and a Bermudian mainsail, B.

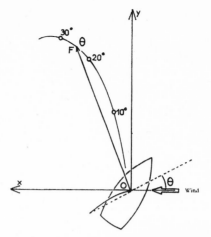

In each curve, you will notice the progressive rise of the force with that of the angle of incidence, then the sudden fall at stalling-point, lastly the steadiness of the force in conditions of turbulence, beyond the stalling angle.

If you will look at the angles which correspond to the various sheeting angles, you will, after a little thought, see that the force is directed:

● behind the perpendicular to the sail for small angles of incidence (e.g. at 10° for sail A);

● then forward of the perpendicular until the critical angle is reached (between 20° and 40° for sail A);

● finally, round about the perpendicular, sometimes a little one side (50°), sometimes a little the other (90°);

● still considering the same sail, when the angle of incidence rises from 39° to 41° the stall happens, and the force drops by 30% in the time the angle increased by 6°.

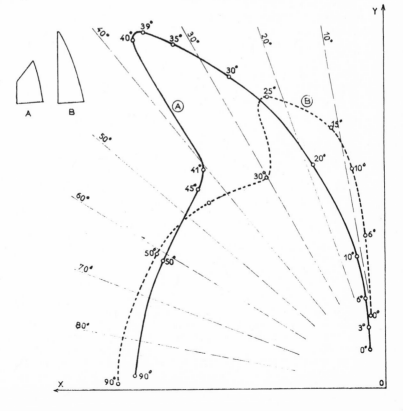

If we compare the two curves, we see the Bermudian sail is far better value when sailing very close to the wind, as it gives a bigger, and a better directed, force at small angles of incidence, hence a far greater propelling component. Thus, for an angle of incidence of 10°, the force is 60% greater, and, by reason of its better direction, gives double the propulsion component (for a boat sailing at 45° to the wind).

We must note that the advantage of the Bermudian sail when on the wind is reversed on other points of sailing; the gaff sail gives higher forces above 25°; and stalls only at 40°; for an angle of 30°, for instance, the force is greater and also better directed.

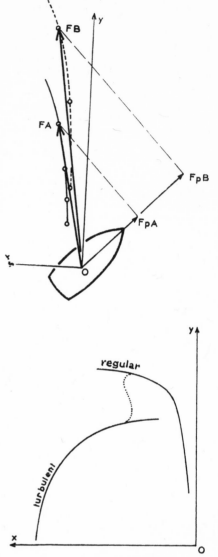

These polar curves appear to contradict what we said about the irreversible nature of the stall. It seems as if, letting *out* the sail beyond high angles, you get, for a given direction, the same forces as when sheeting it *in* from small angles. This is probably due to the fact that, in an experimental wind tunnel, the air flow has some degree of turbulence, which masks the transition between the two states of air flow; and, in this respect, the curves obtained experimentally on a model would represent those obtaining on a real sail only in a wind of extreme violence, a line squall, or similar mass of highly unstable air.

But very probably, in a steady breeze, the curve for a real sail would be ambiguous, and would be unreliable for certain angles of incidence. Without specifically mentioning the stall, Manfred Curry does say farther on:

'. . . an air stream acting on any surface without causing eddies, has an effect 60% higher than that obtaining in conditions of turbulence . . .'

This accounts for an impression you often get; at equal average speeds, a gusty wind will not drive the boat as well as a steady one.

A little farther on, Manfred Curry says again:

'In other words, the ideal sail should *guide or bend* the air stream, and not break it, or interrupt it abruptly, thus forming eddies.'

A book by *Grégoire Imbery* contains results of experiments and trial calculations relating to phenomena concerning sail.

They are very interesting, but not at all easily understandable, and differ from the conclusions we have reached in practice.

Among his experimental results, he notes:

'It is not enough to alter the sheeting of the sail back to the critical angle for the smooth air stream over the sail to be resumed; one must go back to roughly half of that angle.'

We cannot quote these authorities and omit *Ted Wells*, author of *Scientific Sailboat Racing*. This book does not deal exclusively with aerodynamics, but has some eminently practical remarks on the subject. And, in a general way, the author's approach to the subject seems a practical one. We cannot too highly recommend this book, which is packed with good advice.

The influence of aspect ratio

By *aspect ratio* of a sail we mean the proportion of height relative to breadth.

When the height of a sail is increased the forces obtained are greater and more efficient in direction. This is shown by the polar curves above. If A has an aspect ratio of 1, then B, the Bermudian sail, had a ratio of 3.

The inconvenience which offsets this— a lower stalling angle—is a drawback only when well off the wind.

As progress to windward generally decides races, designers have been tempted to use very tall sail-plans. The use of extreme heights is limited by two factors which have nothing to do with aerodynamics:

● the centre of effort is higher, the heeling moment greater, and, other things being equal, the boat heels more;

● the lofty mast is difficult to stay; the spar must be very strong, and the rigging fairly complicated.

These two difficulties very soon cancel the benefits to be had from extreme height; in practice, therefore, figures higher than 3 are very uncommon, 4 practically unknown.

BIBLIOGRAPHY

MANFRED CURRY   *Yacht Racing, The Aerodynamics of Sail*
TED WELLS   *Scientific Sailboat Racing*
GRÉGOIRE IMBERY   *L'Aérodynamique du Yacht*
HERMAN F. WHITON   'Sails are not Jets'
  Yachting, August 1952
HOWARD P. GRANT   'The jet theory of sailing'
  Yachting, October 1960

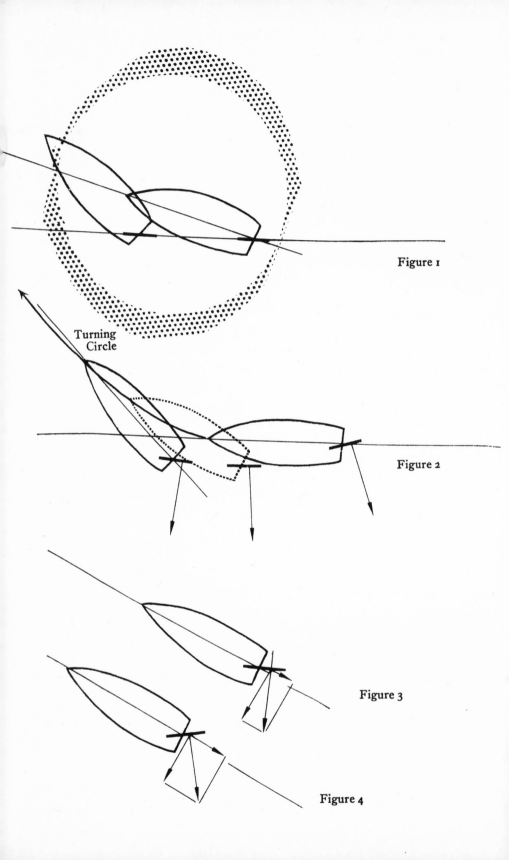

Figure 1

Turning
Circle

Figure 2

Figure 3

Figure 4

how
to steer
a boat

4

the rudder and its action

At the beginning of this course we gave a brief description of the steering gear and explained its action, thus:

> The rudder, flat and thin in shape, tends to move through the water always in the plane of its blade, Figure 1, and moves the stern of the boat round as the tiller is moved.

There is another explanation for this action: if you put the tiller to the left, on a boat which is moving straight ahead, the water meets the rudder at a certain angle of incidence, brings to bear on it a force at right-angles to its plane, and directed to the left. This force impels the stern of the boat towards the left. The boat's bow inclines to the right and moves off in the new direction, Figure 2.

note

● The movement leading to a change of course comes from the stern, which is therefore very definitely displaced towards the *outside of the turning circle,* Figure 2, a thing you must remember when manoeuvring in the neighbourhood of an obstacle.

● The force of the water on the rudder blade can be resolved into:

> a component A, Figure 3 and A', Figure 4 transverse to the boat, which causes the turn;
>
> a braking component, B, Figure 3 and B', Figure 4, directed aft, which applies a brake to the boat. This component increases with the helm angle.

It must be borne in mind that every movement of the rudder puts a brake on the boat's progress.

This is the direction in
which the water meets the
rudder-blade

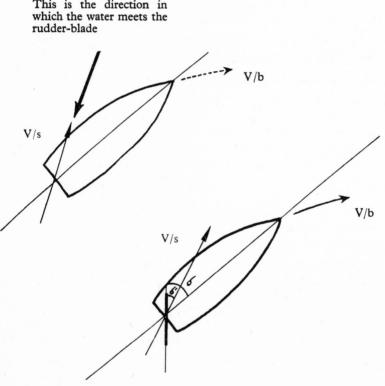

- The behaviour of the rudder-blade in the water is much the same as that of the keel. Thus the force on the rudder varies as:

> the square of the speed,
>
> the angle of incidence at which the rudder meets the water (which is not the same thing as the helm angle, as we shall see).

It is possible to stall the rudder if the tiller is put over too sharply and the rudder meets the water at an angle higher than the critical one.

helm angle, and angle of incidence of the rudder blade on the water

These two angles vary with the rate at which the boat is actually changing direction. Let us see what happens when a boat is turning to starboard. At the moment in question the speeds of different parts of the boat are not the same. We might designate as V/b and V/s respectively:

> the speed of the bow;
>
> the speed at the rudder pintles and gudgeons (or hinges).

V/b is directed to starboard, V/s to port.

The water meets the rudder blade in the direction opposite to V/s, and the angle of attack is, in the drawing, the angle b', definitely less than the tiller angle b.

During the course of the evolution, you may put the tiller over at a large angle without danger of stalling the rudder; but, *to start the evolution*, only a small helm angle is essential.

To start a turn by suddenly putting the tiller hard over is quite disastrous, especially if the boat, having little speed, or being naturally unhandy, answers the helm sluggishly. There is a risk that you will not obtain the best effect from the rudder, and you will certainly put on the brake. In practice, to change course with minimum loss of speed, you must 'go along with' the helm; that is to say, you apply progressive pressure to the tiller, increasing helm as the boat begins to answer, using a steady and continuous pressure; as soon as the boat starts to turn, the helm tends to carry on its movement by itself, and you simply go with it. In the same way, as the boat approaches the desired new course you must bring the helm back to centre gently.

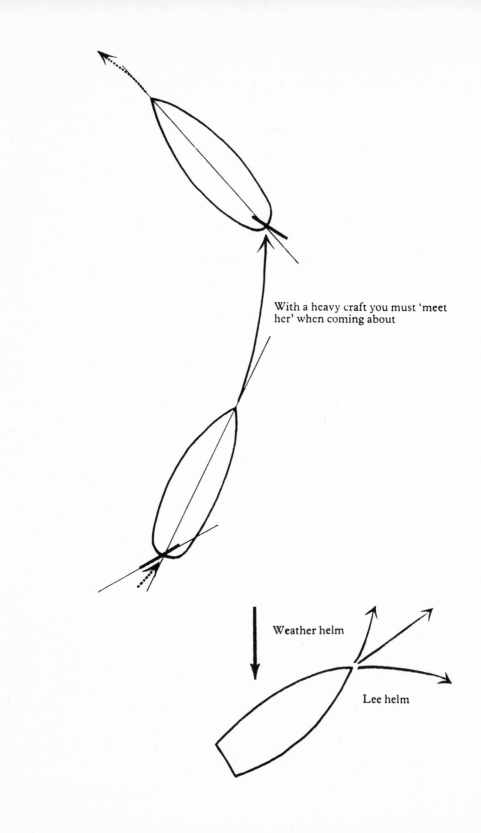

With a heavy craft you must 'meet her' when coming about

Weather helm

Lee helm

If the boat is a natural sluggard, or is barely moving, the evolution will be slow, and so must be your helm movement.

With a handy craft and plenty of speed you can manoeuvre as fast as you like, and the helm may be applied smartly but not viciously. You must in any case avoid jerking at the tiller; never move it other than smoothly and by easy stages.

A large, heavy boat will tend to continue its turn after the helm has been straightened up; that is to say, put amidships. This tendency must be countered, by bringing the helm amidships—and even beyond—before the boat is on the desired new course. This is known as *'meeting her'*.

balance of a boat

the boat's character

Before taking charge of any craft it is well to get to know its natural, fundamental tendencies—its individual character, in fact; and the best way to do that is to get the boat sailing and hold the tiller amidships. Does the boat balance? Three things may happen:

- it may want to luff, when said to *carry weather helm*;

- it may bear away; it *carries lee helm*;

- it may keep its course, and be *well balanced*.

Whether a boat carries lee or weather helm, or is balanced, depends on a great many factors, which we will now examine.

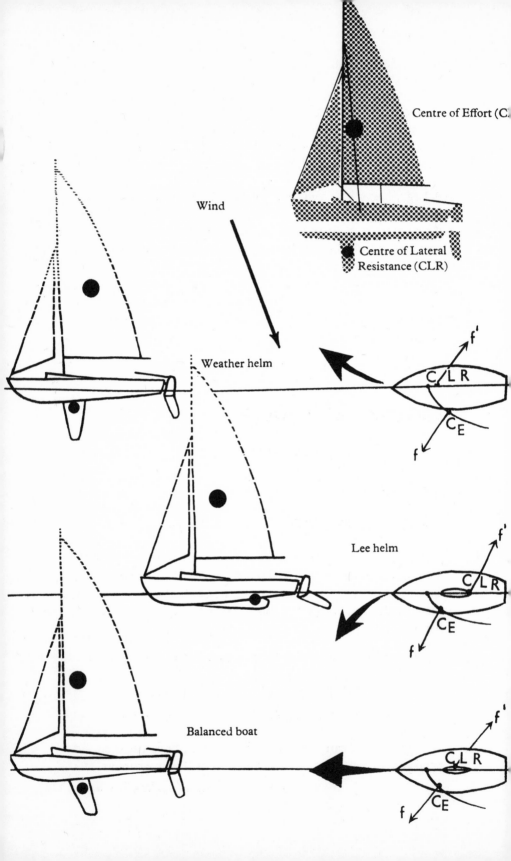

Centre of Effort (C...

Wind

Centre of Lateral
Resistance (CLR)

Weather helm

f'

CLR

C_E

f

Lee helm

f'

CLR

C_E

f

Balanced boat

f'

CLR

C_E

f

theory of centre of effort, and of centre of lateral resistance

● The point of application of the resultant f of all the forces which the wind exerts on the boat is called the *Centre of Effort*, or CE. It is mainly made up of the forces on the sails, but there are also forces acting on every part of the boat which constitute wind-age—upper works, superstructure, crew's bodies, rigging.

● The point of application of the force f', the resultant [1] of all forces exerted by the water on the underwater body of the boat is called the *Centre of Lateral Resistance*, CLR. Here again we have the force acting on the keel (the equal and opposite of the drift component of force f), and the force of resistance to forward movement of the hull (equal and opposite to the propulsive component of the same force f').

● If the CLR is ahead of the CE, forces f and f' form a couple tending to luff the boat, which is then said to carry weather helm. If, on the other hand, CLR is astern of CE, f and f' again form a couple, tending to make the boat pay off, when it is said to carry lee helm. If finally they coincide, or rather, are on the same vertical line, the boat is balanced.

It will be generally agreed that:

> the CE is at approximately the centre of gravity of the sail area;

> the CLR is at approximately the centre of gravity of the under-water body of the boat, including hull and centre-board.

Designers know by experience that for a well-balanced boat the theoretical CE so defined must be a little forward of the theoretical CLR.

This elementary theory does not account for all the phenomena that affect a boat's directional stability, but enables an explanation to be given of some of the practical means we have of influencing that stability.

[1] More precisely, it is a question of the horizontal component of these forces. For this reason, no mention is made of the upward thrust of Archimedes' Principle; it has no horizontal component.

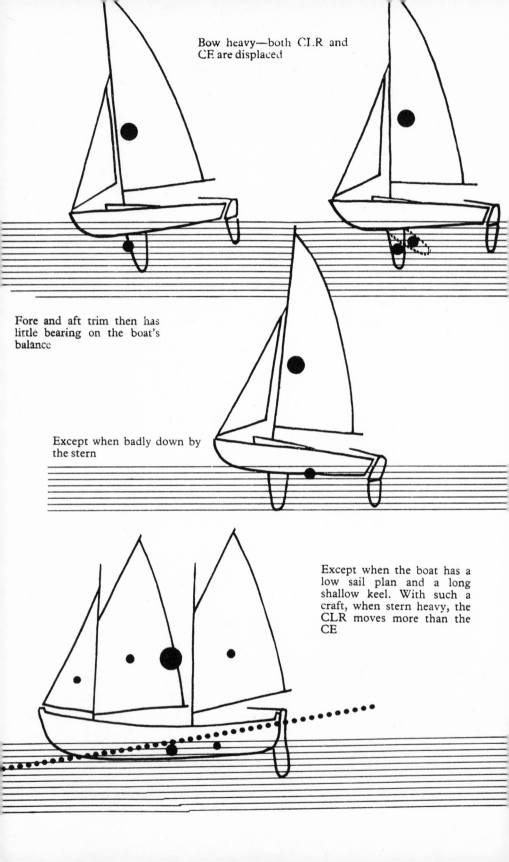

Bow heavy—both CLR and CE are displaced

Fore and aft trim then has little bearing on the boat's balance

Except when badly down by the stern

Except when the boat has a low sail plan and a long shallow keel. With such a craft, when stern heavy, the CLR moves more than the CE

the balance of a boat

If the mast is moved forward, the centre of effort is also moved forward, and the boat carries less weather helm, or more lee helm.

The same result is obtained if the mast is *raked*, or tilted, forward. When the rig includes more than one sail, taking off a sail forward brings back the CE, and gives more weather helm. The opposite holds good—if you *lower* an after sail—more lee helm. The same end is achieved, or almost so, by letting fly the sheet of a sail instead of lowering it. With a sloop, slacking off the jib-sheet makes the boat carry weather helm; slacking off the main sheet, lee helm.

If you can change helm characteristics by slacking sheets off more or less, obviously you get the same effect by the opposite process of sheeting sails in, taking care not to overdo it and cause turbulence.

Juggling with the sheets, therefore, gives you a very delicate control over the CE, and so over the balance of the boat.

But you can also to some degree shift the CLR, whether you have a long, pivoting centre-board or just a dagger-plate.

In the first case, lifting the centre-board begins to take effect, not so much by reducing its surface, as by bringing its centre aft, and, accordingly, the CLR, which causes the boat to carry less weather helm.

In the case of a dagger-plate, you can generally move the plate fore and aft—it has a little play in this direction—and so move the CLR.

Finally, we may mention—only to destroy it—a principle laid down in many books—quite serious books, too—which is, that if you load the bows down you immerse the forward sections more, which results in moving the CLR forward and giving more weather helm. Vice versa, a boat down by the stern will carry more lee helm. Experience generally proves this wrong, which is

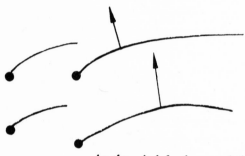

As the wind freshens and the sail's curvature changes, the CE moves aft.

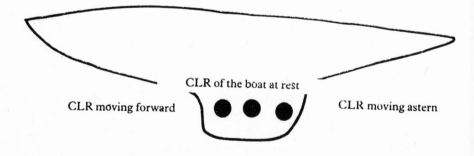

CLR of the boat at rest

CLR moving forward

CLR moving astern

largely accounted for by the fact that the extra load forward has the effect of raking the mast forward too, giving lee helm. Our experience goes to show that the fore-and-aft trim has little effect on directional stability,[1] except, in cases of:

> a boat with a low sail plan, light draught, a long. straight keel (a change of trim then does move the CLR a good deal, while the CE remains nearly stationary);
>
> an extreme stern-heavy condition.

movements of CE and CLR

Movement of the CE and CLR may be caused by other factors quite independent of anything that the crew intends.

centre of effort

Loss of shape in sails will move the CE. In particular, with a freshening wind, cloth stretches, and the flow (maximum curvature) in a sail moves aft.

This also moves aft the point of application of the force acting on each sail, and consequently the CE. Experience does tend to show that a boat carries less weather helm in a strong wind if a means is found to bring the flow back forward.

centre of lateral resistance

This shifts whenever the conditions in which the boat is moving change, whether in speed or leeway.

We will see first how a keel or centre-board works: the point of application of the force which the water exerts on it is at its geometrical centre when the boat is at rest, and moves towards the *leading edge* when the boat is in motion, ahead or astern, coming to rest about 1/4 to 1/3 of the width from the leading edge. In other words, the application point moves ahead when the boat goes ahead, astern when it goes astern.

The whole under-water surface of the boat behaves in the same way, including the keel/centre-board. Its CLR moves back or forward according as to whether the boat goes astern or ahead, and the longer the keel the more the CLR moves.

---

[1] To make it quite clear—'*little effect on directional stability*' does not contradict what we said above, on the influence of trim on a boat's sailing and performance.

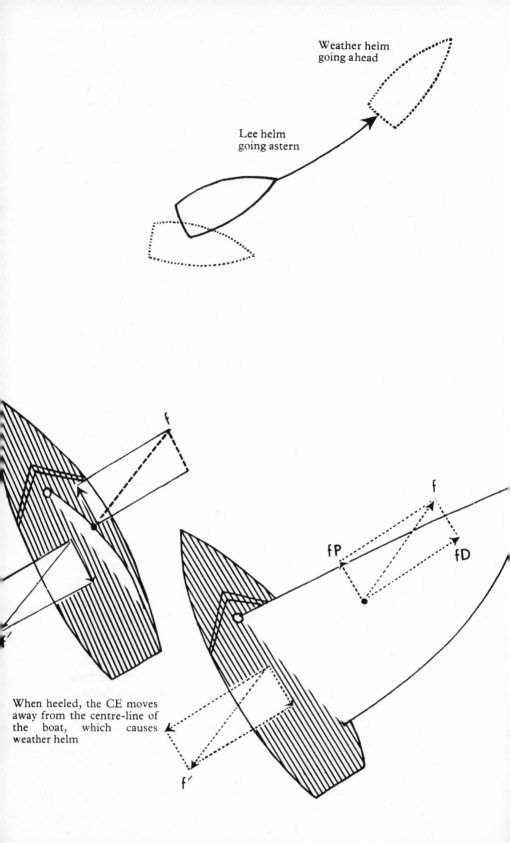

Weather helm
going ahead

Lee helm
going astern

f

f

fP

fD

When heeled, the CE moves
away from the centre-line of
the boat, which causes
weather helm

f´

From this the following facts appear:

- a boat tends to luff when going ahead, and bear away when going astern;

- it is general for a boat to be balanced under normal sailing conditions—under way ahead. (*If anything, it should, however, carry some weather helm; in the event of the helmsman going overboard, it is a great comfort for him to think the boat will luff up and wait for him*); it will generally carry slight lee helm when speed is low, and quite a lot when going astern. To appreciate this, put a centreboard boat head to wind until it starts to go astern; you will see how difficult it is to keep it head to wind.

the influence of heel on balance

When a sailing craft *under bare poles*, that is to say, with no sail hoisted, is moving forward with no heel in smooth water, and no wind, it has no tendency to yaw left or right (unless induced by propellor or screw), as the bottom of the boat is completely symmetrical; when, however, a boat is under sail, experience proves than an increased heel generally gives weather helm.

This can be explained, at first sight, as follows: as the boat heels, the CE moves to leeward, the forces f (wind on sail) and f' (water on keel, etc.), which were originally in the same perpendicular (which was why the boat was in balance), are now separated and form a couple tending to make the boat luff.

This is only a partial explanation of the facts; experiment proves that a boat heeled with no sail tends to want to turn in a direction opposite to that in which it is heeled. This seems to indicate that the under-water shapes in themselves have something to do with the luffing tendency. There is no absolute rule; every boat has its own tendencies:

- most luff when heeled;

- some stay in balance;

- others carry lee helm.

It is not hard to visualize an angle of heel destroying the symmetry of shape of a boat under water which may thus have a tendency to yaw either way.

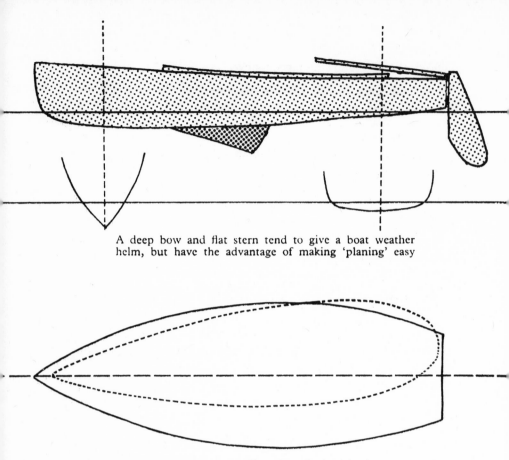

A deep bow and flat stern tend to give a boat weather helm, but have the advantage of making 'planing' easy

Distortion of the waterline when the boat heels

But nobody has ever found a way to explain exactly why a boat carries lee or weather helm when it heels, and it has never been possible to forecast just what helm a given craft will carry.

Designers and researchers have advanced different hypotheses and formulae for designing a craft that will balance when heeled, but they are hardly more than *ad hoc* recipes; none has really stood up to the test of experience. The only thing proved by experience is that a deep and straight forefoot, on the one hand, and a flat and beamy stern on the other, tend to give weather helm on the heel.

Apart from that, we must be content to rely on facts borne out by experience; generally speaking, heel involves weather helm, and in the case of some boats, light centre-board craft in particular, to a considerable degree.

steering and manoeuvring

We make the following distinction between steering and manoeuvring:

Steering consists of guiding the boat in a required direction. The course remains unchanged, except for restoring the boat's head to the required direction after an unintended yaw.

Manoeuvring, on the contrary, involves making a marked change of course. . . .

It seems as though there is a considerable difference between these two things; a boat is easily manoeuvrable to the extent that it changes course with ease, while, to be easy and pleasant to steer, it should hold its course satisfactorily by itself. Actually, a boat may well be easy, both to manoeuvre and to steer. For this condition to hold good, it is necessary that:

the boat does not tend to change course *by itself*,

that it is handy, and changes course easily *at the will of the helmsman:*

and these two conditions are not in the least contradictory.

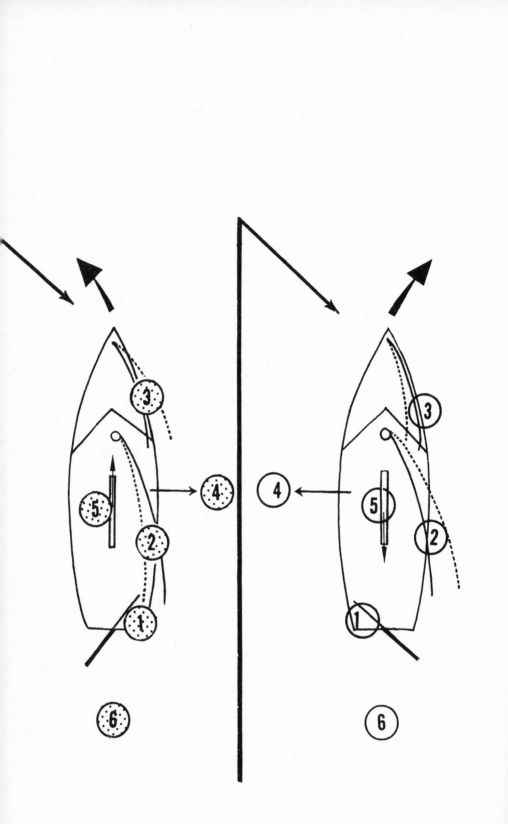

The qualities of a boat in this respect are mainly determined by the designer, who gave the boat its hull shape and sail plan. But the crew, too, have an important part to play; they must devote all their skill to getting the best out of the boat's qualities.

the crew and the boat

- Above all, manoeuvring a boat boils down to knowing how to luff, and how to bear away.

- Steering consists essentially of reducing lee and weather helm. This is why it is now important to go over again the control we have over steering and balance in so far as our present knowledge will take us. We can use one or more of the following possibilities.

to make the boat luff

1. Put the tiller to leeward

to make the boat carry weather helm

1. Sheet in the mainsail
2. Let fly the jib
3. Let the boat heel (naturally)
4. Bring the centre-board forward
5. Let the boat go faster

to make the boat bear away

1. Put the tiller to windward

to make the boat carry lee helm

1. Ease out the mainsail
2. Sheet the jib in
3. Induce a heel to windward
4. Bring the centre-board aft
5. Slow the boat up, or let it go astern

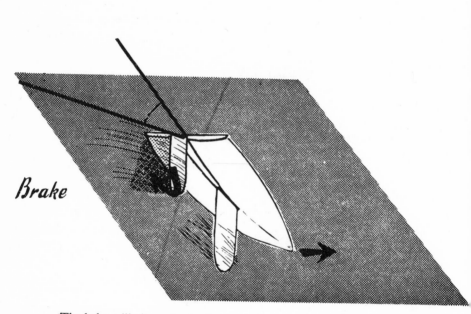

Brake

The helm will always brake the
boat as well as steer it. Every
movement of the helm applies
the brake

steering

Of all the means at your disposal—the tiller, so long as the boat is moving, is the one which gives the quickest results. Therefore the principal means for steering is the rudder, so long as all that is needed are small corrections to the course, or corrections to minor speed fluctuations by a slight change of heading. Such corrections need to be made as early as possible, before the yaw becomes serious, or, when on the wind, before the boat's speed drops too much. But, as we said before, the helm has always, as well as its turning function, a notable braking effect; every movement of the helm slows the boat. It should be used as little as possible, and therefore:

- correct always in good time, so that the least possible tiller movement will do;

- keep the boat balanced, and avoid undue lee or weather helm; try to get it to sail straight with helm amidships, using the latter only for the smallest corrections of course.

discretion in the use of the helm

If the helmsman notices a yaw in its early stages, it is enough to put the boat back on course, to apply a very small amount of helm for a moment, which will slow the boat less than if you wait for the yaw to be big enough to need a large correction. Thus, a good helmsman needs the ability to foresee deviations from the course, but even more important, *the greatest attention* at all times.

It is hardest to learn to use the tiller when close-hauled, because the helm is mainly used to keep the speed steady, and variations of speed are perceptible only after some experience. But, before all else, you must know that:

if you want to luff, because you think you could point slightly higher, do it gently, otherwise you may go so far that the sails shake in a big way (which would stop the boat dead); and stop luffing the second the first sign of lifting appears at the luff; on the other hand, if, through loss of wind or slatting sails, you have to bear away to gain speed, do it firmly and without hesitation; there is no fear that the rudder will slow the boat further. There will be far more braking effect if the sails are left slatting.

When a boat carries weather helm, if you want it to sail straight you must make a constant correction to the helm

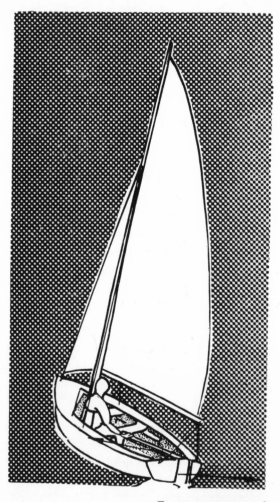

Every movement of the helm applies the brake

balance of the boat

When the boat carries helm—lee or weather—if you want it to go straight, you will have to make up for this natural tendency by keeping constant pressure on the helm, to windward or leeward as the case may be. This is inconvenient in several ways:

> the helmsman tires with the effort; a boat carrying a lot of weather helm may even exhaust him;
>
> the rudder is always acting as a brake;
>
> finally, experience shows a boat so trimmed is much less controllable.

The helmsman has therefore everything to gain by keeping the boat well balanced by the means we are going to indicate.

● Heeling can hardly be controlled by the weight of the crew, except in light centre-board craft; but in these latter the crew's weight must be used continuously to prevent heeling. As a rule boats will stay *balanced* at a quite definite angle of heel, but not a very high one (a few degrees); will carry lee helm when upright, or heeled a little to windward, and weather helm when really heeled to leeward. This property is so important that it is worth while at all costs to keep the best angle of heel, even to the detriment of the sail trim. On a larger boat you must content yourself with keeping the heel to a reasonable angle; a boat of properly balanced shape will sail properly even if overcanvassed; but if heel leads to excessive weather helm, you will do better to reduce your sail area.

● *The centre-board*, if its position fore and aft can be changed, can alter the balance a little, but not generally to any great extent. But it is not to be neglected, especially if the boat carries lee helm in spite of a moderately high angle of heel.

● *The sails* give important control of balance, either by varying their sheeting, or by reducing sail as required.

If it is only a question of a touch on the sheets, it is a good thing to adjust the jib only with a view to getting the best out of it from a propulsion point of view, and to keep the boat balanced by adjustment of the mainsail. This is because the jib sets better than the mainsail, and, on a boat which develops weather helm when heeled, the mainsheet is far more effective in balancing the craft than the jibsheets.

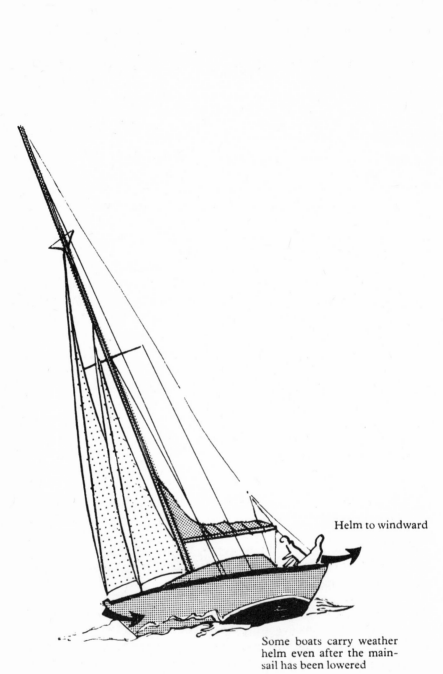

Helm to windward

Some boats carry weather
helm even after the main-
sail has been lowered

- To sum up: sheeting home the mainsail:

> brings the centre of effort aft;
> increases the heel,

two things which make for *weather helm.*

- And, on the contrary, letting out the mainsail:

> brings the CE forward;
> reduces heel

two things combining to give *lee helm.*

- But sheet home the jib:

> brings forward the CE, which gives lee helm, and
> increases the heel, which makes for weather helm.

These two tendencies oppose one another, and tend to cancel out. On light centre-board craft, which, as we have mentioned, carry a lot of weather helm when heeled, handling the main sheet is so easy and so effective that one uses it constantly, not only to keep the boat balanced, but also to steer. On a larger craft this sort of thing is tiring, and hardly ever done; you work through varying the sail area—taking in or shaking out *reefs* [1] in the mainsail, changing jibs, and so on.

What we have already said might be said again here in slightly different form; reefing the mainsail is generally much more effective than a change of jib. The latter will often have an opposite result to that intended; for instance, replacing a small jib with a big one ought to give lee helm; but the increased heel may well counter this effect and more, in which case the boat carries still more weather helm.

In fact, if you have a boat of pretty well balanced shape, the problem is not a big one, and you can leave sail adjustments to their proper function, of giving maximum drive. Unfortunately, if a boat carries undue weather helm when heeled, no sail adjustments may be of sufficient use. In that case, you must either put up with it, or reduce sail, remembering that a boat carrying too much sail forward is not always at its best.

One seldom meets a boat carrying lee helm when heeled; they are very rare (*and very dangerous*).

- Speed, as we have said, gives weather helm; at first sight it might well seem stupid to slow up in order to sail better. It is not, in fact, absurd, and

[1] Taking in a reef consists in diminishing the area of a sail by either rolling it or folding it on the boom. Shaking it out is the opposite.

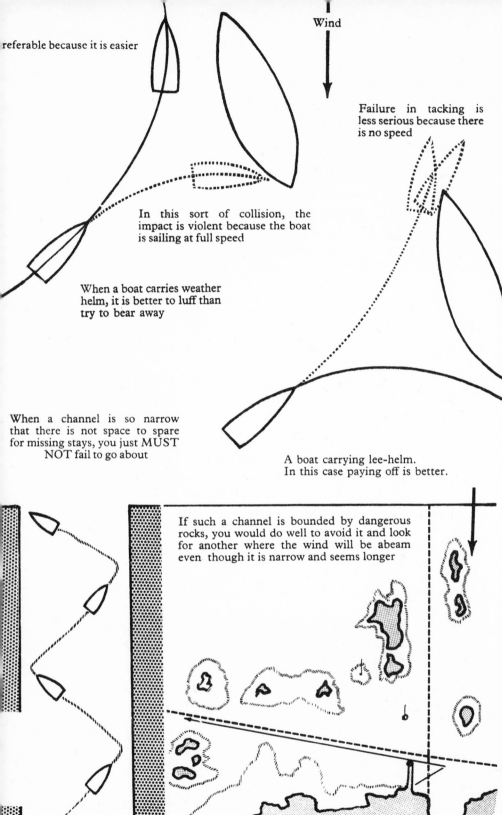

Wind

referable because it is easier

Failure in tacking is less serious because there is no speed

In this sort of collision, the impact is violent because the boat is sailing at full speed

When a boat carries weather helm, it is better to luff than try to bear away

When a channel is so narrow that there is not space to spare for missing stays, you just MUST NOT fail to go about

A boat carrying lee-helm. In this case paying off is better.

If such a channel is bounded by dangerous rocks, you would do well to avoid it and look for another where the wind will be abeam even though it is narrow and seems longer experience proves that it is *sometimes* of advantage when close-hauled to get closer to the wind and sail less fast; the boat carries less weather helm, and the gain in distance made good to windward more than offsets the loss of speed.

manoeuvring

We have explained that a boat is *manoeuvrable* when it is in a state to carry out immediately any evolution desired by the crew. This business of handiness is not easy; whether a boat is handy depends on the boat itself and the manner in which it is handled.

A boat which—assuming correct handling—lends itself to easy manoeuvring, is said to be *handy*. But, however handy a boat may be, it can appear to be the opposite if badly handled. Take an example; a good handy craft, if sailed too close to the wind, has no speed, or next to none, and will not obey the crew in these conditions; the helm is practically out of action. If the crew wants to go about, they will have to bear away and gain speed before they can do so. The boat is said to be un-manoeuvrable.

Sometimes lack of handy qualities may be limited to certain types of manoeuvres. Thus, a boat carrying much weather helm, whether this is an inborn quality, or due to poor sail adjustment, may be quite capable of luffing and going about, while bearing away and gybing are difficult. On the other hand, a boat carrying lee helm may be impossible to tack and easy to gybe.

It might be thought of little consequence for a boat to lack handiness in mid-ocean. However, there's not much hope for anyone who falls overboard. . . .

But it *is* essential to keep a boat manoeuvrable when in a dangerous area and in the neighbourhood of obstructions:

- Entering harbour, you are always liable to find an unexpected obstacle, and you may have to do something on the spur of the moment; the boat must be capable of doing it.

- And when you are tacking through a channel edged by dangerous rocks, you cannot afford not to get round each time, and nothing should be left undone to lessen the risk of being caught *in irons*.

If the crew sits well out, more sail can be carried, and the boat will be handier and have more power

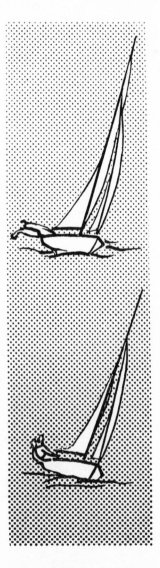

The alternative to the crew using its weight properly—sail must be reduced or left to shake. By and large, power and manoeuvrability will suffer

how to keep a boat handy

Keeping a boat's handiness involves very little:

- carry enough sail—but not too much—in the right parts of the boat,
- maintain speed.

Limited as these requirements are, they do call for a little comment.

- The amount of sail to carry is fixed by the need for speed.

If the boat is carrying too much, it will heel and go off to leeward excessively, head resistance will be high, and the performance of the sails will be poor. Also, the heeling may make it impossible to balance the boat.

Too little sail deprives the boat of its motive power, and speed and acceleration will be inadequate.

If you want to keep the boat entirely handy, you must carry that amount of canvas the boat would stand if it were close-hauled, even though you may be actually on a point of sailing which would permit more canvas without too much heeling. Any emergency might compel you to luff and come up close to the wind; the sail area which was all right with a beam wind may then be altogether too much. Similarly, as we said above, the motive power of a boat is directly proportional to its righting couple (speaking always of sailing to windward).

Now, we have seen that with dinghies this couple depends on the position of the crew; on such boats the crew will hang right out in a fresh breeze if it wants to carry enough sail to go fast. If the crew remains seated inboard, the boat will heel too much and become out of control.

- Proper *distribution of the sail plan* means that the boat will remain properly balanced at all normal angles of heel. It is an ideal which is not easy to attain, and may not go with easy steering. Take the case of a boat not naturally well balanced, which carries heavy weather helm when heeled; with a good breeze, it will heel, and, to make steering easy you may be tempted to carry more sail forward to reduce the resulting weather helm (in other words, you might be tempted to carry a large jib and reefed mainsail). This will make steering easy all right, but you will lose such handiness as the boat may possess; when you luff, and the boat comes upright, it will carry lee helm, and it will be hard to put about. In such a case, you must compromise. Broadly speaking, it will pay to accept a little trouble with the steering when a boat has weather helm, in order to keep it comparatively handy.

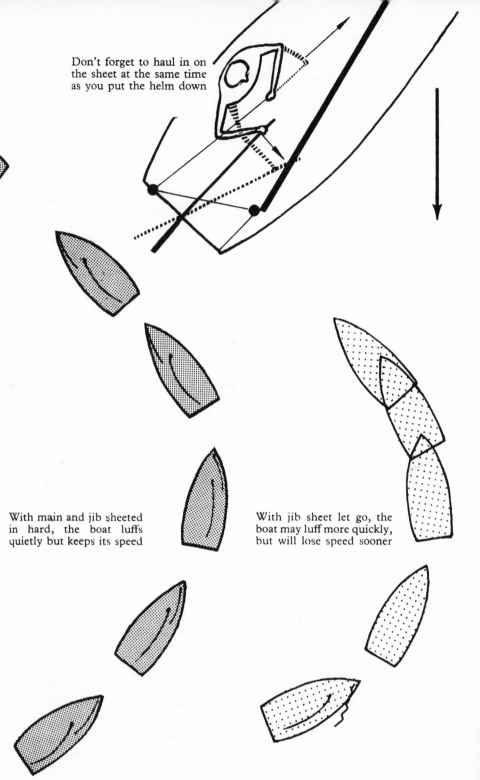

Don't forget to haul in on the sheet at the same time as you put the helm down

With main and jib sheeted in hard, the boat luffs quietly but keeps its speed

With jib sheet let go, the boat may luff more quickly, but will lose speed sooner

● *Speed* is a vital factor. It makes the steering more effective, which is a function of the square of the speed. Suppose the right sails have been chosen, both for area and position, the speed depends on your course relative to the wind direction, and on sheet handling, the two being dependent on one another. We have already spoken of the doubtful value, when beating, of trying to sail too close to the wind; and, when the neighbourhood of obstructions makes it essential to be under full control, you must not hesitate to sail quite full, as far as is necessary to maintain speed; speed must be your first priority in these conditions.

Having gained speed, you must take care over the trimming of the sheets. Very often, they need to be adjusted to within an inch or so, if you are to get the best speed and manoeuvrability out of your boat. Experience only will teach this, but you will avoid a lot of experimental fumbling if you realize the following: if the boat does not pick up speed in a few seconds, something has gone wrong, and you will gain no more speed however long you wait; the cause is generally that the sheets are too hard in for the particular course; or alternatively the sails may be slatting, which you can both see and hear; sometimes you may be pointing too close. Above all, a rough sea, especially a nasty short chop, can cut the speed of the boat a great deal; in this case especially you must avoid getting too near the wind and sheeting in too hard; sails will often pull better in rough weather when they are noticeably lifting.

handling a boat under way

We have already spoken of how careful you must be with the tiller when under way, and will not go over that again. It is useful and sometimes essential to use the steering powers of the sail plan to carry out some manoeuvres.

One will need to use the sheets a great deal more when manoeuvring than when just steering with them always remembering—as we have said before —that the mainsail is far more useful for this purpose than the jib. The main sheet therefore should be worked in conjunction with the tiller by the helmsman; going about, he will sheet in the mainsail to help the boat to luff. Some people are in favour of letting the jib fly at the same time. We think this is a mistake; it should be kept sheeted hard until the moment it starts to come aback. This is because in the first place its effect on the operation is small, and in the second place because, sheeted in, it continues to give drive and a worthwhile degree of speed to help in getting about.

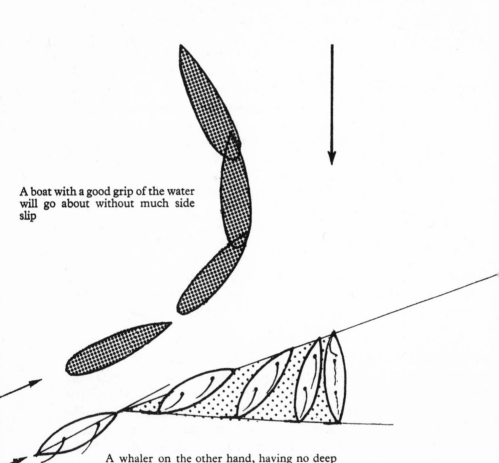

A boat with a good grip of the water will go about without much side slip

A whaler on the other hand, having no deep keel will drift away while going about

You can only make use of the heeling effect on quite small craft, but it can work well with them; so much so that it is possible to carry out all types of evolution solely by moving the weight of the crew, without touching the tiller. Often, getting a centre-board craft off a beach, you have to carry on for a while with the rudder up, and in this case you will use the sheets and your weight. For instance, you have left the shore full-and-by, and have to come about; you sheet the mainsail in hard and increase the heel, when the boat will come about without hesitation, provided it has some speed. Gybing is not so easy; you must give the boat a pronounced counter-heel, start with the wind abeam or even more aft, and let the sheets right off.

drift and heel during a manoeuvre

When the heading of the boat has been changed by the use of the helm there is a tendency to go on in the original direction, drifting. This tendency will be reduced by efficient 'anti-drift' arrangements—keel or centre-board. A boat with a large and efficient keel will go off straight away on its new course.

On the other hand, a boat having no keel, or only a small one, will skid off quite a lot towards the outside of the turn, and will drift a moment before taking up something like the new course. The thing will be even clearer when a boat of this sort—a whaler under sail, for instance, sailing close-hauled, and with a good deal of leeway, wants to go about. The drift caused by the evolution, on top of the normal leeway, will add up so much that, after luffing, the stem of the boat will still carry on in the original direction (see drawing).

The centrifugal force which causes this also sets up heeling. This force of inertia acts centrally on the hull somewhere near the waterline; the force which opposes it acts on the keel, which is normally below the waterline. It follows that these two forces form a couple, which heels the boat to the outside of the turn. This is not to be neglected at speed; it assumes a special importance when luffing, when the centrifugal heel is added to the natural heel of the boat. Thus, a boat running free at a good speed will assume an alarming heel if luffed up sharply.

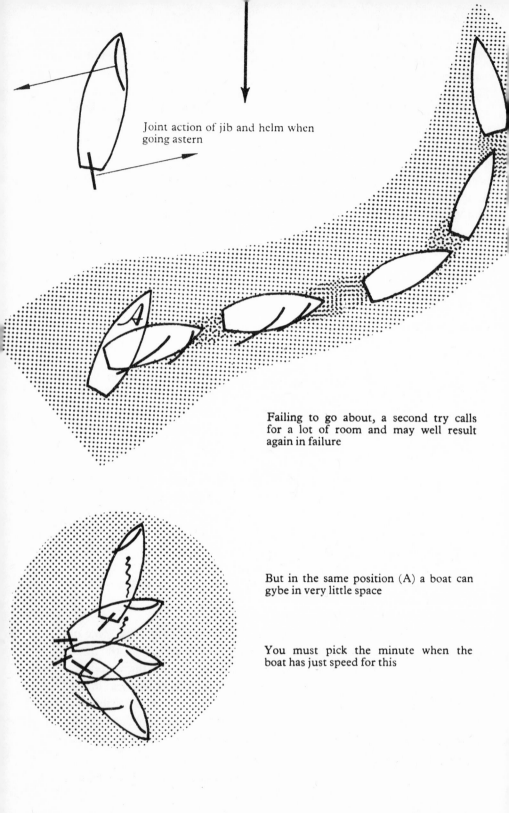

Joint action of jib and helm when going astern

Failing to go about, a second try calls for a lot of room and may well result again in failure

But in the same position (A) a boat can gybe in very little space

You must pick the minute when the boat has just speed for this

particular cases of manoeuvring

We have so far assumed that the boat retains its forward speed during manoeuvres. If the speed drops, or the boat is even going astern, things are quite different; the boat takes on lee helm, the action of the tiller is annulled or reversed, heeling has no effect on steering, if it exists. You then have to use special methods, and they must be co-ordinated. We will analyse a few such cases:

● the boat is almost head to wind, and stopped; it has a pronounced tendency to pay off, as it has lee helm from lack of speed. If you want to stop it doing so, if, for instance, you have been caught *in irons* when going about—stopped before reaching the eye of the wind, you have two ways of continuing:

> pull the jib aback, which tends to bring the boat round, but also tends to send it astern, and so make it carry more lee helm and more inclined to pay off (this will rarely be enough);

> reverse the helm; this, of course, on no account before the boat has sternway and has still more lee helm. Used alone, this is generally too late.

> Use of both of these expedients together, on the other hand, is highly effective. The wind force on the jib combines with the water force on the rudder-blade to set up a turning couple on the boat, which will generally take you through a tack even when you have been caught in irons 5° or 10° off the wind's eye.

● Take now the case where a tack has failed, and none of these methods comes off. One way out is to let the boat pay off, to get speed and try to tack again. This needs a lot of sea-room, and may well fail again.

But, to return to the point of failure, we can see that the boat carries lee helm as it gains sternway, and is quite inclined to bear away sharply, and to gybe. Hence the solution is:

● back the jib, to accentuate the paying-off and sternway;

● put the helm down wind, so as to further the pay-off, with the assistance of the sternway;

● the boat pays off, gets the wind abaft the beam; the mainsail fills, and sternway stops; that is the moment to reverse the helm again, though it will have no immediate effect; the boat, with a lot of lee helm, continues to bear away;

The helmsman wants to luff; the rudder has not the slightest effect, because the boat has no speed. This is because the helmsman had sheeted his sails in too flat

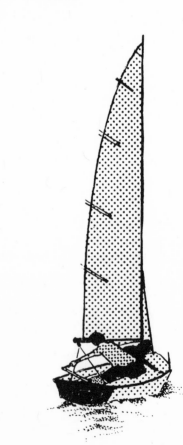

- the boat moves ahead under the now full mainsail;
- the helm is at once and increasingly brought to windward to continue bearing away;
- the boat very quickly gybes, the whole thing having been done almost without forward speed, and therefore in a very small space.

The very rapid success of this gybing is due to the fact that the boat was going astern at the start, which is exactly what we meant when we said a little earlier that 'a gybe is never easier, and never needs so little room, as when you have just failed to tack'. This is true especially for boats with a tendency to lee helm and a tendency to miss stays.

- For every type of boat there is a minimum speed below which any manoeuvre is practically impossible. More exactly, when a boat's speed is down to next to nothing, it has lee helm to the point where it will bear away whatever you do. If a little speed is left, it may perhaps remain balanced, and go straight ahead, regardless of the rudder direction. Often, after a tack, the helmsman tries to steer with his tiller before he has regained speed. His boat pays off too far on the new course, he puts the helm hard to leeward, which applies the brake so hard that the boat cannot get enough speed to give steerage way. In such a case, the only thing to do is to put the tiller back amidships, and let the boat pick up speed in whatever direction it will; then—and only then—will the helm become effective.

To sum up, four factors are essential to the success of any manoeuvre:

- speed and handiness,
- precise handling of the tiller,
- correct sheet handling,
- judicious placing of the crew.

Often, one of these remedies will bring success in a manoeuvre, but often you will have to put several into force. It is a matter of training in their use separately, so that they will become automatic and used without hesitation when the time comes.

In addition, every boat has its good qualities, and also some bad ones which the crew must take the earliest chance of learning.

Knowing its faults the good helmsman:

will never let his craft lose steerage way except possibly when on open water, in which case precautions against losing a man overboard will be redoubled;

will in crowded waters always keep his boat as handy as possible, and, should certain manoeuvres be impossible, will keep away from places where they are unavoidable.

It is very true that the secret of boat-handling consists of never getting into a position where you have to carry out an impossible manoeuvre!

appendix on rudders

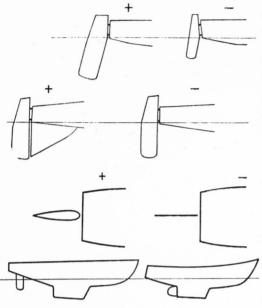

The efficacy of a rudder depends on several factors:

● The pressure of the water on the rudder-blade is obviously proportional to its surface;

● but this pressure is higher if the rudder is hinged on to a fixed fin—quite possibly the keel itself—than if it is out by itself;

● it is higher still if thick and shaped like an aerofoil than if it is flat and thin.

● Next, the rudder has a more powerful and certain effect if it is placed well astern; its power then has greater leverage on the hull.

● Finally, just as for the sail plan, the *aspect ratio* of a rudder is a matter of great importance. The aspect ratio is the ratio of height to width of the blade.

For a given rudder angle—less than the critical angle—and for the same surface, the pressure developed on the rudder will be increased in proportion to the aspect ratio. On the other hand, the stalling angle will drop with an increase of aspect ratio.

The table will give an idea of the stalling angles for thick and suitably profiled rudders:

Aspect ratio	Stalling angle
5	12°
2	14°
1	33°
0.5	45°

From this it will be gathered that full advantage can be gained from a deep and narrow rudder blade only if the helm is handled with discretion.

A boat is said to have good *directional stability* when you can leave the helm to itself and the boat will not go off its course too quickly. Some craft are blessed with perfect directional stability, and you can leave the helm without them going a degree off the course. Others, on the other hand, will yaw off violently the second you leave the helm. Directional stability depends largely on the longitudinal profile of the underwater body—hull, keel and centreboard (if any). It will be very much better if this longitudinal profile is well drawn out and extends well aft. A boat with a long keel, reaching right aft to the stern-post, may be expected to have good directional stability, while one with a thin deep centre-board or a narrow keel placed amidships will be poor in this respect. Sometimes a boat is given only a narrow keel, with a view to less wetted surface, and a fin is added to it astern, to give the desired directional stability.

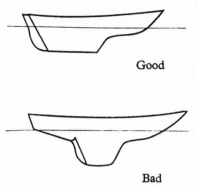

Good

Bad

Directional stability, of course, can normally be had only at the cost of manoeuvrability.

And besides, you have to compromise between the following demands:

● a narrow, deep keel is highly efficient as a preventer of leeway, and is thus of great advantage in working to windward;

● but for getting into harbours where there is little water and, in particular, for taking the ground (intentionally or otherwise) a shallow draft and long keel are blessings (giving good stability when aground).

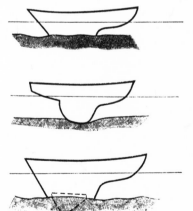

A good compromise is, a fairly long but shallow keel, housing a drop centre-board or plate.

Finally, never forget that directional stability depends very much on balanced sections and a boat's behaviour when heeled.

We have said that a number of craft develop weather helm under heel without going into the reasons, confining ourselves to saying it was a matter of fact, proved by experience and not open to argument.

The exact causes *are* very much the subject of argument; the following is put forward as a general explanation:

That a boat has attained a certain speed resistance to forward motion is mainly the result of wave formation. This slow leakage of energy is due to the fact that a boat, having a certain volume, has to displace the water in front to allow it to have a space to move into; when upright, the shape of the hull is symmetrical, and so is the system of waves caused. But when the craft heels the sections become asymmetrical, different wave formations occur on the two sides of the boat, and the resultants of the forces setting up these wave formations are asymmetrically disposed. They are no longer self-cancelling, and may form a couple making for luffing or bearing away.

It seems a proven fact that imbalance of a boat is bound up with the wave resistance; it is not noticed until a certain speed is reached, and the wave formations become of sufficient size. As the wave resistance is dependent on the shape of the boat itself it is a logical conclusion that directional instability connected with heeling is, in fact, the result of distortion of the underwater sections.

Various devices have been suggested for predicting the behaviour of a boat when heeled, and for designing balanced boats. The best known and most used is the 'Metacentric Shelf System' of Admiral Turner. According to him, it is essential, and sufficient, that the centres of gravity of the immersed parts of the sections should stay parallel to the centre line of the heeled craft, in a longitudinal and vertical plane. This requirement involves a certain symmetry between the sections on either side of this longitudinal plane, and expert opinion is pretty well unanimous that keeping to such conditions gives a fairly well-balanced vessel—sometimes a very well-balanced one. But there certainly are craft which in practice show extraordinarily good balance, in spite of being quite at variance with the principle; which tends to prove that the Turner rule may be sufficient, but is not essential.

Induced rolling and broaching-to

The fact of a boat carrying weather helm when heeled has, apart from being a nuisance, and giving rise to constant braking with the incessant use of helm to correct it, two unfortunate consequences.

On the one hand, this condition is favourable to *broaching-to*; the boat, say on a broad reach, starts on a luff; the heel increases due to the changing wind and to centrifugal force; this heel increases the rate of luffing—and so on; if the helmsman has not acted in time, he finds the boat broaching-to—in an uncontrollable rush up to windward, all the more dangerous in that it generally happens in heavy weather; the boat may end up hard on the wind, with a heavy list, and may well finish by capsizing if the reserve stability is insufficient.

Again, with the wind astern, you may start an intensive roll. The process goes as follows: the boat starts a yaw to port, heels to starboard under centrifugal force, which tends to work up to a broaching-to; the helmsman manages to stop this by violent tiller movement, and the boat goes into a violent starboard yaw, heeling to port. This yaw is dealt with similarly to the first, and so on; the boat goes on, yawing violently from side to side, and rolling viciously. It can be very difficult to get out of the vicious circle, and gybing or broaching-to are imminent dangers. This is called *induced rolling*.

Now, this can be very disagreeable, and even dangerous, if there is as well a rhythm between the boat's natural rolling cycle and the occurrence of two successive induced rolls. This is rhythmic rolling, which we have mentioned when speaking of the hull.

The personality of a boat

Every vessel has its own particular character, depending on the design of the rudder, the arrangement of the keel surfaces, and the underwater shape, balanced or otherwise. It is in accordance with these characteristics that you must handle the boat.

We will make a special study of certain cases, in order to show how we can use such characteristics as our boat contains.

● A *hanging rudder*—that is, one which is hinged on the transom.

This arrangement is common on sailing dinghies. As their anti-drift arrangements generally boil down to a narrow but deep centre-board, you get little directional stability; in return, the rudder blade, by virtue of its aft position, is most effective. Such boats are very handy, and can carry out evolutions under rudder in a very tight turning circle. They quite literally pivot on their centre-boards. But they are not easy to control without the rudder, so this needs to be pivoted so that it can be more or less raised in shallow water. Sometimes, particularly if the boat is one meant for beginners, it has a small fin aft, which increases directional stability. This obviously reduces the manoeuvrability somewhat, but it does enable you if necessary to steer and manoeuvre without the rudder.

Sailing dinghies are generally designed without regard to balance when heeled, the reason being that the crew of such vessels can keep the boat level by using their weight, and that the flat, broad stern which makes for such exciting speeds is not compatible with good balance of sections. It is better, in most peoples' view, to forgo built-in balance when heeled, and to make the special effort called for to keep the boat upright. The effort is essential if you want to get the best out of the boat in the way of speed and handiness.

Hanging rudders are found on plenty of inshore cruisers. With a cruiser, you cannot expect such concentrated attention from the helmsman, nor can the crew be asked to hang over the side all day long. You must therefore go for directional stability, and improve the balance. One way is, for the designer to build in a fairly long keel, for directional stability, and flattened lines forward to improve balance.

● *Rudder continuing a fixed keel*

The shaft, or *stock*, of the rudder goes through the hull by means of a *rudder trunk*, except when the keel goes right back to the sternpost.

(*a*) If the keel is not very long, the boat can be expected to have poor directional stability; this will be aggravated by the fact that the rudder, placed nearly amidships, will have less leverage. Yawing will be hard to control, and with a stern wind steering may be difficult. The turning circle, on the other hand, will be excellent.

Actually, everything depends on balance; if the boat is well balanced, it will be steerable and handy. On the contrary, if it carries a lot of weather helm when heeled, steering will be difficult. Such a vessel, wonderfully manoeuvrable but griping badly on the heel, is hard to steer with the wind aft, and prone to induced rolling.

(*b*) If the keel extends to the transom, directional stability will be far better, and the rudder will have a powerful action—a boat very easy to steer, but perhaps rather hard work to handle. If the boat is in balance, you might get an exceptionally good directional stability —*the Bristol Channel pilot cutter*, for instance.

Peculiarities of balance may lead to craft being very different in their handling qualities; a well-balanced boat will gybe very much better than it will tack, while a craft with a tendency to *gripe* (weather helm), is always ready to go about head to wind. Yet their underwater profile may be very similar.

● *Rudder hinged on a small fin, independent of the keel*

This is a favourite solution for light cruisers; they call only for a moderate sail plan and can make do with a much-reduced keel surface. To improve the

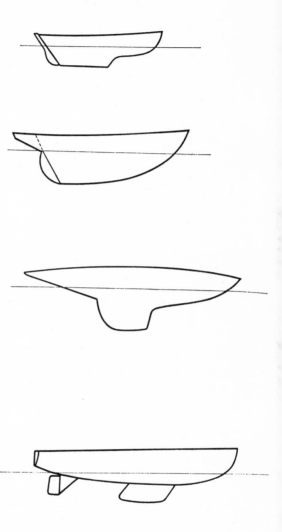

directional stability, which the reduced keel entails, they have a fixed fin astern, on which the rudder is hung.

You get a boat which steers easily, but sometimes to the detriment of handiness.

● *Powered craft*

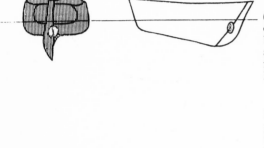

(a) *A cavity for the propeller,* hollowed out in a normal type rudder blade. The boat retains most of the sailing characteristics it would have were no screw fitted, provided the cavity is not too large.

Under power, the slipstream of the propeller leaves the cavity and drives the boat without much extra pressure on the rudder blade. The boat will not turn so well under power as under sail, unless it is moving fast.

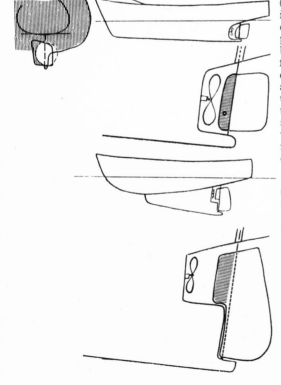

(b) *Rudder all astern of the screw.* This is the usual arrangement with shallow-draft boats designed for running under power alone. The rudder is generally a balanced one, that is to say, part of it is forward of the rudder stock. This both diminishes the effort needed on the helm, and directs a part of the slipstream from the propeller over the rudder, so that the boat will turn without forward speed. But the rudder does not grip the water well, and when the screw is not turning the boat steers and manoeuvres badly under sail.

(c) *A mixed solution:* a combination of rudder hung on the keel, and balanced aft of the propeller. Such a rudder works well under sail or power, whether or not the boat has way on.

(d) *Outboard motors,* as they can send the slipstream in any desired direction, make perfect rudders while they are running. Of course, they have no effect whatever when the boat is sailing or drifting.

Manoeuvring under power

The handling of a motor-boat is quite different from that of a vessel under sail.

In the first place, you must take account of the individual character of the boat, which depends on the relative positions of rudder and propeller. With the type of boats shown above as (*a*), remember, you cannot do anything without forward speed; given this, the boat is probably more manageable with the propeller stopped. With type (*b*) boats, on the other hand, you can hardly steer them at all unless the propeller is turning 'ahead'. Even if stopped, the boat will turn under rudder and propeller together. But even if the boat has forward speed, it will not answer the helm if the propeller is not turning 'ahead'.

Next, the screw has a certain steering effect. The boat behaves as though the screw were rubbing against the bottom of the sea. This because the more deeply immersed blades meet greater pressure of water.

In the usual case of a 'right-handed' propeller, the stern of the boat will tend to turn:

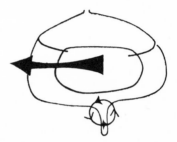

- To the right, when propeller turns 'ahead';
- To the left, when propeller turns 'astern'.

This effect is more marked with a large-diameter screw, when the screw is not deeply immersed, at slow speeds of the boat, and when the propeller is well aft. It is more pronounced, too, when the engine is in 'astern' gear.

Finally, do not forget that wind has its effect on a power boat; the windage is never negligible. Generally speaking, motor-boats have lee helm, and will go off down wind more readily than they will luff; in a strong breeze many power craft will find it hard to come up into wind from a position with the wind abeam. So long as a power craft is drifting with the wind, you must remember that its centre of lateral resistance (CLR) moves as its speed varies; thus, a boat without way on is drifting with the wind abeam; it is better to go astern to pay off, for everything then conspires to make it easy to do so. When moving ahead the boat will be less willing to bear away, for the drift of the boat and the thrust of the screw will join forces to make it luff.

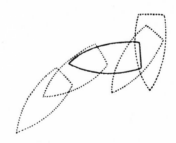

A fact often lost sight of, whereas, in many cases, taking advantage of this property of the boat will help in manoeuvring

boat handling, gear and equipment 5

some general points

In the course of the preceding chapters we have tried to explain how a boat sails, and we hope we have given you the means of understanding the reactions and behaviour of various sized craft. At the same time, this analysing of the subject has led us to separate certain facts which in practice are closely related.

It is therefore necessary, after separate examination of various theoretical aspects, to return to them and look at them as a whole, as they come in real life. In view of the wide practical differences between the various types of craft, we shall for the moment limit ourselves to the case of small boats, the sort that are used for racing or day sailing in sheltered waters where a lookout is kept or where other craft are in sight. Such boats are generally light, unballasted, and have a centre-plate or centre-board, so that an appropriate title for the second part of this volume might be— 'Handling the sailing dinghy'.

All the same, it is an enormous subject, and it would be vain to consider the following chapters as a complete course in the handling of a boat. What we aim at is a collection of exercises in thinking out and solving the problems the subject presents, rather than a collection of individual instructions. We shall look into a number of 'evolutions' in the light of what we have already said—matters which call for understanding rather than instruction.

This will, it is to be hoped, put the reader in the best position to study, understand and carry out every facet of boat handling.

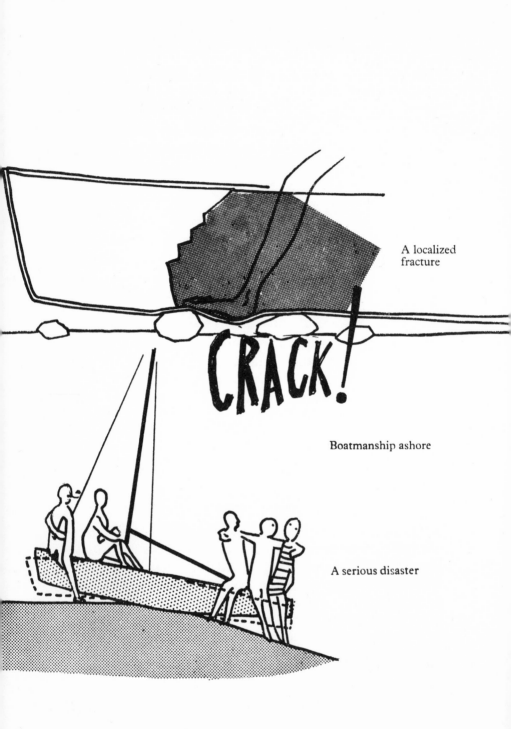

A localized
fracture

CRACK!

Boatmanship ashore

A serious disaster

practical considerations

The beginner is in for plenty of troubles, large and small, if he does not take the precaution of learning a few fairly simple bits of practical knowledge, and some tips for his own safety.

At first sight they will seem of minor importance, but ignorance and inattention will soon transform:

> a peaceful pastime into a source of worry;

> a pretty boat into a useless wreck;

> a harmless sport into a dangerous one.

We will assume you are about to go for a short sail, and will describe at some length how you should set about it and the precautions you should take.

boatmanship ashore

Even the smallest of boats is very tough when seen from the point of view of the worst that sea and wind can do to it; but, out of its element, or submitted to unusual stress, it is quite fragile.

On shore a boat must be regarded as an invalid, at the mercy of the slightest *faux pas* or ill-directed strain, so handle it carefully, treat it as gently as you can, and put it down softly on a level surface. Don't step inside it, and never sit on it while ashore.

inspection of gear

The first thing to do is to check that all gear you are going to need for safe sailing is present and correct.

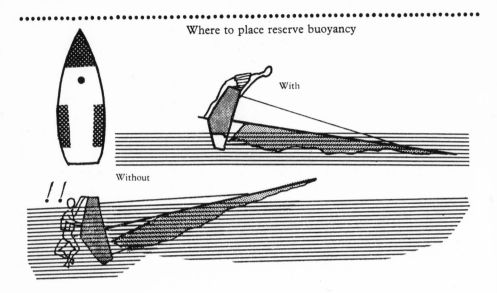

Where to place reserve buoyancy

With

Without

life jackets

Each crew member should have his own reserve buoyancy. There is a great deal of variety—waistcoats, Mae Wests, belts, jackets—and so on; but the object is always to keep afloat a fully dressed person in an emergency.

Here are some fashion plates; the celebrated 1890 model had its heyday with ships of the White Star Line.

reserve buoyancy

The purpose of buoyancy bags or tanks is to keep the boat and crew above water in the event of a capsize, until help comes. Usually well-trained crews will, if their buoyancy arrangements are adequate, be able to right their boats, clear them of water and carry on sailing with no outside help. Such equipment may consist:

of water-tight compartments. Before starting off, check that all plugs, for draining or ventilation, are in place.

of inflatable bags, which must be blown up and suitably lashed.

of blocks of foamed plastics, also properly fixed.

anchor and cable

The purpose of these are to anchor near the shore for any purpose, or to let the crew hold the boat stationary on open water, in case of any sudden accident, while they repair the damage or recover their spirits.

The cable must be made fast inside the boat by its free end, and *flaked down*, that is, coiled down in the order in which it will go out. The anchor should sit on top of the coil, and, of course, be bent (fastened) on to the cable ready for immediate use.

the bailer

Make sure the bailer is there before you set off; you can't do without it—to empty the boat of all the water that gets aboard one way or another—spray and spindrift, the result of a sudden heel when you make a mistake, and so on. While on the subject of water aboard, it is a good thing to cork the *drain hole*—the little hole at the bottom of the transom that lets the water out when the boat is on shore. Nowadays many racing dinghies are fitted with self-bailers, but for general-purpose dinghy sailing the common-or-garden bailer is essential.

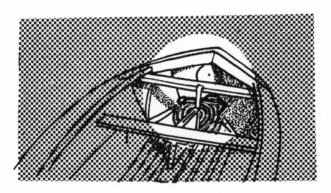

scull or paddle

This is to get you home if the wind lets you down.

Finally, check that you have the gear the boat needs in order to be able to sail:

    Centre-board, or *dagger-plate*, if detachable—*rudder*—*tiller.*

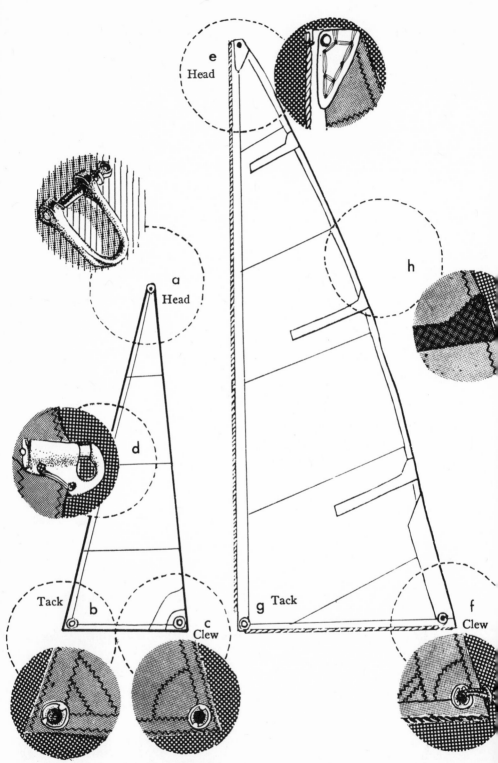

e
Head

a
Head

h

d

Tack

b

c
Clew

g Tack

f
Clew

See page 416 for sail track and slides.

rigging the boat

The word rigging has a pretty wide meaning. In everyday use rigging means getting the sails ready, so that there is nothing to do before leaving except to hoist them. For a sailing dinghy, rigging, though a simple matter, needs close attention—the reward will be in better setting of the sails—and some care, for a sail is easily damaged. In particular, see it does not come into contact with anything which might tear it, or any abrasive substance (sand is a great enemy of sailcloth). When the sails are made of cotton, take care, too, that they don't get wet unnecessarily; if they are damp in parts they will be pulled out of shape. Finally, a lot of damage can be done to a sail by a cigarette, especially to one made of Terylene or nylon. Do not, therefore smoke while rigging the boat.

When you fetch the sails keep them well rolled up under your arm; don't let a corner or a sheet trail on the ground, and don't put them down anywhere but in the boat. Mark the three corners of both jib and mainsail:

tack,

head,

clew.

The drawing will show you exactly how to recognize them.

a Jib head, and its shackle

b Tack

c Clew

d Snap shackle

e Head of mainsail

f Clew

g Tack

h Batten pocket.

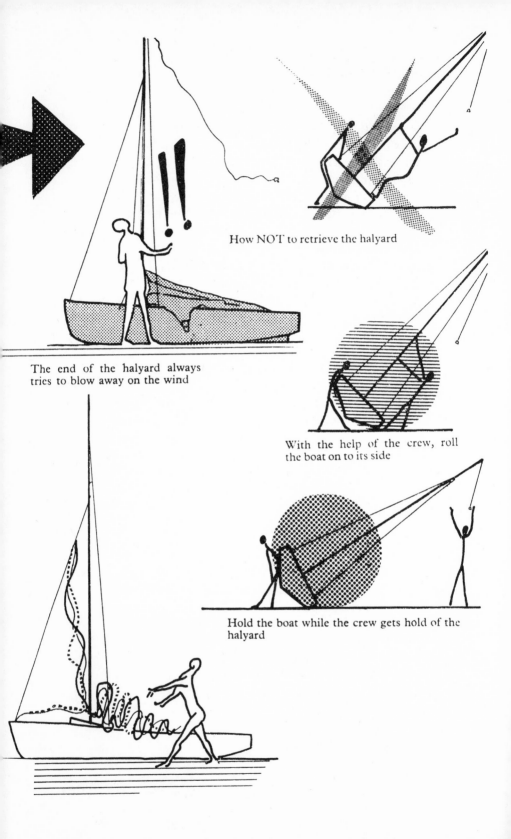

How NOT to retrieve the halyard

The end of the halyard always
tries to blow away on the wind

With the help of the crew, roll
the boat on to its side

Hold the boat while the crew gets hold of the
halyard

bending on the jib

The order of operations is as follows:

Fix the tack down with its shackle.

Starting with the nearest from the tack, clip the piston hanks on to the stay.

Cast off the halyard from its cleat, make sure it renders freely round the sheave and that the two parts are not twisted round one another, nor round the forestay.

Shackle it on to the head of the sail, and make fast the free end the cleat.

In passing, we might mention that the halyard should always either be held in the hand, or fixed somewhere— either on to the sail or on its cleat. The free end of a halyard always tends to fly away in the wind. It is a thing that often happens, and to recover it you have to roll the boat over.

Finally, it is usual to use the cleat at the foot of the mast *on the port side* for the jib halyard. This convention avoids mistakes.

Put the jib-sheets through their fairleads, and make a figure-of-eight knot in the end of each. Generally, the sheets go outside the shrouds, although, on some boats, it is best to pass them between mast and shrouds.

When the jib is ready, hoist it for a moment to make sure everything is clear. See that the tack has not got a turn in it, which might strain it, and that none of the piston hanks is on upside down.

Then lower the jib at once, and don't finally hoist it till the last minute, otherwise it will flap the whole time and the cloth will get frayed and weaken. It will also wear against the mast with constant flogging.

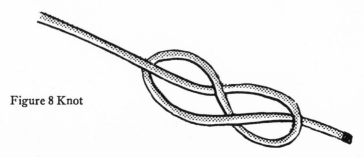

Figure 8 Knot

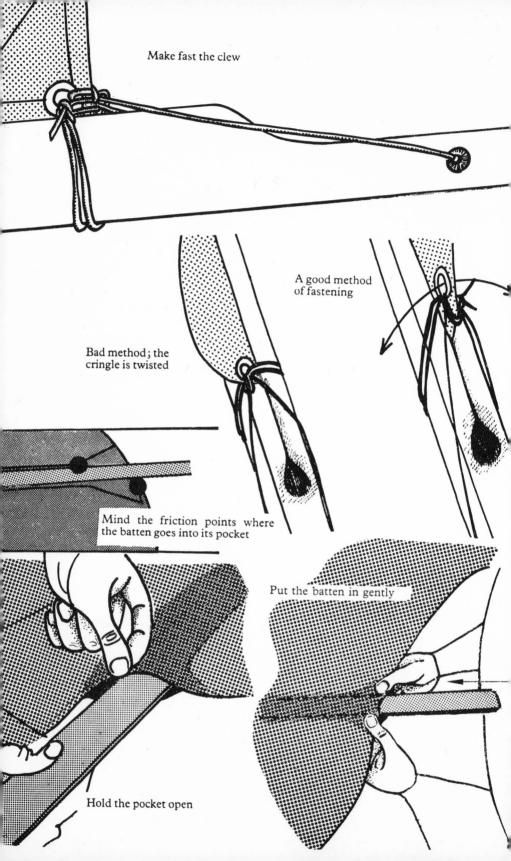

Make fast the clew

A good method
of fastening

Bad method; the
cringle is twisted

Mind the friction points where
the batten goes into its pocket

Put the batten in gently

Hold the pocket open

bending on the mainsail

Find the clew, put the bolt-rope into the boom groove, at the mast end, then pull it right through, one of the crew gently pulling the clew to the after end of the boom, while the other feeds the bolt-rope in at the fore end. The tack must then be fixed on the boom; there is generally a pin to do this, which passes through two tangs on the boom and also the tack cringle which is between them. Sometimes you have to lash the tack down with a stout lacing; you must then be careful not to let the bolt-rope rub against the ends of the groove in the boom, or that in the mast. If the tack is not properly made fast, you will get a frightful series of wrinkles in the sail, fatal both to its performance and to its life, as it will be permanently distorted.

Lash the clew and adjust the tension of the foot, that is to say of the bolt-rope, by means of the *clew outhaul*. The following is what you are aiming at:

The sail must be stretched till a slight wrinkle appears parallel to the boom.

The cringle must be held down to the boom loosely enough to allow a little play, but not crushingly tight.

The process is generally to pass one end of the lashing through a hole in the end of the boom, the other round the boom and through the cringle two or three times, finishing by knotting the two ends together.

Put the battens into their pockets; if the battens rub against the stitching by the mouths of the pockets, it will be worn and weakened, so put the battens in gently. They must not be forced in any way, and should have half a inch or so of endwise play. Finally, when they are in place, mind you don't break them; splinters will soon play havoc with a sail.

Insert the bolt-rope at the head of the sail into the mast groove, having made sure the sail has no turns in it; run the bolt-rope through your hands right up from the tack to verify this.

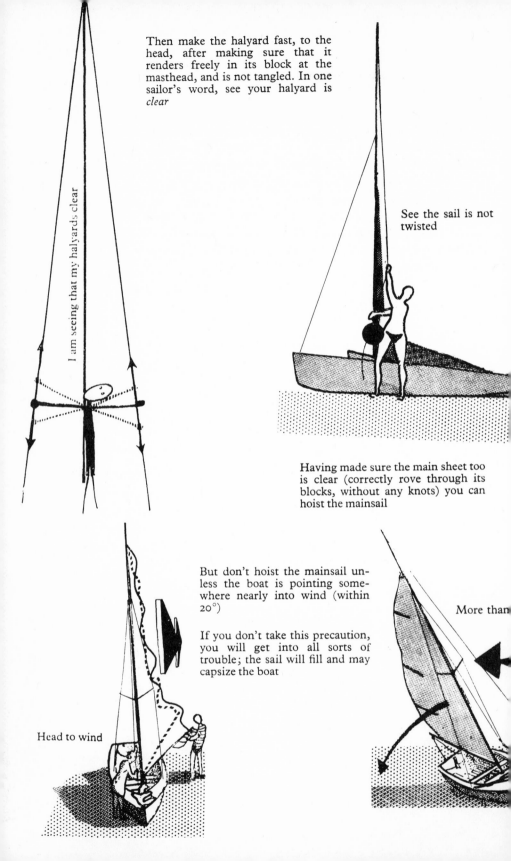

Then make the halyard fast, to the head, after making sure that it renders freely in its block at the masthead, and is not tangled. In one sailor's word, see your halyard is *clear*

I am seeing that my halyards clear

See the sail is not twisted

Having made sure the main sheet too is clear (correctly rove through its blocks, without any knots) you can hoist the mainsail

But don't hoist the mainsail unless the boat is pointing somewhere nearly into wind (within 20°)

If you don't take this precaution, you will get into all sorts of trouble; the sail will fill and may capsize the boat

Head to wind

More than

Before hoisting sail, you will have brought the boat to the water's edge, and placed it head to wind. A few recommendations may be of value here.

Carrying a boat is generally beyond the powers of the crew, who will want extra help. It is tactful to offer someone else a hand first.

Carrying a boat calls for brains more than brawn, and a well-thought-out distribution of available hands makes things simpler.

It is useful if the helmsman of the boat being carried directs matters in person, so that all care will be taken not to ill treat the 'patient', and to put it exactly in the right place, and facing in the direction he wants.

Boat properly launched, floating

The boat may be put down near the water, or squarely in it, but *never half in, half out of water*; it will be rolled about on the beach, and be badly scratched.

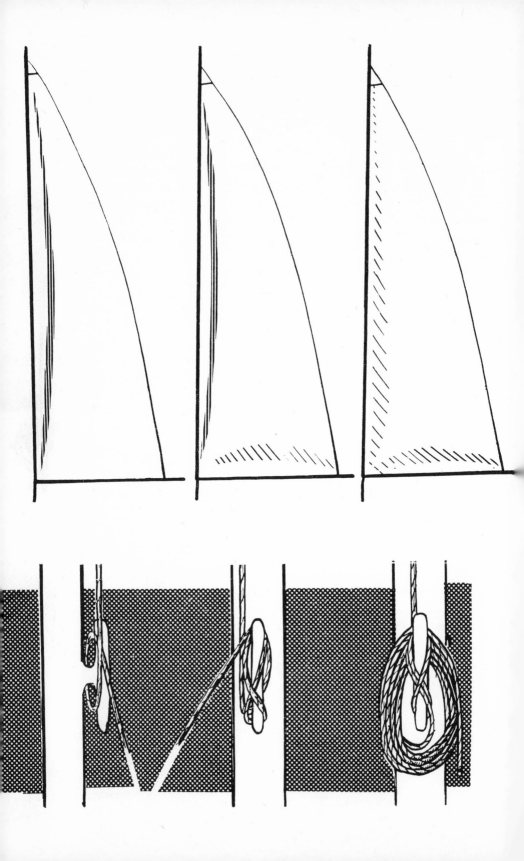

getting under way

When everything is ready, the crew can then:

● put on their life-jackets;

● hoist the mainsail; one of the crew hauls on the halyard with one hand, guides the bolt-rope into the groove with the other. The second man looks after the stern end of the boom till the sail is hoisted (as hard up as you can get it); this simplifies the guiding of the bolt-rope, prevents the boom getting caught under a *thwart* (cross-wise seat), gives the opportunity to see the main sheet is clear, and that the sail will not be sheeted in hard as soon as it is hoisted. Just the same as along the boom, the sail wants to be hauled taut up the mast until a light crease appears parallel with the mast. The halyard is then made fast on its cleat—the starboard one by custom, starting with a round turn and continuing with figure-of-eight turns. It is better not to end up with a half-hitch; in any case, if you do use one, don't tighten it up unduly. The biggest danger is not that of seeing the sail come down with a run when you don't want it to, but, on the contrary, not being able to get it down when you want to, owing to a half-hitch which has tightened up when wet. Finally, the halyard must be coiled and stowed somewhere where it will not get tangled and will stay clear (*many people tuck the coil behind the standing part*);

● take a glance round to see that the centre-board, rudder and tiller are all ready to put in place, or *ship*;

● hoist the jib, which you must heave really taut; make its halyard fast to the port cleat, and dispose of it in the same way as the main halyard;

● put the boat in the water; if you can't get outside help, and the beach is not shingle, it is possible to drag it a short way; but you should lift the forward third of the boat, so that some of the weight is off the ground; don't get aboard until the boat is waterborne.

The method of getting away depends very much on the force and direction of the wind. We will not discuss that for the moment; for one thing it would take too long; for the other, having assumed you are a beginner, we imagine your first outings will be in more experienced company. If this is not so, you must find some charitable soul to hold the boat while you ship rudder and tiller and lower the centre-board.

It might be well to point out here that a boat afloat and under sail can be held by one finger, if it is head to wind and held by the bow, or at least forward of the shrouds. But it will be just like a wild animal if you try to hold it with the wind abeam or astern, or if you try to hold the stern.

under way

Handling a boat properly, and getting full enjoyment from it without running foolish risks, is a matter which calls for a lot of attention. But a few sails in fair weather might well give a contrary impression; at such times everything seems easy, and boats, being intelligent creatures, take the necessary decisions for themselves. The beginner should beware of these very fallacious ideas.

From the very beginning avoid the habit of wandering about at the will of your boat; always have an objective, and force yourself to attain it. This will bring home the real difficulties, and will make you the quicker in overcoming them.

If you take the easy way out, and let the boat be carried about by the elements in a carefree way, you will probably have a rude awakening one day, not to say a wet one.

While giving the matter your whole attention, it is fatal to concentrate on a single point of detail; a ceaseless watch must be kept on:

> wind force and direction;
>
> sail trim;
>
> speed of the boat;
>
> balance and heeling;
>
> position of obstructions and of other craft;
>
> your own position.

wind force and direction

As the sailing of a boat depends entirely on wind direction, the crew must always know it as nearly as possible.

The behaviour of the sails is the best indication; in any case, on any point of sailing between close-hauled and a reach, the moment that they start to lift gives warning that the wind is too fine on their leading edges. A momentary easing of sheets will let you 'feel' how close you are to the wind.

Little ripples on the water—not waves, or even wavelets, but ripples an inch or so high, are always moving in the direction of the wind. With the wind aft, they are a better guide than the sails, which will not lift, even when eased right out.

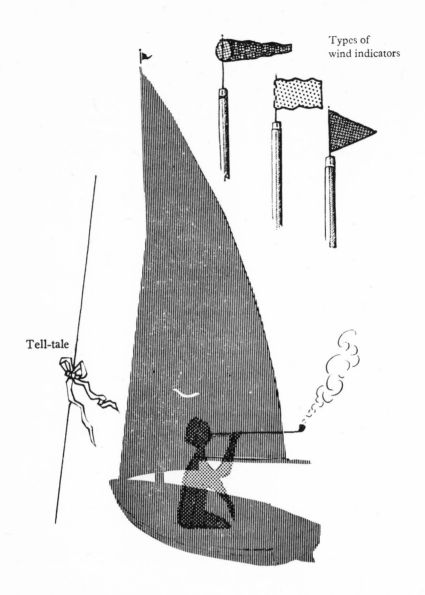

Types of
wind indicators

Tell-tale

On all points of sailing, a wind indicator at the mast head, or tell tales (ribbons, strands of cotton or light wool) on the shrouds, or again tobacco smoke, which works in the lightest airs, give the most positive guidance, but are all liable to be disturbed by a neighbouring sail.

The force of the wind has much less influence on the boat's sailing; it determines the strength it will take to steer and to handle the sheets. Still, if the wind blows up too much, the boat will be hard to hold, and a simple mistake might lead to a capsize. So, if the wind does get up, don't hesitate to come back before it gets too strong and things have got out of control; this is particularly important if you are sailing where immediate help is not certain if you capsize.

sail trim

We have seen that the sails must be sheeted in just hard enough to keep them from lifting. If they do, you will lose driving force; if they don't, it might be that they are sheeted in too hard—in which case they will set badly, and may even be a danger. Remember—the sheeting of the jib and mainsail are interdependent; a jib sheeted in too hard will make the mainsail lift near the mast and slow up the boat.

The best way of checking that your sails are properly sheeted is to let out an inch or two of sheet every now and again, or luff a point or so, and see if they lift. The beginner especially should do this quite frequently; as experience comes, he will sheet his sails correctly by instinct.

With a wind anywhere abaft the beam, you can no longer 'feel' the wind, as the sheets are right out and boom and mainsail are hard against the lee shroud. There is now no idea of the best sheeting, and we get no information on wind direction from the behaviour of the sails. It does not matter too much; you can always run off, right to a wind-astern position, without touching the sheets. But it is annoying; you can get past the wind astern position—sailing *by the lee*—without realizing it, and do an involuntary gybe; a risky matter in a fresh wind. With this in view, you would be well advised to avoid sailing right before the wind, and avoid gybing in a strong breeze.

While sheets only need slight adjustment so long as the boat holds its course, when you change the point of sailing you must make such bold sheet adjustments as the situation needs, a matter of feet rather than inches. While speaking of sheets, we might say—so that you do not start bad habits—that beginners tend to deal too coarsely with the sheets when it is a matter simply of feeling for the wind, and to be too niggling when adjusting them to a new point of sailing.

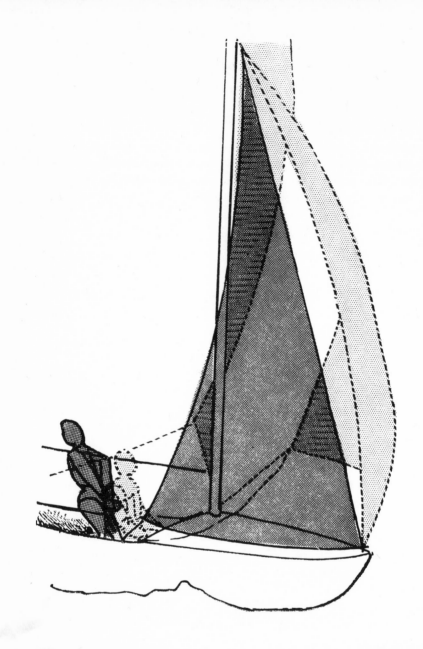

One very positive pointer to sheet control—sheet trim must depend solely on the behaviour of the sails; the pull on the sheets is no guide at all, and depends only on the point of sailing and the wind force. Thus, close-hauled in a fresh breeze, the jib-sheet hand has to pull pretty hard on the sheet, while in quiet weather and with the wind aft, it takes no effort to sheet it in, and the pull of the jib is so slight that you may have to help ease the sheet out through its fairlead. Beginners tend to go too much by the pull of the sheet; they sheet in too hard in a light wind, and not enough when close-hauled in a fresh one. Forewarned is forearmed.

the speed of the boat

Even though you may not be racing, always keep a good speed on your boat. A boat sailing slowly, owing to poorly trimmed sails, or to being pointed too close to the wind, is sluggish on the helm, and will get in irons sooner or later, which may be dangerous. Speed may be said to be a safety factor, and you must be able to estimate it and know how to improve it. Unfortunately, this calls for a lot of experience, and a few essentials are all we have room for here:

- The look of the wake, the noise of water under the bow, give a good idea of the speed; but readiness to answer the helm is the best sign as to whether a boat has enough speed or not.

- If you have not enough speed, look at the sails; you will see:

  either that they are not lifting, in which case they are probably sheeted in too hard;

  or that they are lifting; you must sheet in and shift your weight outboard, so as to keep the boat level.

- If the boat drags in a slight or moderate wind, with the sheets correctly trimmed, you are probably pinching, or pointing too close to the wind; pay off a point or so, trim the sheets 'as required' and the boat will get moving at once.

trim and heel

The fore-and-aft trim for best speed and handiness is generally that at which the transom is just on the waterline. This is not easy to gauge from inside the boat, and it is best to ask the crew of another craft how your trim is. You will soon get to know the best place to sit. But, to start with, every time you have to move for some manoeuvre, you will end up too far aft; this can be avoided if you know about it. Just so as not to make

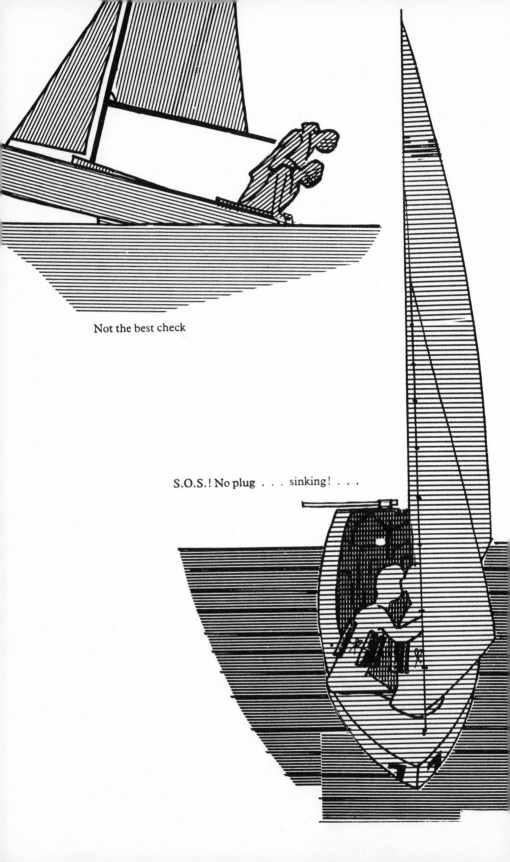

Not the best check

S.O.S.! No plug . . . sinking! . . .

yourself look silly, it might be well to remember that it is no good leaning over the stern to see if the transom is sitting on the waterline, because doing so upsets the trim. And besides, if you *have* forgotten to put in the plug, there is no need to panic—if you are sitting in the right place, the boat will not make a single drop of water.

Heeling, too, has a great deal to do with the sailing of the boat. With excessive heel, a boat will gripe badly, and will give a great appearance of speed—it is only an appearance—and will be hard to pay off from the wind. With an abnormal heel, to windward the boat will carry lee helm and steer badly. Broadly speaking, the best performance is with a light heel of a few degrees to leeward, the test being that the boat should carry on straight with the tiller neutral. (Many prefer slight weather helm, which is a safety precaution.) If the boat luffs unduly, lessen the heel; if it bears away, increase the heel.

Of course, at each change of point of sailing, and each alteration of sheet trim, the crew must move in or out from the centreline; close-hauled in a fresh breeze, your weight must be as far to windward as ever it will go.

The following is a repetition, but it is so important we have no hesitation in making it:

> When the wind is puffy, you must be on the move constantly if your sheet trim is to be right. But it is tiring, and, besides a squall may be too much for you, and your weight alone may not be enough to keep the heel reasonable. So think of the mainsheet as a safety valve, and let it fly as soon as the heel gets out of control; the effect is immediate. But you must still get all the control you can by your combined weights.

positions of obstructions and other craft

It is always well to avoid collisions with anything; it is always bad for the boat, and sometimes dangerous for the crew. Collisions generally arise through carelessness, more rarely through bad seamanship, quite exceptionally through unavoidable accident. Therefore, keep a constant watch on the movement of all the different obstructions relative to yourself. A continuous lookout will warn you in time of impending accident. In which case, set about avoiding action in good time so as to avoid panic.

The coast, or a rock, are usually easily avoided obstructions, by reason of their size and immobility.

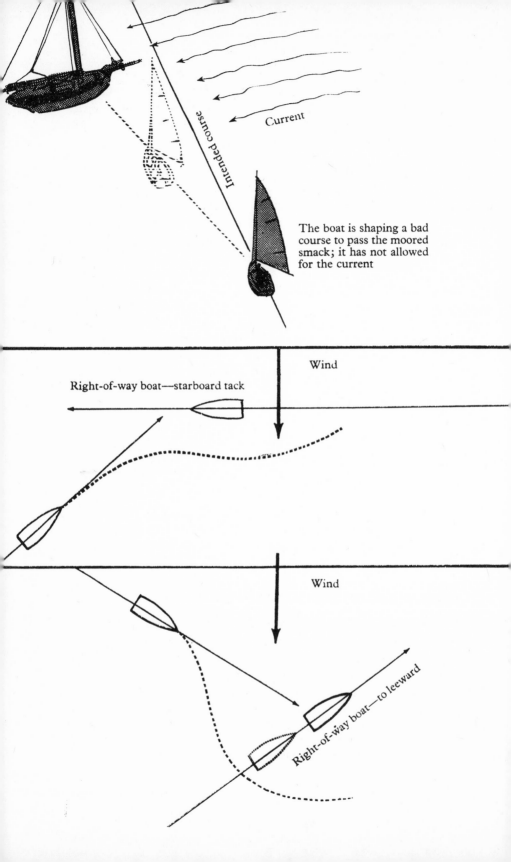

Current

Intended course

The boat is shaping a bad
course to pass the moored
smack; it has not allowed
for the current

Wind

Right-of-way boat—starboard tack

Wind

Right-of-way boat—to leeward

A boat on a mooring is more deceptive. If there is a current it will behave as though it were under way, but it is not a bit of good expecting it to take avoiding action. Cross its bows only at a respectful distance; it will be head to current, and the current will carry you down on to it.

A boat under way, in the hands of a crew on the lookout, or supposedly so, may eventually take action to avoid you. There are simple rules for the avoidance of collisions, when such seems likely:

> the craft on port tack gives way to the one on starboard tack;

> of two craft on the same tack, the one to leeward has priority, as it is pointing closer to the wind;

> motor-boat gives way to sailing craft.

You must know these rules, and should give way as laid down in them, but don't be too sure the other chap will give way to you. He may

> not have seen you (hail in good time);

> not know the rules;

> not know what to do about it (remember your own early days);

> not be in a position to manoeuvre;

> or just be a clot.

So, even though you have right of way, if you can pass astern of a boat under way rather than ahead by a slight change of course, don't hesitate to do so.

And when you do change course, right of way or not, make the change *boldly* and *in good time*.

Racing yachts. Racing yachts and dinghies are subject to the 'rule of the road' when meeting other vessels, but it is correct etiquette for a non-racing boat to keep out of their way. The racing rules may differ from ordinary sailing rules in many ways, the principal difference being that a racing yacht on the starboard tack has right of way over other racing yachts on the port tack under all conditions, even when the starboard-tack yacht is running and the port tack yacht is close-hauled.

position of your own craft

Don't forget that the sea is large, and that boats move fast; don't get too far from the place you are going back to, and if possible stay to windward of it. In any case, don't lose sight of it, and don't get out of the field of vision of the watchers allotted to your sailing ground.

The impact could easily distort the boat's bottom

- If the water is shallower where you come ashore—on the beach, or on a river bank—and if you have a dagger-plate as opposed to a pivoting centre-board, bring it up in good time; if it hits the bottom, it may jam, and will probably damage the boat. The same applies to a drop rudder. If this happens to you, the first thing is to jump out and attend to the boat; then heel it over to clear dagger-plate or rudder.

- Come alongside the wharf, or run up on the beach, as slowly as you can. If you cannot do it somewhere between a beam wind and full-and-by, your boat will arrive at full speed. Unless the wind is very light, you should lower the mainsail beforehand, and then the jib.

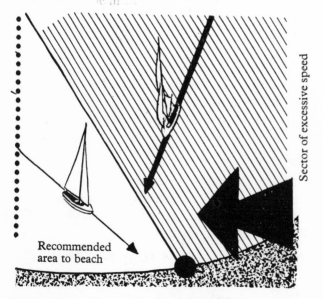

Sector of excessive speed

Recommended area to beach

return to shore

Beaching is, for a boat, a thing for which it is not designed; there is a risk of damage if certain precautions are not taken.

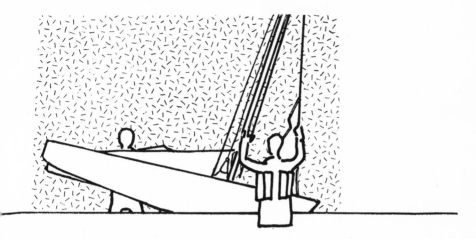

● Stop the boat with the hand as far as you can:

>Coming to a beach, step out before the boat touches bottom.

>Hold the boat off from the quay or stage by hand, and don't let the boat bump against it.

● Lower the sails—if you have not already done so—and that will be easier if you are head to wind.

● Finally, don't leave your boat half afloat, rubbing on the sand; or scraping against the quay. Pull, or better carry, it out of the water at once, unless the prevailing wind might keep out on an anchor, or unless the walls of the quay are provided with fenders soft enough for a small boat.

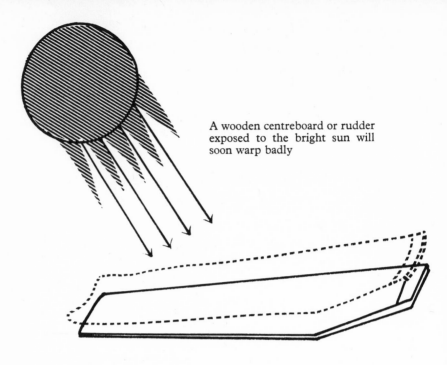

A wooden centreboard or rudder
exposed to the bright sun will
soon warp badly

Your day's sailing is only finished
when you have left the boat perfectly
ready to take the sea again

unrigging the boat

Unrig your boat calmly and carefully, whatever sort of state of excitement an enjoyable trip may have induced.

- Get the battens out gently.

- Don't lose hold of the halyards; make them fast to their cleats carefully.

- Getting the mainsail off the mast and boom grooves, pull gently; if you meet resistance, investigate the cause rather than use force.

- Leave the tack and halyard shackles on board rather than on the sails.

- Take the sails and put them away at once; if they are cotton, hang them out to dry; if synthetic fibre, put them away damp or even wet rather than put them in the sun.

- Empty the boat of any water that may be in it. Take out the plug, or—if there isn't one—use a sponge. If the boat has water-tight buoyancy compartments, take out the plugs to let them air. Check whether they are leaking.

- Carefully remove all dirt from the boat—seaweed, sand and so forth.

- Coil down the main sheet, and the anchor cable if necessary.

- Stand the rudder and dagger-plate somewhere where they will be out of the sun, which will warp them.

- Check all the equipment which should be in the boat.

- Leave the boat on a soft flat piece of ground, and chocked up so that the wind will not be able to shake it.

You will not be able to remember all these practical details after one reading. And it is not suggested that you sail with the book in one hand and the tiller in the other. But, the better your preparations, the more you will get out of your boat.

Read these pages again and again after your first few sails.

the points of sailing | 6

running

definition

A boat is said to be running when it is sailing dead down wind; but the conditions we are going to describe apply to the behaviour of a small boat with the wind 20° to 25° either side of the dead aft position.

general remarks

On this point of sailing the sails have to be trimmed at right-angles to the centre line of the boat, the main sheet is out to its maximum, boom and sails hard against the shroud on one side; the jib can often be *goosewinged* on the opposite side, its sheet held out by the crew, or extended by means of a whisker-pole or a boat-hook.

If the wind is really dead aft, it does not matter which side the main boom is on; but, if the wind is coming even slightly from one side or the other, the mainsail should be to leeward, the jib to windward.

behaviour of the boat with wind aft

In the conditions just described, the wind will necessarily be in a state of turbulence when it meets the sails; its force will therefore be less than when on, for instance, a broad reach, where, with the same sheeting, the air flow is steady. It follows that the boat does not go so fast right off the wind as on a reach, and again from that it follows that the boat speeds up if you luff. This acceleration on a luff is one of the most marked characteristics of the behaviour of a boat when running.

With such a wind direction and a suitable sail trim, the force on the sails is to all intents and purposes along the fore-and-aft line of the boat; its transverse component is slight, if it exists at all. Having no tendency to

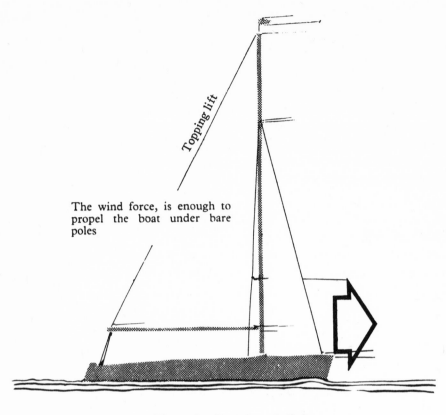

Topping lift

The wind force, is enough to propel the boat under bare poles

The mainsail tends to luff the boat, which is partly counter-acted by the jib

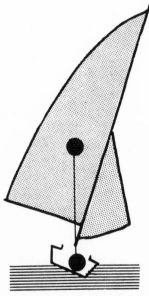

Heeling the side opposite the boom, stops weather helm

heel, there is no need for any sitting-out by the crew, who should distribute their weight between the two sides of the boat; running is the one point of sailing which is physically restful. There is no tendency to make leeway; the centre-board is useless, and may be raised. Still better, speed is not in itself necessary for straight steering without yawing; sail may be shortened, or even removed altogether; the effect of the wind on bare poles is enough to propel the boat. You can keep going in such conditions quite slowly, whereas, you will remember, you cannot work to windward except at a certain minimum speed.

In the course of the last chapter we studied how the force exerted on the sail varied with the angle of incidence of the wind, and we saw that, once the critical angle of stall is passed, this force is practically unvarying in intensity, and stays roughly at right-angles to the sail. From this it seems that, when running free, a variation of 20° to either side of the optimum would only diminish the propulsive force by 5%. Sheet regulation is not therefore of great importance, and has practically no effect on the speed of the boat.

The mainsail, and, of course, the force it has working on it, is mostly out to one side, which tends to make the boat luff, even when there is no heel. The jib opposes this tendency, boomed out on the other side, but the latter, with its smaller area, cannot altogether counteract this. The only way of preventing weather helm is to heel the boat to weather, that is, on the side opposite to the boom; this is doubly effective; the hull tends to pay off, while the sails being nearly perpendicular to the keel, no longer try to luff the boat. It might in passing be mentioned that weather helm is preferable, as it offers some protection against bearing away suddenly and involuntarily gybing; if it were carrying lee helm, the boat would go into an involuntary gybe at the least lack of attention by the helmsman.

A deformation of the mainsail, known as *twisting*, has much influence on the boat when running, especially in a strong wind. Here is what happens; the lower part of the sail is pinned down by the boom to its proper shape; but the upper part, being relatively free, tends to give way before the force of the wind, and is said to twist. The sail assumes a sort of spiral form, more or less pronounced according to the strength of the wind; the upper part may twist far enough so that it is flapping if the wind is strong enough. The first effect of sail twist is to reduce the propulsive force, so much less sail surface being presented to the wind. See page 258.

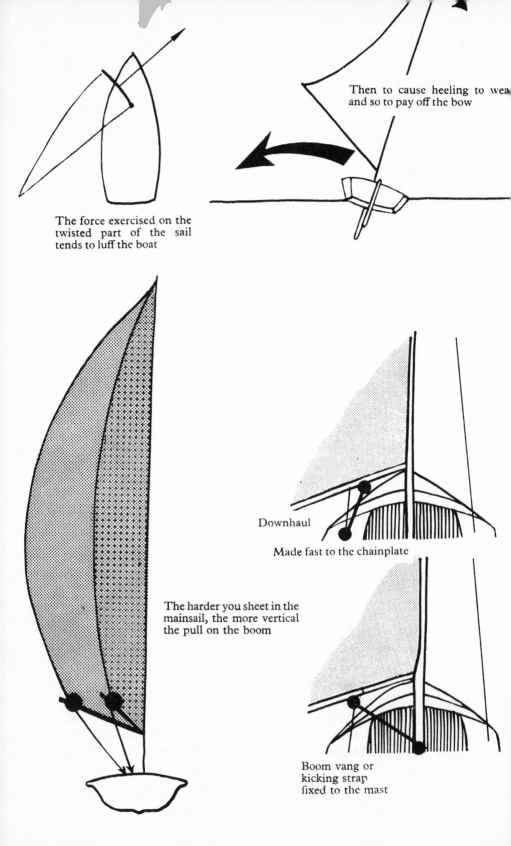

The force exercised on the twisted part of the sail tends to luff the boat

Then to cause heeling to wea and so to pay off the bow

Downhaul

Made fast to the chainplate

The harder you sheet in the mainsail, the more vertical the pull on the boom

Boom vang or kicking strap fixed to the mast

Next, in the upper part of the sail a force is developed, directed to windward (opposite to the boom), which, in the first place, tends to luff the boat, but which may also give rise to a roll to windward, and consequent paying-off. A twisted sail, therefore, has the effect of producing considerable difficulty in steering; also, if the sail is twisted suddenly as the result of a squall, the sail may go by the lee, and the result will be a gybe—generally a Chinese gybe—as the boom tends to rise vertically up the mast as it carries the bottom half of the sail over on to the other gybe.

It might be said that twisting of the mainsail is not confined to running. You will get it on all points of sailing other than when close-hauled; but when nearly on the wind, the harder the mainsheet is sheeted, the closer the boom lies to the centre line of the boat, and the more vertical is the pull of the sheet. The leech of the sail is thus kept tighter, and has less tendency to twist. Moreover, twisting in these cases only affects the set of the sail, and does not cause any tendency to do an involuntary gybe.

Twisting can be practically eliminated by fitting a *downhaul* or *kicking-strap*, an arrangement for holding down the boom even when right out athwartships. The most effective type of downhaul for off-wind sailing consists of a tackle of simple form, between the boom and the *chain-plate* (to which the shroud is fitted). The drawback is that if you want to gybe, or even sheet in a little, you have to unrig the downhaul.

A tackle between the foot of the mast and the boom at about 45° from the vertical is a little less effective, but much more convenient; you make it fast, and need not touch it again, no matter what the point of sailing or what evolutions are carried out. The drawback of this is that the jib man is always getting tied up with the tackle; each time you go about it gets in his way.

At first sight, the reader might think it would have been better to wait for the paragraph on 'managing the boat with wind aft', to talk of kicking straps. But the latter, besides increasing speed and diminishing the danger and likelihood of gybes, have a fairly important effect on the boat's steering, which is what we are now going to discuss.

When on the subject of stability, we had occasion to talk about rolling, and how the sails largely act as shock-absorbers in damping down rolling. That is very true when they are sheeted in on the wind, but when running free they have no damping power on a thwartship force. A long series of oscillations will be started by every little momentary heel when running—a movement by one of the crew, a wave, twisting of the mainsail, and so on. If the boat is one that carries weather helm when heeled, these oscillations will affect the steering, and tend to make it yaw to alternate sides.

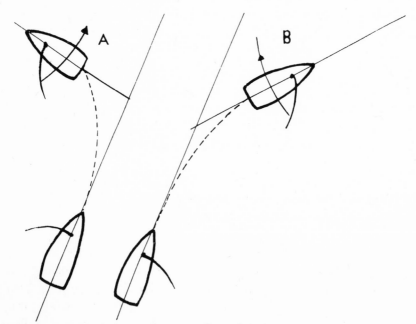

A, with sail set to leeward has to pay off much more than B in order to gybe, A is therefore in less danger of an involuntary gybe

Apart from *induced rolling*, it may be said that rolling and yawing are chronic diseases of a craft running; a mere nothing will start the rolls, and they are quite a job to stop. The boom vang can play a most important part to this end; by eliminating sail twist it removes one cause of a roll building up, and therefore indirectly improves steering. In fact, experience teaches that, with a strong breeze, a good boom vang will work wonders on controlling a light centre-board craft, making it much easier to handle and more predictable in its behaviour.

To recapitulate what we have said on sailing with the wind aft:

- The boat does not go very fast, but has no tendency to heel or to make leeway.

- The trim of sheets is not so important.

- But the directional stability is poor, and in a strong breeze rolling and wild yawing will be experienced.

- This is the more trying, as a yaw is liable to develop into either an involuntary gybe or a broaching-to.

- This situation is much improved by a good kicking strap or boom vang.

- This point of sailing is physically restful, but, on occasion, distinctly wearing on the nerves.

managing the boat with wind astern

choice of gybe

When the wind is dead aft, as we have seen, the mainsail may be set on either side, and you can change your gybe at will. But as soon as the wind ceases to be dead aft you can distinguish between windward and leeward. It is always best to set the mainsail to leeward, because there will be less risk of gybing involuntarily; more exactly, to get the boom across, you would have to make a bigger alteration of course than if you were *by the lee*, that is, boom to windward. The propulsive force, too, is a little more when the sail is to leeward; it is slightly more at right-angles to the wind (the shrouds will not let it be quite so), and it does not mask the jib. This is why, when the mainsail is to windward, one is said to be sailing *by the lee*.

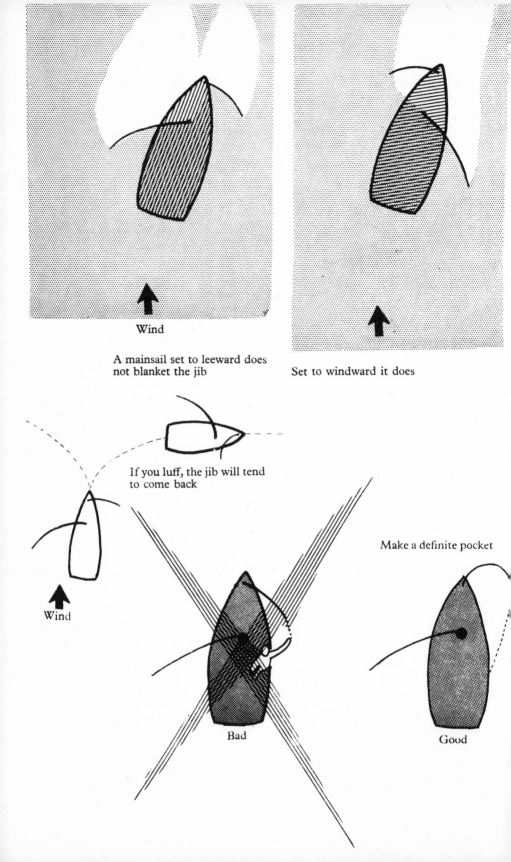

Wind

A mainsail set to leeward does
not blanket the jib

Set to windward it does

If you luff, the jib will tend
to come back

Wind

Make a definite pocket

Bad

Good

The most important thing about sailing with the wind astern is to be on the *right gybe*. How is one to be sure of this ? Sheet the sail in, and see which gybe it wants to go on; that is the way to be sure. But take care you don't luff while you are doing it, or you will get the wrong answer. The jib's behaviour will be another pointer; if the crew have no difficulty in keeping it out on the opposite side to the mainsail, all is well. If you luff now, it will have a tendency to be taken aback. If, on the other hand, you pay off, it will deflate, collapse and be very much disturbed owing to the backdraught from the mainsail. These two symptoms are unmistakable in a good breeze, but may not be so reliable in medium or light airs. If you have no boom vang, the sail will twist a lot, and the boom will tend to rise when you get by the lee. Look out! A gybe is near.

sail trim

Supposing you are on the right gybe, how do you handle the sheets ?

As for the mainsail, ease the sheets out as far as possible, push the boom out if necessary. The order is 'square off the boom'. It must be right up against the shrouds, and the sail against the crosstrees.

Harden the boom vang as much as possible, unless the wind is light, when the weight of the boom will be enough to stop the sail twisting. It might be noted that the best time to make the boom vang fast is before you start off, when the sail is slatting with the wind ahead and the boom amidships.

The jib, whether held out at arm's length by the crew (a tiring business), or by means of a jib-stick or paddle, should not be flat. Let it fly as far forward as it will, and form a pronounced bag. It may not seem to be setting too well, but it will draw better like that than if kept flat. Let the clew go up as high as you can, too.

the position and behaviour of the crew

Your position fore and aft must be about the same on any other point of sailing, if you want to keep the right trim, with the transom on the waterline. But in a strong wind the boat does tend to bury its nose, and to make up for that you could move a little aft. As there is no heel, you would well sit one each side, the same distance from the centre line. The more inboard your weight is, the more inertia the boat will have in the thwartship plane, and there will be less tendency to roll. All the same, you should keep

When the centre-board is right up, the boat skids at every yaw, which causes loss of speed; with a little board down there will be less yawing, and no skidding

The jib hand to windward, looking after his sheet; helmsman to leeward

as still as you can; every movement tends to start a roll and put on the brake. If you have no jib-stick, the crew should always be to windward, holding up his jib-sheet, and the helmsman will sit to leeward, by the boom. At each gybe you will have to change sides, and that will cause a roll unless you are very gentle with it and time your move together. In light weather, or when repeated gybes seem probable, it may be better to set the jib without the jib-stick to avoid having to move unduly. It is unnecessary to change over a boom or jib-stick at each gybe—the crew can perfectly well manage the jib without it at a distance.

centre-board

Strictly speaking, when the wind is aft, the centre-board is of no value. You can raise it and reduce the wetted surface. But without the centre-board you don't steer so well. Each yaw makes the boat skid somewhat, which has quite a noticeable braking effect. With a fresh breeze or a chop on the sea, put the board down a bit (say a quarter); this is essential then, as accurate steering is necessary to avoid a gybe, and especially broaching-to.

As soon as the wind draws away from dead aft, the boat has a tendency to leeway, and a little centre-board will stop it, increasing the resistance.

It may quite definitely be said that a little too much board is far better than too little, except in a perfectly smooth sea and light airs. Even then, don't delude yourself:

> the centre-board is only 10 to 15% of the wetted surface;
>
> friction resistance, due to the wetted surface, is only part of the total resistance.

speed control

Running is certainly the point of sailing at which it is hardest to keep control of the boat's speed; the matter is out of your hands, and speed is dictated by the elements, the force of wind and the length of the boat.

You can't go at the speed of the wind, in a light breeze, because there would be no propulsive force; the relative wind on your sails would be nil.

In moderate winds the boat's speed reaches a maximum, for there won't be enough power for planing, unless the boat is very light and carries a lot of sail.

With a strong breeze, you might plane, but that would mean that your boat was carrying too much sail, and the slightest yaw would be fatal. In fact, except for a boat which is *intended* for fast planing, speeds above the

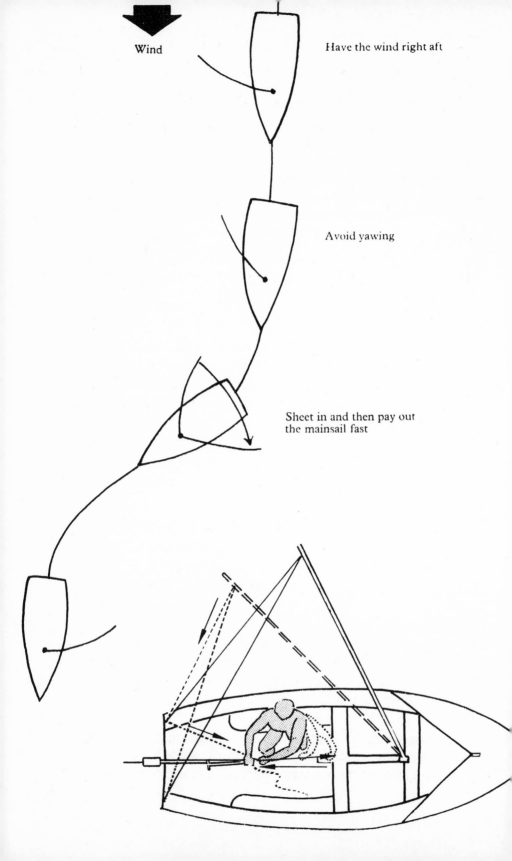

Wind

Have the wind right aft

Avoid yawing

Sheet in and then pay out
the mainsail fast

critical one with wind dead aft mean that the wind is such that the boat would be out of control on any other point of sailing.

Therefore:

● In a light wind your boat, whatever it may be, will go up to 80 or 90% of the wind speed. That is, in a 5-knot breeze a normally sailed boat will attain about 4 knots, while a very light and somewhat overcanvassed boat will do 4½. Note that the first craft will have a relative wind speed of 1 knot, and the second a relative wind speed of ½ knot; half the force.

● As the wind rises your boat will reach its critical speed and no more.

Which being so, there is little you can do about it.

For maximum speed, trim the boat correctly, harden the boom vang, let the sails right out—so long as they do not get by the lee—and, particularly in light weather, keep as still as you can.

You have not got many means of slowing the boat. Upset the trim, start a roll, yaw from side to side; it will not affect things very much. Sheeting all sails hard in would certainly slow the boat, provided the wind were light. If not, it would not do much good, and might be very dangerous.

To stop completely, you would have to leave this point of sailing and luff up, till the wind is ahead of the beam.

gybing

A little farther back, talking of the choice of gybe, we supposed you to know how to gybe. We did talk about it in Chapter 1. But it seems a good thing to return to the subject with some practical remarks.

The most difficult thing, is that you must get the wind right aft, and keep it there while you haul in the main sheet. The jib, or the ripples on the water—take a glance aft—will show you just when the wind comes dead aft as you pay off. At that point it is advisable to note a point ahead on which to steer.

When your course is steady, dead down wind, you can sheet in the mainsail. The boat now carries heavy weather helm, and calls for firm pull on the tiller to windward, opposite to the boom. The moment the boom goes over, everything is reversed, and the boat tends to luff on the new tack. To avoid that, let the sheet run out fast, just checking it towards the end of its run; at the same time, helm to windward (for the new course).

This is the normal procedure when the wind is not too heavy, and you have no boom vang.

Two variations may be mentioned:

If the wind is slight, there is no fear of twisted sail, of the boom climbing the mast, of a Chinese gybe; the crew picks up the boom without more ado and pushes it over.

If you have a boom vang, there is nothing to fear from a Chinese gybe in the heaviest of weather. You can gybe with a light heart; pay off firmly till the wind is aft—the boom comes over with a bang, but the sail cannot get hung up anywhere. The only things to be careful of are—have the sheet clear for running out, and take early and correct action against the tendency to broach-to, which will be more marked now than with the normal method.

Now let us look at the movements of the crew; we are running on the starboard gybe, the helmsman sitting to leeward, to port, the crew busy with the jib to starboard. As far as possible, it is better that neither shifts *during* the gybe, because it is not easy to time their moves together. It is quite feasible with a light breeze; the helmsman pushes the tiller over with his right hand, while the sheet slips through this hand and is gripped by the left. After the gybe, helmsman and crew changes places if they like, smoothly and without fuss.

If there is much wind, you must both be ready to counteract a sudden heel, produced by a hard luff before or after the sail goes over. With this in mind, during the critical time crouch with one foot each side of the boat, ready to sit out; the crew facing aft and neglecting the jib for the moment; the helmsman, too, facing aft, can watch his wake better, and his wind and his boom; and he runs much less chance of getting tied up in the sheet. If there are other craft, or obstructions in the neighbourhood, he must obviously look out forward, but he cannot actually face forward, because he has to haul in the sheet; in this case he will throw astern each coil of the sheet as it comes in, so that he cannot possibly get it tangled with his feet. The great danger in a gybe is not being able to pay out sheet fast enough if the boat starts to broach-to before or after. Note now, then— and we will come back to it later—that you cannot do better than to get the habit of easing sheets automatically the moment an abnormal heel starts as well as anything else you might do to restore the situation.

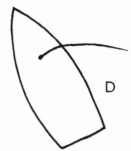

D

Then gybe again and try to do better next time

C

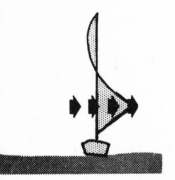

Only remedy: gybe back again

. . . a Chinese gybe

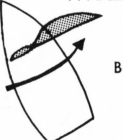

B

makes a mess of it and does . . .

A

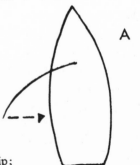

Trying to gybe ship;

dangers of running free

The risks you run with a stern wind, non-existent in light weather, increase both in seriousness and frequency with the rising wind. They comprise involuntary gybes and broaching-to.

The danger of an involuntary gybe is twofold; there is a chance of its being a Chinese one, which may tear the sail; the only thing to do is to gybe back as soon as possible on to the original tack. Next, there is a risk of a violent broaching-to following an accidental gybe, which is the more dangerous as the crew may be unprepared to take counter measures against the sudden heel; a capsize may well result.

This is why we recommend to beginners that they should avoid running in heavy weather. The risk is that through an error of judgment in estimating the direction of the wind they will find themselves sailing by the lee all unawares, and, so unstable is the boat's behaviour, that they could easily lose control. You cannot, obviously, gybe if you are unable to keep the boat exactly before the wind.

A violent luff when gybing, just before or just after the boom comes across, when the boat is off balance, is dangerous in itself only because the helmsman in such a case tends instinctively to freeze on to the main sheet, or because the sheet has got tied on to something, and will not run free at the critical moment. In either case, you are as often as not in for a sudden capsize.

Now, we have said that a boom vang makes things very much safer, and diminishes certain risks and their consequences. An experienced crew will have no hesitation in using one. For a crew of beginners, there are snags; the crew will keep on getting entangled in it. So, for novices, we do not recommend a boom vang; they will just have to shorten sail in a fresh breeze.

There is one more danger attached to running free; you have little *freedom of action*.

The crew has no control over the speed of the boat; it is like being in a car with no brakes and the throttle jammed open. If you want to stop, you must do at least a 90° turn.

And then, you cannot just turn without thinking. An extemporized gybe, without a few seconds' thought, is not a thing to be lightly undertaken. The only thing is to luff up; and that, to start with, will increase your speed. One other resort, lowering the mainsail, is, on this point of sailing, a difficult job and not without risks to your gear.

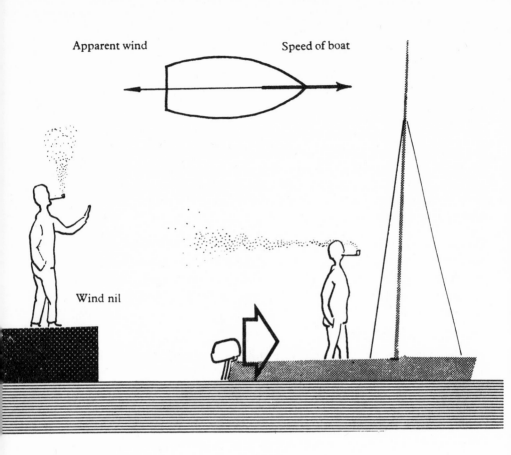

Apparent wind   Speed of boat

Wind nil

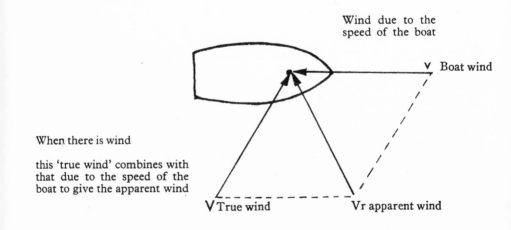

Wind due to the speed of the boat

v Boat wind

When there is wind

this 'true wind' combines with that due to the speed of the boat to give the apparent wind

V True wind   Vr apparent wind

reaching

definition

The field covered by reaching as a point of sailing is not altogether clear, so we will make an arbitrary rule; the following instructions will apply to the sector between wind $22\frac{1}{2}°$ forward of abeam and wind $22\frac{1}{2}°$ from dead aft. The field is a pretty big one, and we will on occasion distinguish between a *close reach,* a *beam reach,* and a *broad reach.*

general remarks

On a close reach, that is, with the wind just forward of abeam, the sails need gently sheeting in, or they will lift. A little farther off the wind they will keep full, even with the sheets right out—at least, the mainsail will; the jib may not be out to the full extent of its sheet even with the wind right aft.

The sails are generally working in the best conditions on this point of sailing; the air flow is smooth, and *pressure is at its highest*; the boat sails well, at maximum speed.

It is next essential to consider the difference between the true and the relative winds.

true wind and apparent wind

The force and direction of the wind are not the same for a stationary craft as for one under way. For an explanation of this, look at the case in the drawing; the wind is a flat calm, that is, there is no motion as between the air and the water, while the boat is moving, propelled by an engine.

Obviously, in this case anyone in the boat will feel a wind of force and direction equal and opposite to those of the boat. This is the *relative wind,* or the *apparent wind.*

Suppose now that a wind is blowing, that is, the air is in movement over the water, its speed and direction being represented by vector V; that is the *true wind.*

The relative wind Vr which will be felt by the crew and the sails of a boat under way will be the resultant of the real wind V and of the wind v due to the movement of the boat. Naturally it is the relative wind that we have to think of when we deal with the action of the wind on the sails, and what often complicates matters is that that depends on the speed and direction of the boat's movement.

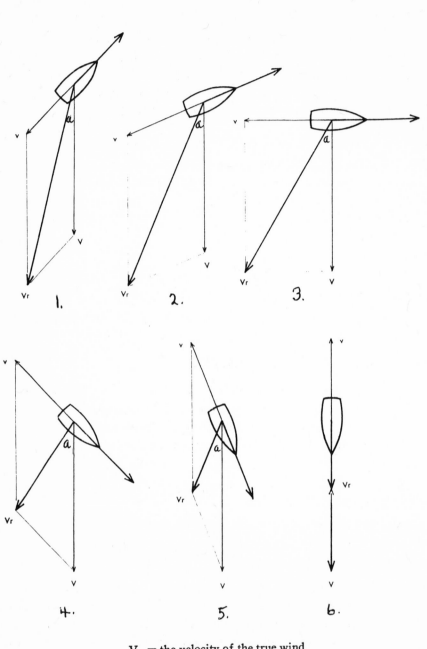

1.

2.

3.

4.

5.

6.

V = the velocity of the true wind
v = the boat wind (due to boat speed)
Vr = the velocity of the apparent wind

To illustrate what we have been saying, and by way of excusing ourselves for a diversion from the subject-matter of the present chapter, we will show the direction and force of the apparent wind for a boat on different points of sailing, the true wind blowing at 8 knots, V.

Point of sailing	v Speed of boat	Vr Speed of apparent wind	a Angle of apparent wind
1. Close-hauled 45° off wind	3.8 knots	11 knots	14°
2. Full-and-by 22° forward of beam	4.6	10.7	23°
3. Beam reach	4.8	9.3	31°
4. Broad reach 45° aft of beam	4.6	5.7	35°
5. Broad reach 22° from aft	4.5	4.2	24°
6. Wind aft	4.3	3.7	0°

The speeds indicated for the boat on the various points of sailing have been chosen arbitrarily, but are reasonably realistic.

Conclusions:

● The apparent wind is always forward of the true wind. In other words, you must always sheet the sails harder when the boat has speed than when it is has not, and for a given point of sailing and true wind the faster the boat goes the harder you must sheet in.

● The speed of the apparent wind is greater when close-hauled, and less with the wind aft, than that of the true wind. From one extreme to the other, it varies in the case quoted from +30% to −50%. This explains why the wind always seems stronger when close-hauled; the apparent wind *is* stronger.

● Lastly, the angular difference in the directions of the true and apparent winds is greatest when reaching. This is why the matter has been discussed here rather than elsewhere. On these points of sailing every variation in the boat's speed brings a noticeable variation of direction of the apparent wind.

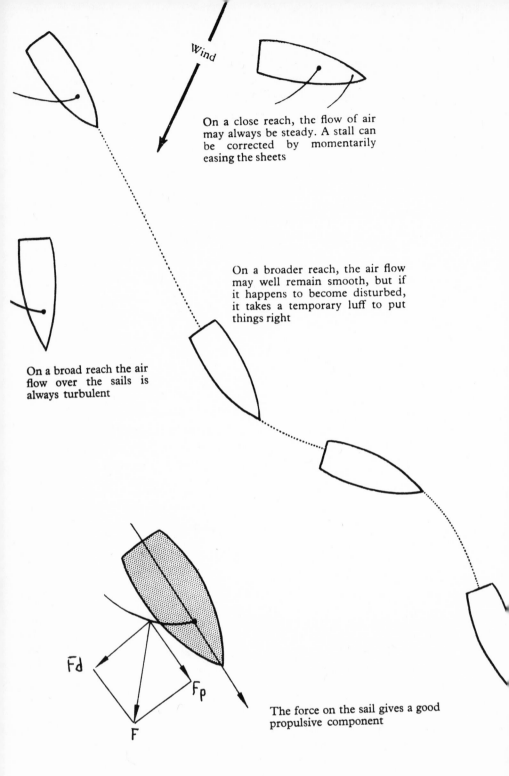

Wind

On a close reach, the flow of air may always be steady. A stall can be corrected by momentarily easing the sheets

On a broader reach, the air flow may well remain smooth, but if it happens to become disturbed, it takes a temporary luff to put things right

On a broad reach the air flow over the sails is always turbulent

Fd

Fp

F

The force on the sail gives a good propulsive component

behaviour of light centre-board craft on the reach

There is one point common to all the different shades of reaching; this is the point on which sailing is easy and fast. The pressure on the sails and the propulsive component may rise very high, but the drift component stays low.

But, between the extremes of close and broad reaching, there are great changes in the air flow over the sails, thus:

On a *close reach* air flow may be smooth; one can sheet the sails so that they are just not lifting. Should a stall occur, you can easily get back to a smooth flow without changing course—simply by letting the sheets off momentarily till the sails start to lift.

On a *broad reach*, right up to the limits of wind aft, the mainsail flow is always turbulent, even though it is hard against the shrouds. The jib sometimes has a nice smooth flow.

Between these two points of sailing there is a point at which the mainsail flow is precariously smooth; precariously, because, if it becomes disturbed accidentally, you can't let off more sheet because of the shrouds. In this case, you must luff to put things right, then pay off again with a good air stream until it is again stalled by some accident.

In each of these cases the boat behaves in a peculiar manner, which we shall look into in turn.

the close reach

As the air flow is smooth, the pressure of wind on sails goes up as they are sheeted in, drops as they are let out. Similarly, the pressure drops with a luff, rises as you bear away.

These reactions are those you get on points of sailing closer to the wind than this; the crew gets used to them from the first; to stop heeling, you either luff or ease sheets.

This force on the sail is high when the air flow is smooth, and the more the sheets are eased the higher is the driving force. Experience, in fact, shows that it is on a beam reach that you get the highest propulsive force and the

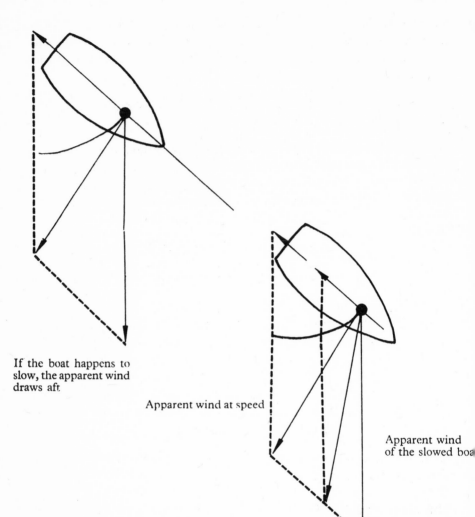

If the boat happens to
slow, the apparent wind
draws aft

Apparent wind at speed

Apparent wind
of the slowed boat

highest speeds; on a broader reach the air flow is not so good; on the points of sailing nearer the wind the propulsive component is too low.

The transverse component, in relation to the wind force and the sail carried, may be high if you are sailing in a fresh breeze and overcanvassed. Possibly the crew must go to the limit in sitting-out. A close reach is not a restful point of sailing in these conditions, but it is an exciting one; the effort of sitting out is rewarded by a much higher propulsive force, and much higher speeds, than you ever get close-hauled. Now, the high transverse force in this case may make you wonder if you ought to have the centre-board right down. Actually, no; on this point of sailing good propulsive power offsets the high side thrust and also the speed is high. Broadly speaking, half centre-board is enough.

the broad reach

The air flow is disturbed, and the behaviour of the boat is much the same as with wind aft; it does not go very fast, the exact adjustment of the sheets is of no importance, heeling and leeway are slight. Lastly, a luff tends to increase the heel, and not to diminish it, as it does on a close reach. The only difference from wind astern is the better directional stability; though the boat gripes badly, it has no tendency to bear away or gybe.

intermediate points of sailing

When the air flow is trembling at the threshold of turbulence the boat behaves oddly, for a sudden stall can occur at any time.

To explain this, start, in imagination, with a beam wind, and pay off steadily. The boat moves fast, and the relative wind is noticeably different from the true one, in direction if not in force. As you pay off, the pressure on the sail increases, the boat accelerates, the apparent wind differs still more from the true in direction, and begins to lessen in force (see above for the difference of speed of the apparent wind between a beam wind and a broad reach). As you bear away, even with the mainsail right out, you reach stalling-point, and, when it comes:

> sail pressure drops;
>
> the boat slows up;
>
> the apparent wind draws astern;

and, with this apparent wind, it is not possible to get back to a smooth airflow, except by luffing momentarily to restore order. Here we find what Manfred Curry calls the *dead point* with wind aft. Note that this authority

The axis of the force acting on the sails goes aft of the CLR, giving weather helm

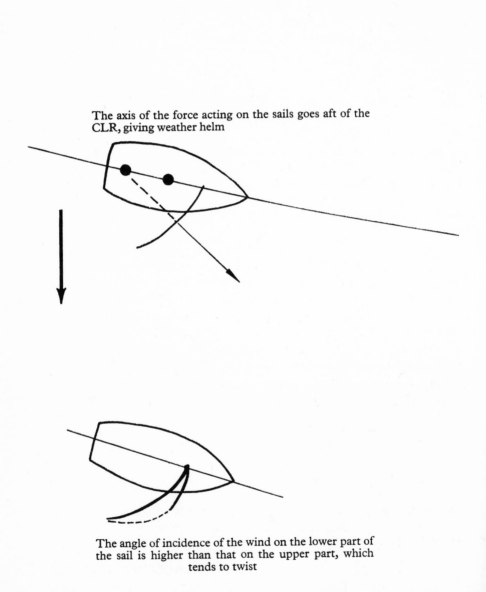

The angle of incidence of the wind on the lower part of the sail is higher than that on the upper part, which tends to twist

passes straight in his applications from a wind abeam to a wind astern; this dead point occurs on what we have called a broad reach. Manfred Curry makes no attempt to go into the causes of the phenomenon, the interplay of disturbed air flows, and of relative winds, but prescribes the same cure as we do—luffing.

This stalling, this dead point, is particularly abrupt when the boat is exceeding the critical speed for then the sheets have had to be hardened in to follow the relative wind; the abrupt cessation of the heeling force can capsize the craft *to windward* before the crew can come in from their sitting-out positions.

Without going as far as that, and even in comparatively calm weather, you will often see two boats on the same reaching course, with sheets at much the same angles to the centre lines, going at quite different speeds; the one, having come on to this point of sailing from having been on a wind aft course, has kept its disturbed airflow, and is travelling slowly; the other, which paid off from a beam wind, without losing its smooth air flow, is much faster.

Of course, the first is quite certain to be unable to accelerate, unless he luffs up for a moment, while the second has no assurance that a stall will not upset his very uncertain air flow, which is giving him his speed.

Finally, still on the topic of the behaviour of a reaching boat, we must mention two things, true for every aspect of this point of sailing: the weather helm, and the twisting of the mainsail.

The primary cause of this weather helm is that the axis of the force acting on the sails moves aft of the centre of lateral resistance. But, too, the slightest heel gives a tendency to luff, a large tendency because the boat is sailing fast. It is therefore most important when reaching to keep the boat upright, if you want perfect control.

This twisting is important, especially when the air flow is steady, because the sail pressure is high, and because the pull of the main sheet is not now vertical. In practice, there is less danger than when running with wind astern, but, from the point of view of sail performance, the twist is a disaster. In point of fact, the angle of incidence of wind on the mainsail varies all along the luff; this being so, the bottom part of the sail is sheeted too hard, while the top lifts; only the centre of the sail is working properly. A boom vang, if it is powerful enough, gives a pretty constant angle of incidence all along the sail's luff.

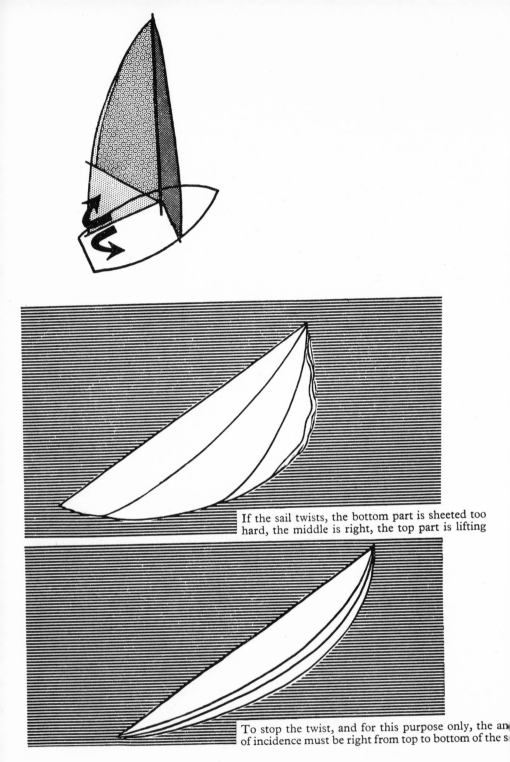

If the sail twists, the bottom part is sheeted too
hard, the middle is right, the top part is lifting

To stop the twist, and for this purpose only, the an
of incidence must be right from top to bottom of the s

See 4th paragraph, page 233.

boat handling on a reach

sail trim

We have just explained that a powerful boom vang is essential to get the most out of a sail. So far as possible, stick to the idea we put forward right at the beginning of the book—'The sail-boom assembly can pivot round the mast *like a door on its hinges.*'

If you don't achieve this, you can't really adjust your sheets to a nicety; some part of the sail is always at a wrong angle of incidence. If, as a beginner, you took our advice and forgot about boom vangs, the delights of planing speeds are not for you. Don't let that worry you; your boat will get along quite nicely without one.

The next important question is what is the best trim for the sheets. You can't give a very exact answer, because so much depends on the air stream. When it is steady—sheet in; the air pressure and the propulsive force go up. But, at the first signs of turbulence, ease out—boom up against the shrouds—or at least out to the point where obvious lifting tells you the airflow is smooth once more. It would seem then that sheet trim must often remain an open question; the air flow may deteriorate without warning. The best way to tell if a touch on the sheets will improve the driving power or not, is the heel—or, should we say, as you have already (we hope) got the habit of correcting the heel by your weight—the tendency to heel. So long as sheeting in increases the heeling force, sheeting in will pay. But you need experience—and good 'hands'—to pick the moment when your sheets are best sheeted. We will give some simpler methods.

In practice, even if you have set up a boom vang, some twist will persist, leaving the top of the sail the last to stop lifting. Experience teaches that it is of no value to sheet in more than will stop this lifting at the top, except possibly in a moderate breeze when the boom vang has enough power really to stop all sail twist. In fact, if you sheet in hard enough to stop lifting at the top, stalling will start in the lower part of the sail—even sooner possibly if you have no boom vang, as the angle of incidence of the wind is higher at the bottom.

It all boils down to one simple recommendation: sheet in just hard enough to quieten the sail. Only sheet harder if you have indications that you will get higher speed from it.

Sometimes circumstances will combine to make your chosen course one producing unstable air flow; even if the mainsail is eased right off, it will

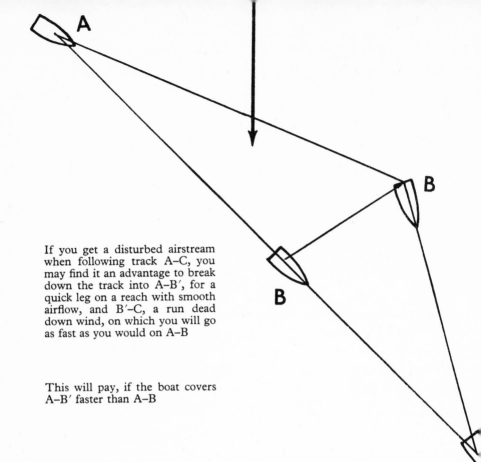

If you get a disturbed airstream when following track A–C, you may find it an advantage to break down the track into A–B′, for a quick leg on a reach with smooth airflow, and B′–C, a run dead down wind, on which you will go as fast as you would on A–B

This will pay, if the boat covers A–B′ faster than A–B

then pay to make a brief luff from time to time. You might even find it advantageous to break down a leg of your journey into one closer reach, where you will move very fast, and a run with the wind right aft, when your speed will be as high as on the broad reach with a poor airflow.

position and behaviour of the crew

Your position athwartships depends on the point of sailing and the force of the wind. Your boat has to be kept upright, or at a low angle of heel; in any case, you should not let it heel to the point where it gripes badly.

On a broad reach, or in fine weather, you need not go to great lengths in sitting out, and you will have no trouble finding where to sit to accomplish this.

On a close reach, with a strong breeze, you will have to sit out, sometimes quite energetically if you want to sheet in hard enough to get the best out of your sails. You can, of course, always stop a sudden excessive heel from a squall by a gentle luff, or, more effectively, by letting fly the main sheet.

If you stall, and the boat suddenly heels to weather, you must get back to the centre of the boat at once. This is easier said than done—the boat keeps slipping away under your weight. It is very effective in this case to luff up; the pressure on the sails rises at once.

Fore and aft, it is the speed which governs your position. Trim should be normal at a moderate speed. If there is plenty of power in the sails, a shift aft might start the boat planing. It's worth trying, but don't keep on if it does not work. To trim a boat down by the stern is of no value except to start planing.

So far as concerns the position of the crew in fine weather, everything we said when discussing running applies here; move as little as you can. In particular, if you have managed to bear away on to a broad reach (without a stall, because your speed gives you almost a beam apparent wind), do not lose sight of the fact that your good air flow hangs on a hair; the least thing, a slight jolt on the boat, for instance, will stall you and will kill the boat. Some crews who keep calm manage to keep their boats moving in light airs at a speed which is quite disheartening to their rivals, who make their boat drag its feet by their own fidgeting.

centre-board

There is not much to say on this subject. There is no need to lower it

Wind

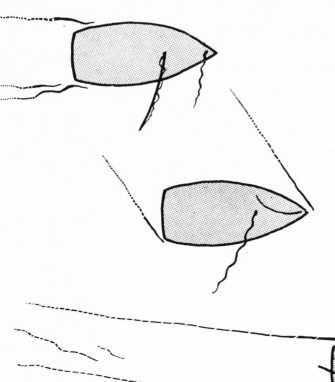

With sails slatting, the boat slows up, but it is not good for the sails

With the jib hauled a'-weather, the boat stops almost dead, but there is a lot of drift.

Hove to, jib sheeted a little to windward, the boat retains some speed. There is no leeway and no heel, and the sails are coming to no harm. The tiller must be kept to leeward.

fully, even for a heavy wind. But take a look at your wake from time to time, and see that you are not making leeway—the wake should lead away straight from the stern—and if there is any doubt drop the board a little too much rather than not enough. If it is a pivoting, long centre-board, as opposed to a dagger-plate, bringing it up half-way or even more brings back the CLR, which is a good thing, and eases the weather helm.

control of speed

To slow up, let the sheets off; this does not apply when on a broad reach, as they are already right off, but on a close reach you can slow the boat up considerably, though you cannot stop it; the mainsail will hold a little drive with a beam wind, even when sheeted right out. The shroud will keep it at a small, but not negligible, angle of incidence. With the wind abeam, you can nearly stop by backing the jib hard, but note that you will drift off to leeward as soon as you stop, as well as tending to pay off. To stay in one place as far as possible, keep your mainsail sheeted in fairly hard to keep a little speed, so that you can steer and keep the wind abeam.

If the boat starts an unwanted plane, you can always stop it by shifting your weight forward a little, and it will come back to normal speed, unless you are carrying far too much canvas. If that is so, luff up gently.

dangers

There is no special danger about a broad reach, though you should remember that sailing with sheets too hard is the main thing to avoid. A luff could then capsize you, if you did not instinctively let fly the sheet. You may remember the information you have just acquired—that 'a luff diminishes heeling'. But this does not apply if you are already sheeted in too hard. A less obvious risk is that of capsizing to windward when a stall has interrupted a burst of speed. If, when you are sitting out on a reach, you suddenly feel the boat sliding away under you, luff up at once. It is not the natural thing to do; if the same thing happens when you are close-hauled, the thing to do is to pay off.

Liberty of manoeuvre is greater on a reach than when the wind is astern, at least so far as the boat's head is concerned; you have not got the threat of a gybe to stop you bearing away. But remember—on a broad reach gybing is not so far away, and beware when your jib collapses. But you have less control of speed; you have no brakes, so, with a beam wind, sheeting out may be your only means of slowing down.

Wind

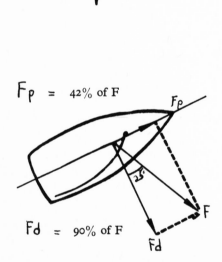

F_p = 42% of F

F_d = 90% of F

from a beam reach to full-and-by

What we are about to discuss refers to the times when the boat has the wind between the beam and the point at which you must compromise between course and speed—the point, in fact, where you can definitely just lay your objective without having to tack.

general remarks

In passing from a beam reach to full-and-by, you obviously have to sheet in. The drift component, giving heel and leeway, therefore causes the apparent wind speed to rise. If the propulsive component, though less, remains ample for the boat to continue sailing easily, it is none the less a fact that the drift component reaches its maximum for a given wind force when you are sailing full-and-by. Suppose that, when full-and-by the total force F on the sails is exerted at $25°$ forward of the beam, which is fair enough, the drift component is then 90% of F, the propulsive component 42%.

behaviour of the boat between a beam reach and full-and-by

We have just shown how large the transverse component is; when therefore the wind is fresh the crew must sit out with all their might; and the centreboard must be right down. The boat will not, though, carry too much leeway; as we saw above, the force on the sail still includes a fair propulsive component, which will keep you moving.

On these points of sailing there is hardly any problem of air flow. It always ought to be smooth, and if you happen to disturb it by sheeting in too hard, it is perfectly simple to ease the sheets a little and settle the air flow again. Stalls hardly ever happen in practice, except in a light breeze, and when the crew lose touch with their 'feeling' of the wind.

As the air flow is smooth, the boat reacts normally to sheet and helm in a luff; pressure on the sails, and, consequently, heeling, rise when you sheet in, drop when you luff or let out sheet.

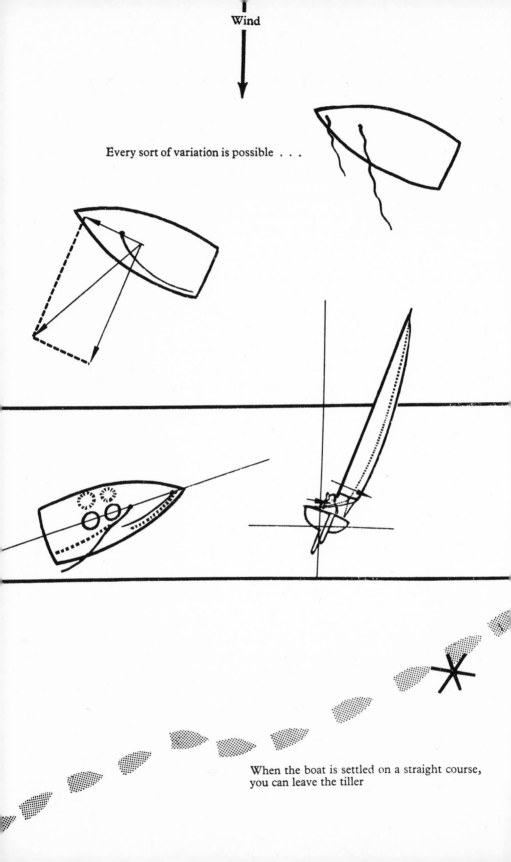

Wind

Every sort of variation is possible . . .

When the boat is settled on a straight course, you can leave the tiller

As well as giving fine control over sail pressure and heel, the sheets let you control the propulsive component from nil to a pretty high value, according to where the sails are, from sheeted in hard, to the point where they flap. So you have plenty of control over the speed of the boat, without having to change course. When full-and-by, then, the boat will not play any tricks. But, before we go on to recommendations on boat management, there are one or two possible points from which value may be got. You can, on the one hand, organize things so that directional stability is perfect and the helmsman can leave his helm; again, you can slow up and practically stop without the sails shaking themselves to pieces.

First, think what happens to the boat when you depart from the usual sheeting and trim, and do the following three things:

> let the mainsheet out a little;
>
> sheet the jib in rather more;
>
> move your weight, to heel the boat 15° or 20°.

The result will be:

> the centre of effort comes forward, and the boat takes lee helm;
>
> the heel makes the boat gripe, or rather, makes up for the tendency, imparted by the unusual sheet trim, to pay off;
>
> and so the boat maintains its course on its own.

Actually, if the boat starts to luff, the sail lifts more, the pressure on it diminishes, the CE comes forward, and heeling lessens; these two things give lee helm, and the boat bears away.

If, on the other hand, the boat starts by bearing away, the mainsail fills, heeling increases, and the result is a luff.

Now if, in practice, you have carried out the above ideas in your sheet trim and weight distribution, if you steer straight *just for a moment*, the course will stay steady, and you can leave the helm; the boat will carry on gently and quite straight. The crew can then, so long as they do not disturb the heel (don't rock the boat!) devote themselves in peace of mind to other things, such as bailing, making running repairs, filling a pipe, taking a snack, changing places, shipping or unshipping the rudder, and so on— something you find it hard to do on other points of sailing, beyond a beam wind.

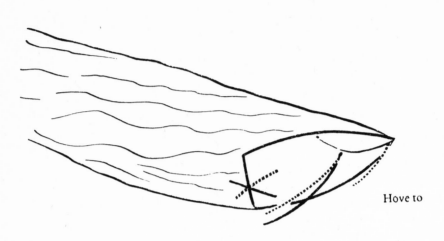

Hove to

This has the advantage of freeing the helmsman from his tiller without the inconvenience of leaving the mainsail to flog, though the latter does not inevitably happen, and it may flap gently.

If you adjust your sheets as follows:

ease the mainsail out a little;

back the jib,

the result is to slow the boat up considerably, and to stabilize its course to a certain degree. Generally, though, this will not be enough to set the helmsman free; steering has to go on, but it may be possible to lash the helm in a fixed position. All this results, as well as slowing up the boat, in diminishing the heeling force; the jib is in disturbed air and under moderate pressure only; the mainsail, in the disturbed draught from the jib, is nearly blanketed and has hardly any drive; it naturally lifts a bit, but not nearly so much as in the last case. This is an excellent way of calling a halt, for instance to take a breather during a hard beat to windward, or to bail, there is no need to sit out and the boat will look after itself. This is known as *heaving to*.

the boat's behaviour, between beam reaching and full-and-by

There is not much to say on the subject, and any beginner should sail very easily on these points of sailing, without any difficulties or serious dangers.

sail trim

The mainsail has very little twist, but what there is does not improve the available power, for the same reason as when broad reaching; the angle of incidence is bound to be wrong somewhere along the luff.

The boom vang is not very effective, as, with the greater wind pressure, what little twist remains is hard to remove. You will get rid of twist better with a main-sheet traveller, an arrangement which makes the point of attachment of the sheet on the transom movable, so that the pull may come, not from the middle, but from the corner of the transom. The block on the transom is fitted to a runner either sliding along a wire span, or on a track. The twist is dealt with very efficiently, as the pull of the sheet is much more vertical for a given boom angle.

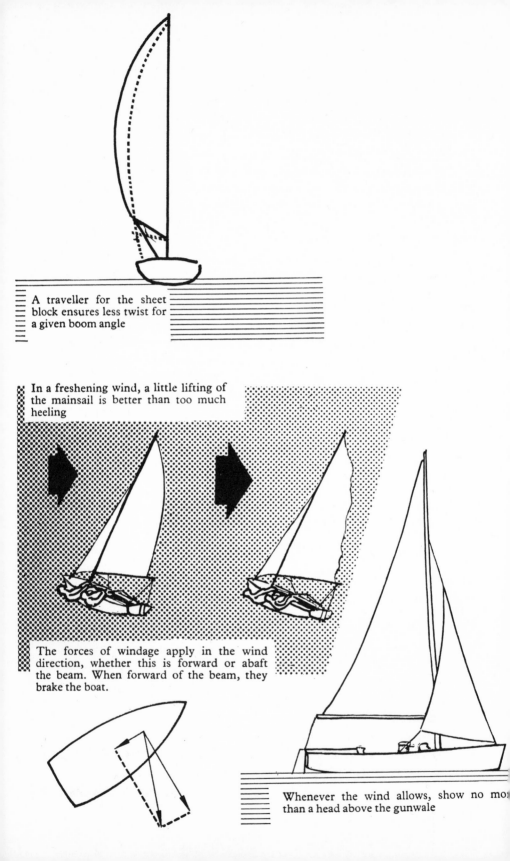

A traveller for the sheet block ensures less twist for a given boom angle

In a freshening wind, a little lifting of the mainsail is better than too much heeling

The forces of windage apply in the wind direction, whether this is forward or abaft the beam. When forward of the beam, they brake the boat.

Whenever the wind allows, show no mor than a head above the gunwale

This is just mentioned in passing; many craft are not fitted with a sheet traveller (or *horse*); it must have a fairly long travel to be of use on this point of sailing.

To end with a note of warning on sheets, you must remember that when you sheet in you increase the wind pressure on the sails, but not necessarily the propulsive component. It is not at all certain, therefore, that you should sheet in right up to the point of maximum pressure, that is, the stalling-point. In practice, especially if you have no boom vang or sheet traveller, and the mainsail twists, it will not pay to sheet in more than just stops the tops of the sails lifting.

position and behaviour of the crew

The thwartships position of the crew is governed by the need to keep the boat level. When sitting out is no longer enough to keep the boat upright, with sheets properly hardened, you must choose the lesser of two evils; let the boat heel or let the sails lift. Experience tends to prove that a lifting sail reduces speed less than an unduly heeled boat. The jib must stay sheeted hard, to avoid undue weather helm.

From the safety angle it is much better to slack the main sheet a little; as soon as you begin to find yourself tolerating heel, you are dulling the instinct which tells you to ease sheets automatically every time the boat heels—an instinct which is essential for sailing when there is a good breeze.

So far as fore-and-aft trim is concerned, there is no hope of planing when full-and-by. You might slightly exceed the critical speed, to which end your weight a bit more aft could help. Apart from which, normal trim.

Avoiding jumpiness on the part of the crew is not so essential as when reaching, but it does help when the wind is light.

Lastly, when the wind if forward of the beam, as it is here, don't forget that all *windage* provides a braking effect. It will therefore pay to make yourself as small as you can from the windage point of view; if the lightness of the wind permits, you should hide away in the bottom of the boat.

centre-board

As we have said previously, the centre-board must be dropped more than half-way when reaching.

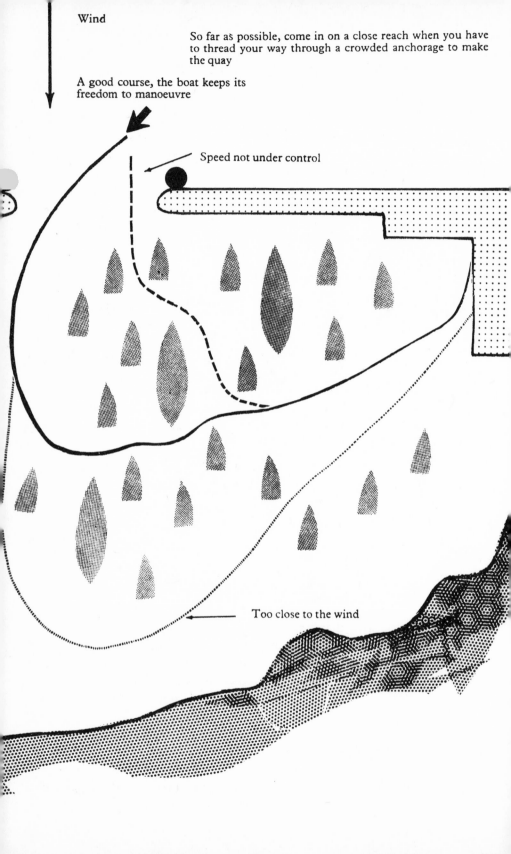

Wind

So far as possible, come in on a close reach when you have to thread your way through a crowded anchorage to make the quay

A good course, the boat keeps its freedom to manoeuvre

Speed not under control

Too close to the wind

speed control

We have spoken on this subject, too, under the heading of the boat's behaviour, and we now recapitulate the means you have.

You can slow your boat up, with great accuracy and with instant effect, by easing the sheets out more or less. At the same time, you must shift your weight inwards; the two things are easy enough to co-ordinate. If you want to speed up again, reverse the process, and the boat will gain speed as quickly as it lost it.

Do not use this method except for a very temporary check; for longer periods the sails will come to harm from too much flogging. To stop suddenly haul the jib aback.

And, if you want to hang about for a lengthy period, it will be better for your gear, if you heave to.

dangers

They hardly exist—at least, much less than on any other point of sailing. With sheets well eased off, or hove to, you can *ride out* temporary excessive wind forces, especially thunder squalls.

One thing you should note, though; not that it is an immediate danger, but it may edge you into a dangerous situation bit by bit. It is when full-and-by that the boat is at its wettest; it is going fast, and butting into the seas; spray comes aboard in quantities. It is all right if you bail in time, but you must do it, before you accumulate a dangerous lot of bilge water.

the special safety of this point of sailing

Between full-and-by and a beam reach, you have the greatest freedom to manoeuvre. You can alter course as suddenly as you please and can control your speed exactly.

This is the point of sailing on which you may cheerfully pass through a narrow passage with reefs, shoals and what not on both sides. And it is the point of sailing on which to engage in all kinds of precision manoeuvres; coming alongside, or letting another boat come alongside under way, fishing something out of the water, picking up a mooring, and so on.

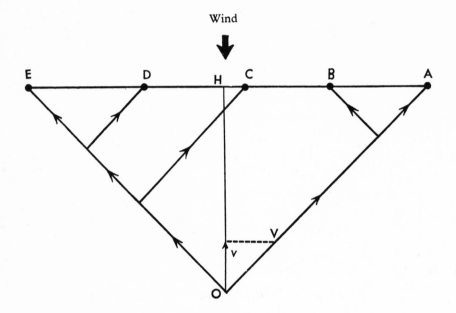

close-hauled sailing and making to windward

We would define close-hauled sailing as being necessary when a boat cannot with certainty reach the objective desired in one board; there is consequently a compromise between speed and course.

general remarks

As you cannot make direct for your chosen destination, and have to proceed by boards or tacks, the problem comes down to gaining to windward. Thus, for instance, points A, B, C, D all on one line at right-angles to the wind direction are, *for a sailing craft*, equidistant from point O; the windward distances between O and any of these points are the same, having the common feature OH, the distance to be made good up wind.

The '*speed made good*' is used to describe the velocity v with which a sailing craft goes to windward; it is the projection of the speed of the craft V on to a line parallel to the wind direction.

To get to a point up wind, a sailing craft can make two long boards or an indefinite number of short ones. It has the utmost liberty as to how to make them, and, subject to the one condition, of not carrying on longer than necessary on one tack, the only thing the helmsman has to worry about is so to adjust his course and speed to obtain the biggest gain to windward.

The two extremes he has to compromise between are:

- pointing close to the wind to shorten the distance covered;

- bearing away to increase the speed.

The factors which influence the gain are not only the course followed, but also the way the sails are set and their trim; the choice of trim and heel, the distribution of weights, the method of giving and keeping speed by minor deviations from course, and so on. It is therefore a matter of experience; it is acquired gradually, by practice in general, but more particularly by sailing in company with other boats, whether as the result of a casual meeting, or in an

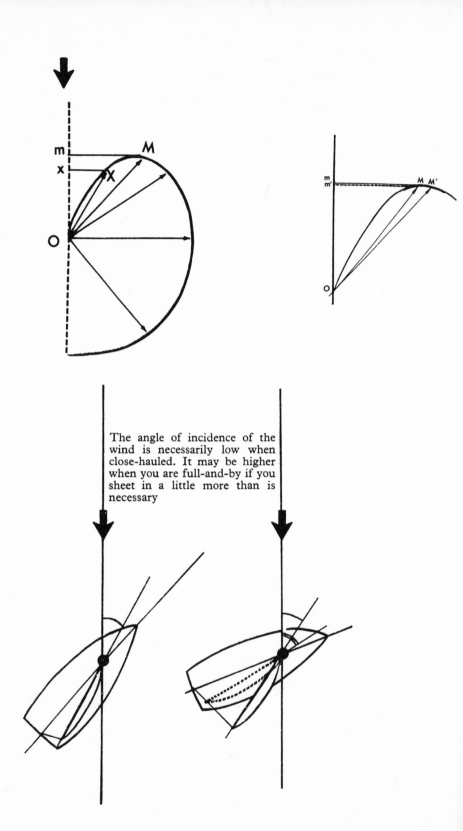

The angle of incidence of the wind is necessarily low when close-hauled. It may be higher when you are full-and-by if you sheet in a little more than is necessary

organized race. Such comparisons are so necessary to learn to sail properly on the wind that we venture to suggest that a helmsman can never expect good results if he does not from time to time yield to the spirit of competition, and give himself up to the racing urge.

Important as experience is, it does seem worth while to make one theoretical remark which has its bearing on the problem.

Trace the curve of the distances run on different courses in a given time, by a perfectly handled boat starting from point O. The distance covered depends on the course, increases as one bears away from the wind, reaches a maximum with a beam wind, drops a little on a broad reach and running. The gain for heading OX is Ox. The maximum gain Om is got on the heading OM, M being the vertex of the curve.

The important thing to note is that a heading OM', deviating a certain amount from OM gives a gain Om' differing only to an infinitesimal extent from the maximum gain Om. That amounts to this—the best heading is not really a very critical matter, and that deviations several degrees on either side will make very little difference to the gain, always *on condition* that the boat is perfectly handled as regards sails, heel, etc.

In other words, when beating, the main preoccupation of the helmsman should be, not so much to keep exactly to the best course as to keep his boat at its best speed on the selected heading.

how the boat behaves close-hauled

On this point of sailing the behaviour of the boat is governed by two facts:

- the sail pressure is high;
- this force breaks down into a large drift component, Fd and a small propulsive one, Fp.

On the first point, we should say that the force is high, but certainly not at the highest possible value, for the angle of incidence of the wind on the sails must be low. Actually, the highest pressure is got just before stalling point, when the sail is sheeted much harder in than necessary to stop fluttering; this cannot happen except when the boat is farther off the wind than close-hauled.

As the force on the sail is less close-hauled than full-and-by, generally speaking heel is reduced by luffing. See diagram, page 36.

Speed and leeway—the two eternal opponents are always working for one another's destruction

The following description of the boat's behaviour is based on the splitting of the force on the sail into:

- a high leeward component;
- a low propulsive component;

and these lead to the following characteristics:

- a strong tendency to heel, and to make leeway;
- comparatively low speeds, in contrast to other points of sailing, and poor acceleration.

The leeway made depends largely on the speed; as a general rule therefore, ability to sail close to the wind is a most valuable characteristic, as the driving power tends to dwindle away and the thwartships component remains intact.

Speed and leeway are two eternal opponents, and are always working for each other's destruction; as speed goes up, leeway drops; every increase in leeway reduces your speed.

When on the subject of the action of water against the keel of a boat we went into the matter of how a momentary braking or accelerating effect could have lasting effects on these two elements of speed and drift; a purely temporary check may result in a lasting slow-up. Which is the more annoying, because you get a false impression of speed from undue leeway.

On such a point of sailing as full-and-by, or a close reach, the boat picks up its speed as soon as sail is trimmed; not so when close-hauled; you will not get the best possible results just by setting the boat's head on the best course and trimming the sheets as required; you must build up a reserve of speed and give the boat a little way from time to time; it cannot accelerate, however perfectly you have trimmed the sheets, without a little help.

The speed of a boat, on its best windward heading, in a good breeze, is round about 80% of the critical speed—say 3.8 knots for a 13-ft boat with a Vc of 4.7 knots. Going back to the curves of resistance to forward movement above, we see that at this speed:

- the total resistance is not very high compared to that at Vc;
- friction resistance accounts for a large share of the total.

This explains why a dirty hull is such a much bigger handicap when sailing close-hauled than at any other point of sailing; the fouling increases the friction resistance then preponderant.

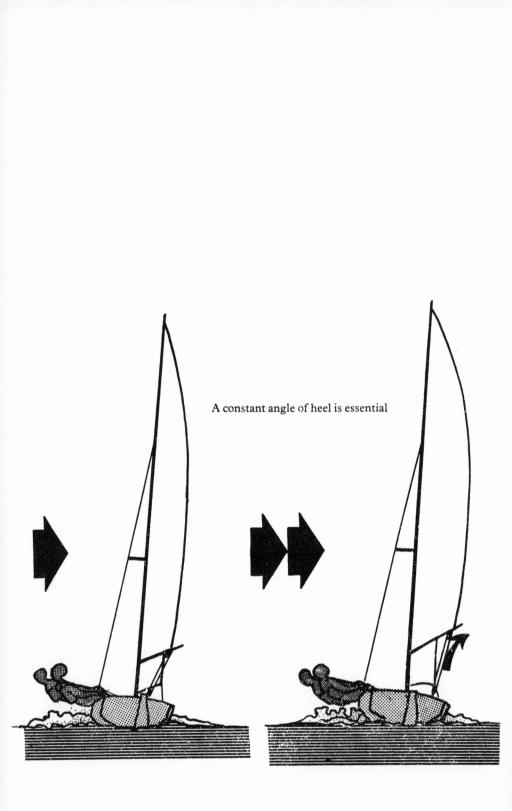

A constant angle of heel is essential

the boat's handling close-hauled

choice of heading when tacking

As we have said, broadly speaking it is not vital to keep exactly to one course; the trim of the sails is far more important.

Quite simply, you can point closest in a wind of middling strength. You cannot point as close in a light air, or in a choppy sea.

And we saw, too, that the best course depended on the boat, and in particular on its sail plan; a flat sail will enable you to point higher than a sail with a lot of flow. Don't forget that when you follow our advice and compare your own close-hauled sailing with that of someone else; a difference of flow in the sails may account for differences in the behaviour of the two boats, without necessarily signifying a better performance of one as against the other. A dirty boat, too, must be sailed fuller than a clean one; but, of course, it will not gain so fast to windward, other things being equal.

It never pays, as it sometimes does on other points of sailing, to sheet the sails a little harder than necessary to stop lifting; you lose nothing by letting them lift very slightly, rather than sheeting them in too hard. Doing the latter cuts down the propulsive component.

Still, with a fresh breeze, the most common mistake is not to sheet in enough; the cause may be physical weakness, idleness, or the fear of heeling too much. This last fear is not unreasonable, and we shall see that it is, in fact, never a good thing, and often dangerous, to let the boat heel as it wishes. But the crew must go to great lengths to sit out enough to let the sheets be hardened in to the best point without heel, but the time will always come when it will not be possible to sheet in so hard in a rising wind without heeling too much.

Here is the dilemma; put up with sails lifting, or with too much heeling? Both for safety's sake, and for performance, the answer is let the mainsail—and only the mainsail—lift just enough to keep the boat upright.

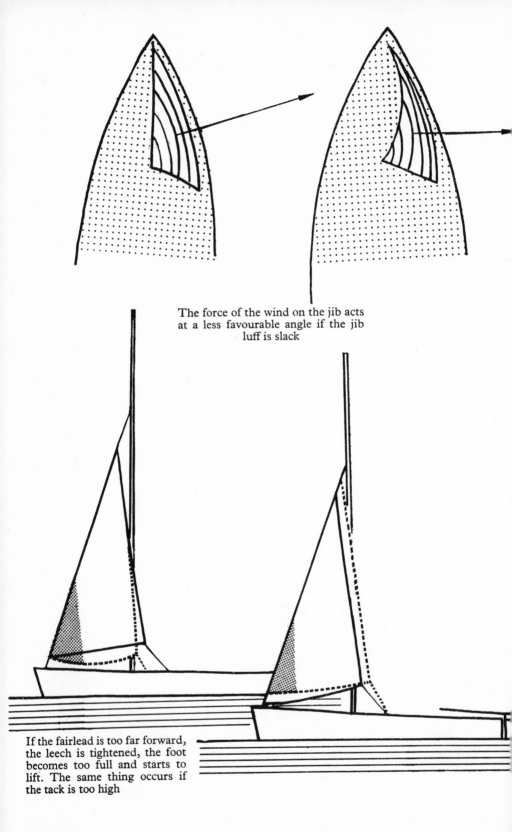

The force of the wind on the jib acts at a less favourable angle if the jib luff is slack

If the fairlead is too far forward, the leech is tightened, the foot becomes too full and starts to lift. The same thing occurs if the tack is too high

Here is another problem: the boat pitches more or less violently in a moderate breeze and a choppy sea, the mast jumps fore and aft, and the whole sail plan shudders and lifts on each downward plunge. This is because the alternative movements of the mast keep changing the apparent wind, leaving the sails first sheeted too hard, and then lifting. What is the thing to do in this case? Sheet block and block? Or put up with momentary lifting? Broadly speaking—only experience can be a real guide—the best solution is to sheet in so that the sails will lift for maybe a third of the pitching cycle. You would have to sheet in block and block to stop them altogether, and run off the wind as well, which would be most unfortunate, as they would be sheeted too hard almost all the time. The term *block and block* or two-blocks means hauled in so hard that the blocks meet or almost meet.

Anyway in such a case, it will be very difficult to find the best heading and sail trimming without having an identical craft sailing in company for comparison.

trimming the jib

Except in the lightest air, the jib luff must be kept as taut as possible. Let us look at what happens if it is slack. The leech keeps its original shape pretty well, the luff falls away to leeward, and the centre part of the jib acts as if sheeted in much harder, or at least sets far more on the centre line of the boat than it should; the sail balloons out, and tends to curve to windward towards the leech. The force on this part of the sail is therefore directed much more athwartships, and gives much less propulsive effort, with, of course, the same, or an even greater, leeward element.

A jib with a distorted luff gives as much heeling force as a properly set one, and much less pull.

Experience proves that a taut luff for the jib has a great effect on the efficiency of the sail in a good breeze.

There are two ways of attaining the desired tautness:

- set up the shrouds;
- sheet in the mainsail.

We shall see later that these two remedies call for distinct styles of sailing.

Another point is—the lead of the jib-sheets must be right. With the fairlead too far forward, the foot is too full, and, when you luff, the jib will lift first at the bottom. If the lead is too far aft, the top of the jib will be the first to lift. The best fore-and-aft position of the jib-sheet fairlead is that

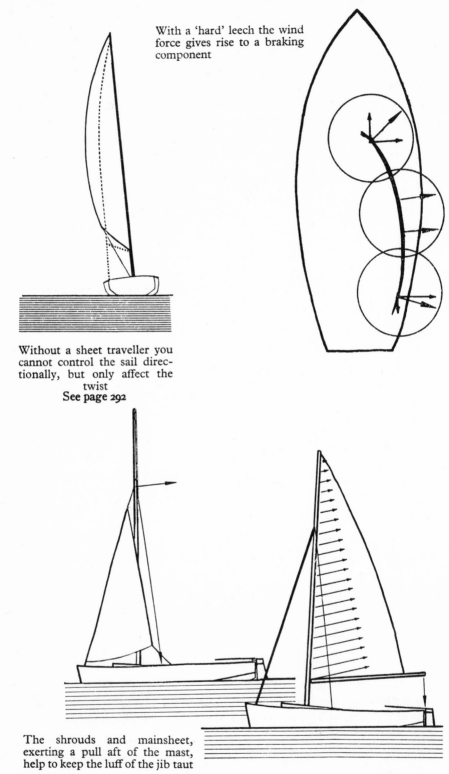

With a 'hard' leech the wind force gives rise to a braking component

Without a sheet traveller you cannot control the sail directionally, but only affect the twist
See page 292

The shrouds and mainsheet, exerting a pull aft of the mast, help to keep the luff of the jib taut where the jib starts to lift at the same time over the whole of its height, or starts to lift at the top just a little earlier.

adjustments to the mainsail

When the boat is fitted with a traveller for the main sheet, it must be used with discernment. By its use, you can have a sail sheeted flat with no twist on any course; it is only necessary to move the traveller along its rail or wire, as necessary.

With a non-adjustable sheet block, on the other hand, you have no real control over the sail's setting, for when you sheet it in more or less it is only the twist that you are working upon.

You will adjust the slider according to the course the boat is following; the object will be to sheet the sail flat enough to avoid twist without bringing it in more than is necessary to stop lifting. Of course, the fresher the wind, and the less close the boat is able to point, the farther out on the transom should the sheet block be.

Another important point is the flow in the sail:

- *in extent*, it is controlled by the amount the foot of the sail is tightened on the boom; the sail is flattened as the bolt-rope is stretched.

- *in position*, it is controlled by the halyard; the tighter the halyard, the nearer the mast will be the point of maximum flow.

With a light wind it pays to let the sail have its maximum flow, so the bolt-ropes are not pulled tight.

In moderate weather you will get to windward just as well with a sail moderately full as with a flat one; but remember, you do not sail the boat in the same way in these two cases; sail free with a full sail; point close with a flat one.

And lastly, in a strong wind the sail should be as flat as possible; and, as the flow tends to move out towards the leech of the sail, harden down the halyard to retain it in the best place. With a synthetic fibre sail, don't be afraid to haul it taut, as it will not be pulled out of shape; but a cotton one, if hardened to the point where wrinkles appear, may set right for that occasion, but only at the expense of its future; you may be distorting it permanently. Finally, still speaking of heavy weather, a good boom vang will serve a useful purpose in limiting the twist when you have to let fly the sheet for a passing squall.

You will have to balance the heeling couple, arising from sail and centre-board (FF′) by the righting couple arising from weight against water thrust; this couple you set up and adjust by moving the crew inboard or out

$$FZ = PX$$

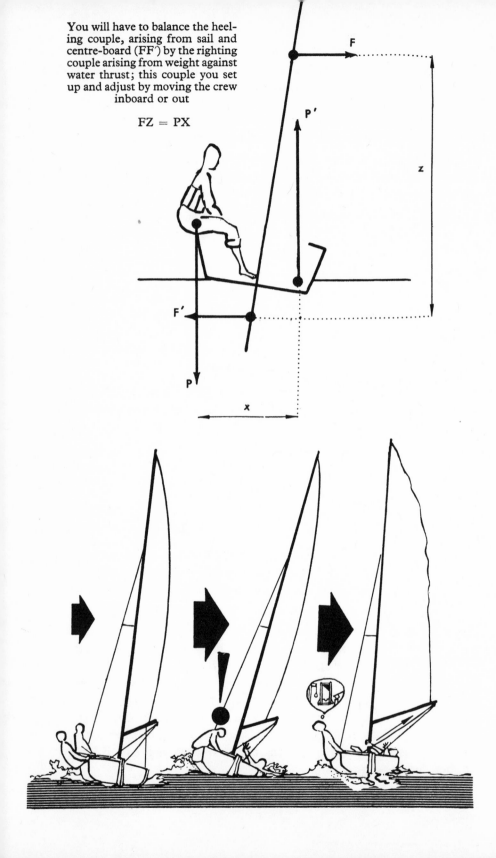

control of heel

In light or very light airs it will pay to heel the boat a little, to avoid lee helm, to lessen the wetted surface, and to help the sail into its proper shape by virtue of its own weight.

Apart from this one case, heeling is always harmful; the centreboard loses its efficiency, resistance to forward movement grows, the boat gripes and calls for a great deal of helm, which puts on the brake . . . and so on; not to mention the risk of a capsize if the heeling becomes excessive.

The best sailing-point of a boat is generally at a very slight angle of heel, at which the helm is perfectly balanced.

To keep this ideal angle of heel, you must balance the heeling couple of the sails by the righting couple of the boat, the latter being created by moving the crew's weights. Light variations of heel, due to wind fluctuations, can be smoothed out by varying the boat's heading very slightly as necessary.

With a variable wind you will have to keep on juggling with all the factors that affect the heel. If a squall blows up, for instance, there are several methods open to you to keep the heel low:

- let fly the sheets;
- sit out farther;
- luff.

And here are the advantages and the drawbacks of each of these:

Letting the sheets out, or rather letting out the main sheet, is the quickest in bringing results; you can let go at once, without any effort, and let out as much or as little sheet as you need to give control. The main sheet acts as a safety valve; the helmsman who has got the instinct into his head to let fly whenever the boat heels too much, is protected from the consequences of sudden gusts and of a crew who slips and falls down to leeward. The reverse of the medal is that when the squall has passed you must sheet in again, and that does call for hard work. You will soon get tired doing this in very fitful winds.

Sitting farther out is a bit slower, for it doesn't take effect until the crew is in the new position—and has no effect at all (even perhaps, by reaction, a negative effect) while the move is going on.

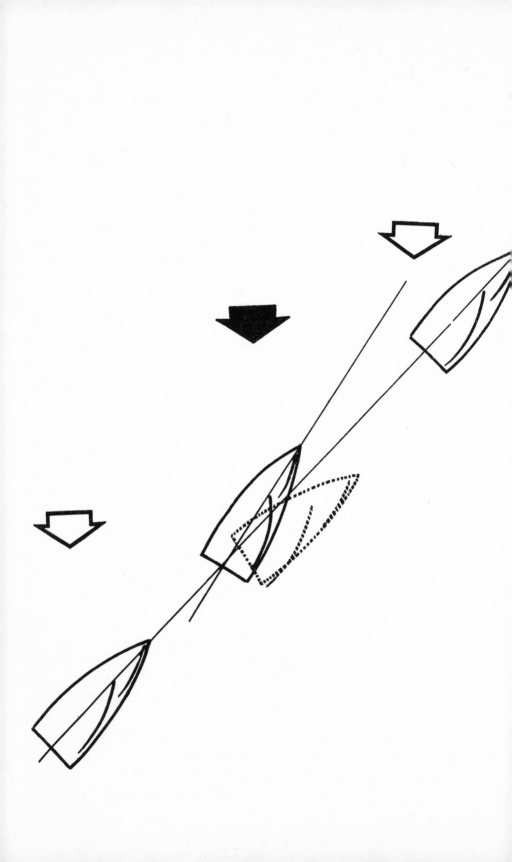

And lastly, luffing is a little slow in taking effect, but is less tiring. It is not easy to judge the extent of luff needed, and you run a risk of losing speed and control or getting taken aback if you go too far.

So the field for each of the suggested remedies is:

- *Letting fly sheets:* the quick and safe way to be used whenever the boat starts to heel, whether or not you do anything else. You can get back some of the sheet you paid out at the first onset of the squall.

- *Sitting out more:* potent but slow in results; do it for the longer-lasting squalls.

- *Luffing:* for use with discretion, to prevent extra heel before it happens, or rather, at the first onset of the squall.

In practice, it always pays to sit out as far as you can; the motive power depends on the boat's righting couple. But easing sheets and luffing are such different ways of going about things that they involve radically different styles of sailing close-hauled in a fresh but variable breeze.

To go into them in detail:

first means of neutralizing a squall

Keep the jib well sheeted in, then slack off the main sheet as soon as the boat tends to heel.

Later, pay off a bit to keep speed; this is easier, as the main sheet has been let out.

As soon as the squall has passed sheet in again on the mainsail.

Naturally, the better the crew sit out, the less sheet you will have to give out and the better you will keep your speed.

If the crew remains sitting out in the same position, you will not lose driving power if you only veer main sheet as necessary; but on one condition—that is, that the jib continues to draw normally, and that its luff does not sag in the squall. If the sail does twist, the jib balloons and loses much of its power. So the rigging must be well set up.

When the squall comes, luff-up and harden in the sheet

The wind pressure drops, but keeps a small propulsive component

If you let the sail flog, you will reduce the wind pressure, but its direction of effort changes most unfavourably

This means of control is virtually essential, when one is confronted with light planing craft such as the Uffa Fox types.

It is effective in correcting the tendency of such boats to carry excessive weather helm when heeled.

It has the drawback of being very tiring for the helmsman, who is constantly hauling back the sheet he has let out. On the other hand, undue accuracy is not called for; the boat will behave very well close-hauled without; it may lose its speed for the moment, but is quick to get it back.

It is the easiest remedy to apply, the most certain, and, as a result, the first to be taught to a beginner.

● As soon as you have a little experience, and have your boat well under control, you can forestall a coming heel with the appropriate luff, without touching your sheets.

This is what the trained crew does.

The real originator of this method was the American, Ted Wells, several times world champion in Snipes.

It applies particularly to a heavy craft—like the Snipe—which does not lose way too quickly; but it can be perfectly well used on very light boats.

It calls for a sensitive touch and skill. You must feel the coming squall before the boat heels. The sails must be flat in proportion to the wind force. To estimate the amount to luff, you must use real judgement, or you will come up too far and risk being taken aback. And, of course, you must be sitting well out, and prepared to veer sheet if the heel comes in spite of everything.

You end up very close to the wind, but without serious loss of speed.

This fact, that the boat carries its way, is surprising, but this is the explanation:

when you sheet home hard and luff, the sails are almost lined up with the wind, and the pressure on them does not rise much; this explains why heeling remains slight.

But the propulsive component dwindles, and the boat only continues to move forward because the resistance to forward movement dropped sharply with the fall in speed; very little driving power suffices to keep up this reduced speed.

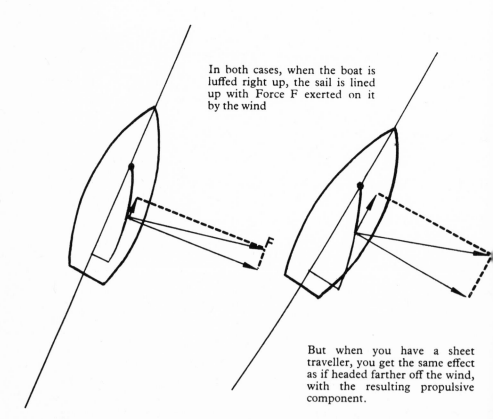

In both cases, when the boat is
luffed right up, the sail is lined
up with Force F exerted on it
by the wind

But when you have a sheet
traveller, you get the same effect
as if headed farther off the wind,
with the resulting propulsive
component.

See upper left sketch
on page 284

A good boom vang would be equally
effective

The difficulty is obviously to sheet in enough, and to make a small enough luff not to get caught aback. Obviously, if the boat was slowed up too much, it would start to make leeway, the resistance to forward movement would go up, which again would slow it up . . . a vicious circle which would end only when the boat was stopped dead, when it would immediately get out of control.

This does not stand out too clearly on paper, but it does give the results of experience and technique. It is known from experience that it is possible with practice to point so close as to make up for the loss of speed it causes.

It is a good way of dodging a squall, and lets you carry a lot of canvas in a fresh breeze without excessive heeling or flapping sails.

- Get up speed while sailing normally, with enough slack in the main sheet not to have too much heel;

- sit right out;

- then at the same time, luff and sheet hard in.

The boat will gain to windward very much faster than by conventional sailing.

Certainly, sailing conditions do tend to be unstable; if you do begin to lose speed, the boat will go into the vicious circle we have described.

Now and again, when you get an abrupt loss of speed, you must relent, ease sheets and bear away to collect the speed you need. As you get more experience, this need becomes less frequent.

To maintain a good drive/drift ratio, too, a sheet traveller is useful; you can keep the sail flat without bringing it too much to the centre line of the boat. The sail can be 'lined up' with the wind without luffing excessively. The fresher the wind, the more the boom needs to lie over the quarter when sheeted in.

The most important thing is, to be in sympathy with your boat, and, particularly, to keep it at the angle of heel at which it is in perfect balance; this gives you the best sensitivity of helm to allow a quick luff or pay-off as the wind demands.

Balance of the boat must be thought of in terms of something balancing on a needle's point. The slightest breath makes it pivot. So it is with the

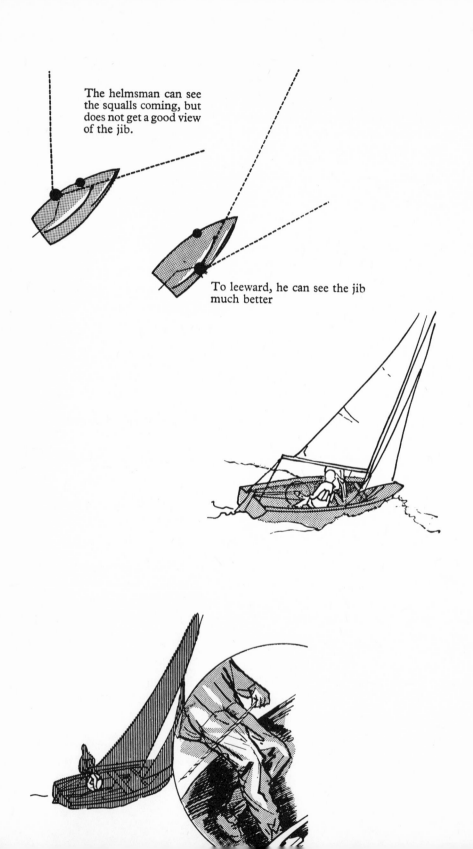

The helmsman can see the squalls coming, but does not get a good view of the jib.

To leeward, he can see the jib much better

boat when in this state of hypersensitivity; you can hold the tiller between two fingers, and the boat will follow the wind by itself, luffing and paying off at the slightest alteration of heel.

This method is most efficient, the boat keeps dry, which is an excellent thing, and it is certain in action if you get the habit at the start of easing the main sheet at the first sign of heeling.

To conclude, there is another very valuable thing; the flexibility you can have in the rigging. Everything can be left with plenty of play, and the main sheet will look after the tension of the luff of the jib.

position and behaviour of the crew

It is quite feasible in light weather for the crew to sit one on each side of the boat, and the problem arises, should the helmsman sit to weather or to leeward? To windward, he can see where the light puffs are coming from, but does not get a view of what the jib is doing. To leeward, he will see his jib nicely, and will sail the boat better, but a lot of people do not like this position. The best way is to make yourself learn to steer equally well from the windward or the lee side; this avoids the helmsman and crew having to shift their weight at each tack.

In light weather, too, it is feasible for the crew to disappear inside the boat to a certain point and reduce windage.

With a rising wind, the crew will sit out farther and farther. One might recommend:

- keep your weight as mobile as possible in a thwart-ships direction; always have your feet apart one on each side of the boat, and don't get one behind the other;

- if you have *toe-straps*, only put one foot under the straps, and the other as far as possible underneath yourself; like this you will have most control over the placing of your weight, and there will be less risk of being thrown off your balance if a sudden lurch throws you towards the centre of the boat. And, don't forget to see the straps are in good condition. It would be too bad if they were to break.

- the crew should always be a little farther out than the helmsman; the pair will cause less windage if one is in the lee of the other;

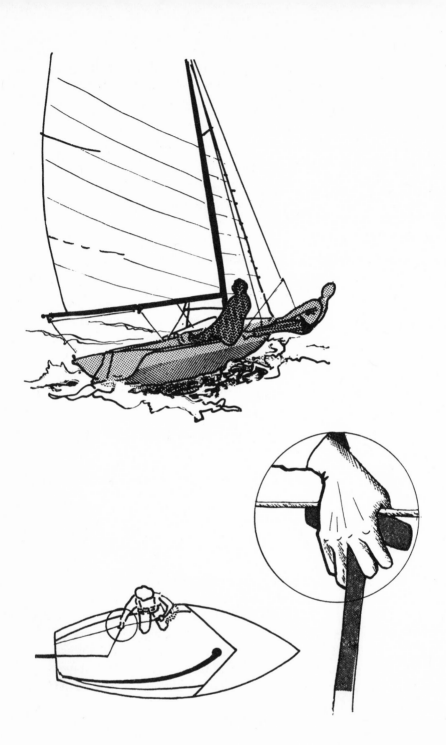

- Using a *trapeze* is rather less tiring and much more effective than sitting out with straps, but it's an acrobatic business, and good training is essential. The helmsman has to be used to keeping constant heel angle.

The longitudinal trim, of course, needs attention, and, especially when there is a lop on the water, it pays to keep the fore-and-aft inertia low; the crew should sit close together, when the boat will climb over the waves better and be stopped less.

The jib hand will not generally find it difficult to hold the sheet— it will even be a means of support for him when sitting out; but the helmsman has to handle tiller and sheet, and fiddle a lot with both. The *tiller extension* is a nearly universal arrangement these days. It lets the helmsman do much more sitting out; it is hinged to the tiller, or better, has a sort of universal joint attachment, so that he can turn it in any direction. If the sheet comes to him from the transom, he can hold tiller extension and sheet in one hand and hang on with the other. It is quite feasible to steer and sheet independently of one another with one hand. Still, in the ordinary way, and as there is not a great length of sheet to deal with, it is best to steer with the aftermost hand and use the forward one for the sheet.

speed control

You can regard the boat as having good brakes when close-hauled, but poor acceleration:

- easing sheets will slow you at once;

- but hauling in again will not result in quick acceleration. To get up speed again quickly, you really have to pay off and let drive for a moment.

going about, or tacking

We talked about this in a general way in chapter 1. We have also had occasion to mention it here and there, particularly when on the subject of manoeuvring. The success of a tack may be judged by the amount of lost time it causes. Time may be lost because the evolution is made too slowly, or because the boat has lost speed.

The best way to go about is to set about it at a reasonable rhythm, not going to the extreme of an abrupt turn, ruining the speed, nor to that of such a slow turn that the boat stops before it is head to wind.

Let us recall what you have to do to ensure getting round successfully:

- you must *use the helm* gently, avoiding any abrupt handling of it;

- the sheets must be handled with accuracy, that is: the jib sheeted in till the moment when it lifts, then let fly at once; the mainsail sheeted in block and block;

- the weights must be shifted in time with the evolution, to keep the boat upright; but, as the turn starts, it will help to increase the heel a trifle.

- the boat must have enough speed.

Actually, all these points do not need to be perfect to enable you to get about, but perfection in one or two of them does help to make up for deficiencies in the others; you can, for instance, get about with practically no speed if your handling of tiller and sheets is right, and you don't have your weights in the wrong places. And, when faced with a difficult tack, you have to use every means there is; so train yourself to use each of them separately, so that you will really know what the effect of each is.

Some practical ideas may well be given, as to the co-ordination of helmsman and crew.

It is most convenient for the helmsman to tack facing aft; for instance, starting on the port tack:

- he brings up his right foot and puts his left foot forward (or gets ready to, if sitting out);

- he makes sure his sheet is nicely coiled down between his feet and the stern of the boat;

- he pushes the tiller to leeward with his right hand while he hardens the main sheets right in with his left;

- he gradually crouches down—on both feet—and is exactly amidships when the boat is head to wind;

- he starts to get over to the other side as soon as the boat starts to heel and puts the tiller back, turning the extension aft;

- he changes hands on sheet and tiller, and starts sitting out gradually.

Note that:

- the helmsman's feet did not move;

- that he can see what the boat is doing all the time; as soon as he looks up, the boom acts as a giant wind indicator and tells him where he is with regard to the wind, and what to do with his tiller:

- the heel of the boat regulates the movement of his weight, and tells him to ease sheets if need be.

The drawback to this way of doing things is, that for a moment he loses sight of what is going on ahead. If he is in a jostle of other craft, or if, as an instructor, he has to watch the crew's actions, he must face forward. In this event, he will put his right foot forward and his left towards him. Helm and sheet change hands behind his back, which is the difficulty of *this* method.

It is essential to know how to go about at a moment's notice, one way or another as necessary. You are more likely to succeed if you know how to do it without foot faults; fumbling your feet stands a good chance of throwing you off balance or getting them tied up in the main sheet.

With no boom vang, the crewman may prefer to face forward for the turn. However he does it, he moves his feet the same as the helmsman; while his foot movements are dictated by the amount of heel, this has nothing to do with his sheet handling; the jib must draw as long as it can.

In passing, if the helmsman and crew do the turn, one facing forward and the other aft, they are liable to bang their heads together, or against something else.

dangers of this point of sailing

Close-hauled sailing is safe enough, because the boat answers well to helm and sheets, partly because the sailing calls for more effort than on any other point. There is therefore no risk of carrying on comfortably without noticing a rising wind—which may happen, and often does, when running; if, for any reason, you then have to luff, you will find that a boat hitherto docile has become unmanageable, owing to being overcanvassed. If the boat is hard to manage close-hauled, any other point of sailing will ease matters for the crew.

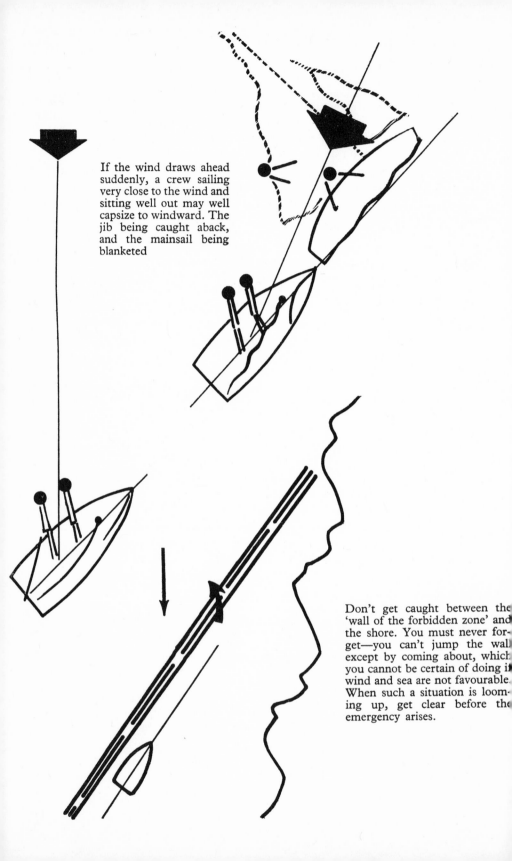

If the wind draws ahead suddenly, a crew sailing very close to the wind and sitting well out may well capsize to windward. The jib being caught aback, and the mainsail being blanketed

Don't get caught between the 'wall of the forbidden zone' and the shore. You must never forget—you can't jump the wall except by coming about, which you cannot be certain of doing if wind and sea are not favourable. When such a situation is looming up, get clear before the emergency arises.

When the wind is unsteady, there is obviously a risk of capsizing on being hit by a squall, but it is not a grave danger if the helmsman is well trained to ease sheets at once as soon as the heel becomes excessive. It has to be a pretty sudden squall to capsize a craft before a helmsman who is doing his job can let fly his sheet. On inland waters, a by no means negligible risk is that of seeing the jib taken aback suddenly when you are sitting out; the boat, suddenly relieved of the weight of wind in the sails has a very good chance of capsizing *to windward*. This may well happen when the wind draws ahead, or as a result of going too far with a precautionary luff. It is the sort of thing which happens to the best-trained helmsmen.

And finally a more general danger is due to lack of sea-room and to hindrances to free manoeuvre.

The boat lacks manoeuvrability in the sense that, sailing slowly, it is not quick to answer the helm. It may be that when close-hauled it has not—just for the moment—enough way on for an unexpected evolution. You must just avoid pinching too close to the wind when in the middle of a lot of other boats or obstructions. The following are examples of hindrances to manoeuvre:

- as regards direction, you can't luff without stopping, or else you must go about, which, as we have seen, may not be feasible;

- as for speed, it is easy enough to slow up, but almost impossible to accelerate again without bearing away;

- if the wind heads him, the helmsman *must* bear away;

- if wind and sea conditions are such as to make going about difficult, you must keep sea-room when coming up to an obstruction, so that, if you fail to get round, you can try again, or find another answer—gybe.

From all this it appears that when close-hauled the helmsman needs to pay a lot of attention to obstacles, and act as far as possible in such a manner that they will not set him any difficult problems; nothing harder than slowing up or paying off.

One of the cardinal principles of safety is, never to go too close to windward of an obstruction. It applies to all points of sailing, most of all when close-hauled.

And, when you have got yourself on the wind into an area full of obstructions, you must train yourself to keep well off the wind, to be sure of keeping your power of manoeuvre.

The problem of getting aboard

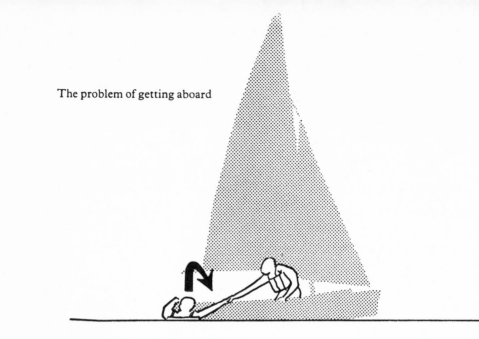

The best solution here would be
to go back and start again

because

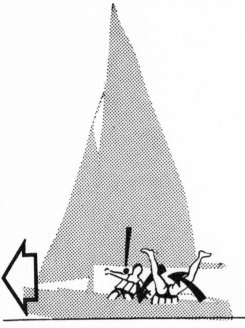

getting aboard this way, even
with the crew's assistance, generally ends up with a belly-flop on
the floorboards

handling a boat | 7

setting sail from a beach

There is often very little water at the edge of a sandy beach. It is a good thing to walk into the water carrying the boat rather than drag it, especially if there is any surf. If the boat has not got a lifting centre-board and rudder they will have to be shipped well out from the beach, and then the problem will arise of getting yourselves aboard. Being wet through up to the waist before you start is no great pleasure. So it might be considered preferable to start right from the beach.

At first sight, sailing without a centre-board and a rudder appears an impossible job, unless you have a following or at least a beam wind. But if the wind is on shore, you don't have to set sail necessarily from a straight beach. It will be well worth while to look for an alternative, such as a creek which will permit of a beam-wind take-off.

Before we go on to a practical study of the three conditions for setting sail, beam wind, stern wind and head wind, we will look into some general instructions.

team work

It is a good way to begin the job by a clear explanation to the crew of what is going to happen. If you are the helmsman, leave nothing to chance; the crew may have quite different ideas on the best way to proceed. If you are the crew, and are still at the stage when you mix up sheets and halyards, port and starboard, windward and leeward, do make a point of getting clear on matters that you are not sure about.

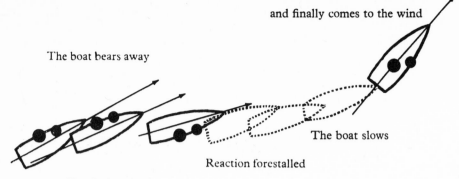

and finally comes to the wind

The boat bears away

The boat slows

Reaction forestalled

You induce heel

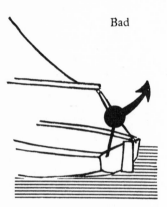

Bad

Harsh helm application

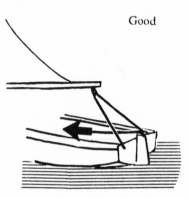

Good

A firm steady hand on the tiller

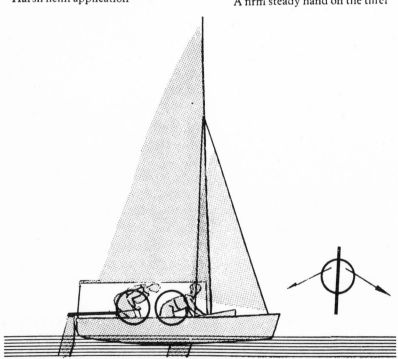

In any case, when the two members of the crew really understand what the problem is, a lot of explanations will be unnecessary, and there is every chance of success. Teamwork by both is essential; and it has the happy effect of keeping everyone in good humour, whatever happens.

behaviour of the boat

The boat has no, or practically no, centre-board down, the rudder has no, or practically no, effect.

Centre-board or dagger-plate, there is little difference in the effect; a pivoting centre-board dropped an inch or so gives lee helm; and, as we have said, the boat will not stand any sheeting in of sails in the ordinary way as if it was in deep water, when it has no centre-board. To counter the drift, you must have speed; and how are you to get that without sheeting in? Simply by not attempting to sail too close to the wind.

sailing without rudder

Little skill is called for to sail in shallow water without the rudder. You will soon get the idea if you do a little training in deep water in steering by means of the sails and by arranging your weights, but remember the following points:

● The boat has a certain degree of inertia, and will not answer to your efforts at once.

● In steering, the mainsail is more use than the jib, so use the jib for drive and the mainsail for steering.

● As control of heeling is needed quickly and constantly, the positions of the crew are a little different from the usual ones; the helmsman, crouching a little to dodge the boom, with feet apart, looking forward, just behind the crew, who will be in the same position, ready to alter the heeling, and to handle the jib. The crew can then jump out at once if the boat goes aground.

It brings to mind the behaviour of a bicycle when it is going too slowly; it is no time to put up your feet and take your hands off the bars; you must be ready to go to one side or the other, or jump out fast.

● You can use a scull or paddle to steer; but the helmsman must not get so involved with his paddle that he can't look to his sails, or where the boat is going.

Look! No rudder!

We will now go into the three ways of getting off a beach: wind astern, wind abeam and wind ahead.

wind abeam

It is a fairly simple matter to get away from a beach in a beam wind, that is to say, with the wind blowing along the beach.

On this point of sailing there is good speed and little leeway.

It is possible to manage the sheets so that the boat will hold its course without a rudder. To do so, here is the procedure:

> jib sheeted normally, just enough to prevent lifting; mainsail well out.

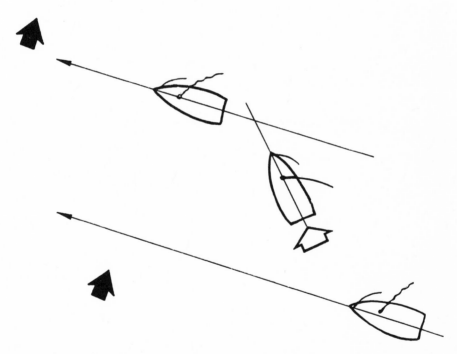

What happens? The boat tries to pay off under the influence of the jib, off to a broad reach; then the mainsail fills, speeds up the boat and makes it luff up to lifting point; then the whole thing starts again. Give it a slight heel so as not to fly right off the wind. Beware of too much speed; speed causes weather helm, and without your rudder might find yourself head to wind.

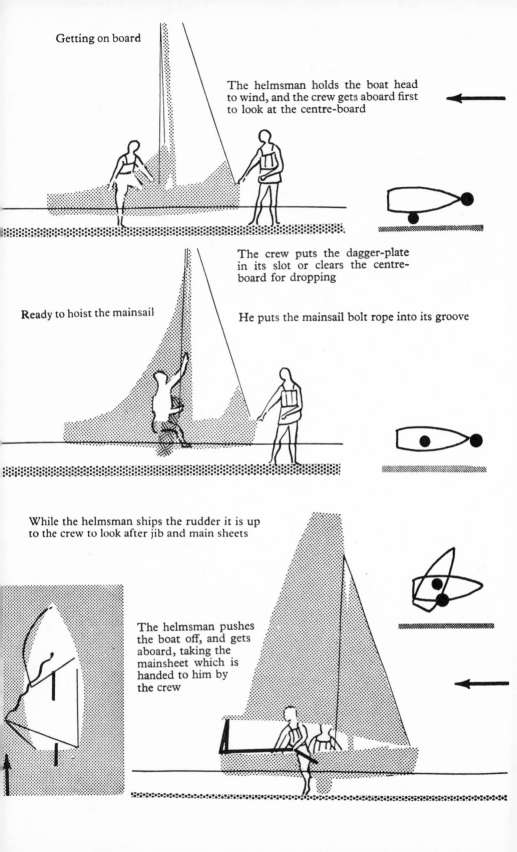

Getting on board

The helmsman holds the boat head to wind, and the crew gets aboard first to look at the centre-board

The crew puts the dagger-plate in its slot or clears the centre-board for dropping

Ready to hoist the mainsail

He puts the mainsail bolt rope into its groove

While the helmsman ships the rudder it is up to the crew to look after jib and main sheets

The helmsman pushes the boat off, and gets aboard, taking the mainsheet which is handed to him by the crew

The boat rides the rollers best with a beam wind. But too much speed may be a nuisance; the boat may fail to rise to the wave, and ships a lot of water

lind you don't both get out on the lee side; ke boat will be out of balance, and will spin und and make for the beach; if you both :t on the weather side, the same thing will ippen, except that you will gybe and make r the beach instead of tacking

At a moderate speed the boat rides the waves and goes over it comfortably

To get away from the beach at this point of sailing, just let the boat go. The only difficulty will be to go slowly enough

Remember, if the beach is backed by a sand-dune the wind will increase very quickly as you draw out of its lee

To get aboard;

Put the boat in stern first, and hold it head to wind while the crew gets aboard

Wade in holding the boat, so as to give it room to turn

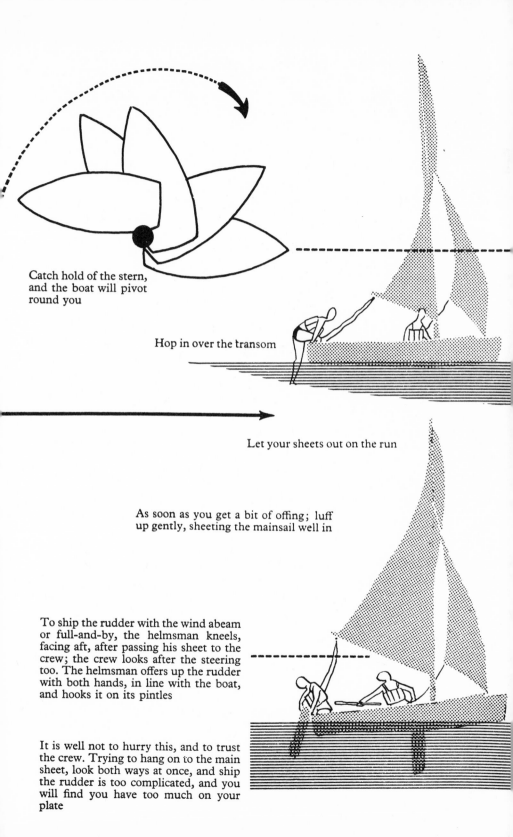

Catch hold of the stern, and the boat will pivot round you

Hop in over the transom

Let your sheets out on the run

As soon as you get a bit of offing; luff up gently, sheeting the mainsail well in

To ship the rudder with the wind abeam or full-and-by, the helmsman kneels, facing aft, after passing his sheet to the crew; the crew looks after the steering too. The helmsman offers up the rudder with both hands, in line with the boat, and hooks it on its pintles

It is well not to hurry this, and to trust the crew. Trying to hang on to the main sheet, look both ways at once, and ship the rudder is too complicated, and you will find you have too much on your plate

wind ahead

Setting off from a straight beach into the eye of the wind is practically impossible. With little centreboard down, you can't really get up any speed until you are full-and-by.

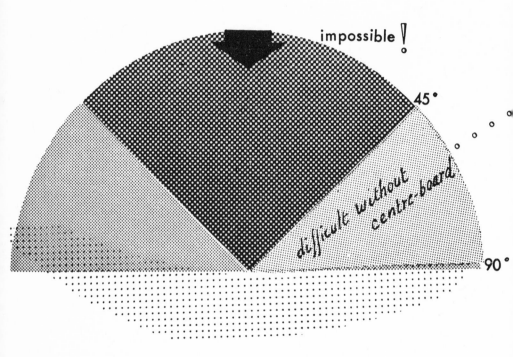

And we have said nothing of the surf! You must then find somewhere (a little point, a hard, jutting rocks, or similar) from which the boat can leave on a close reach, with the possibility of coming to a broad reach to get up speed and then luff again; a point which will be beyond the surf, and will give you a chance to get the centre-board down quickly.

A The first thing, in this case, is to make up your mind *which tack you will have to go out on*. Nearly always you will find one better than the other—the wind is rarely right on the beach. But there will generally be one position on the beach better than any other—the *windward* end.

For instance, with a little beach with a rocky point (of different lengths) at each end:

● if the wind blows from A or C, you would take off from *a* or *c*, which would give you a beam wind in those respective cases. It will be rather more ticklish to leave from *a*, as the larger rocky point will involve an early tack;

● if the wind is from B, it will not be so easy; you would do best to leave from *b*, hard under the rocks, as far to windward as you can get.

Two points:

> ● the best point from the wind aspect will generally be the same as that where rollers are smallest;
>
> ● if you choose your place carefully, you are pretty much in the same position as with a beam wind.

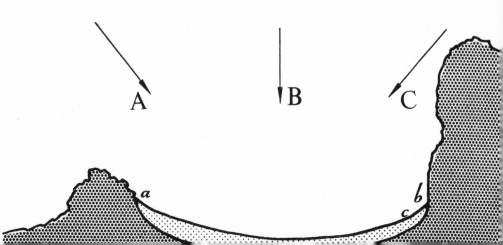

B Here, then, is the way to set about it:

● the boat is put in the water, bows first, and the helmsman holds it abreast the mast. The crew gets in first, puts the dagger plate (if fitted) into the trunk, and takes his sheet;

● the helmsman wades forward, drawing the boat with him, and need not get wet much higher than the knees. The crew starts to put the centre-board or dagger-plate down, passes the main sheet to the helmsman, and sheets the jib home;

● the helmsman gives the boat a good shove off, and jumps in as it goes by;

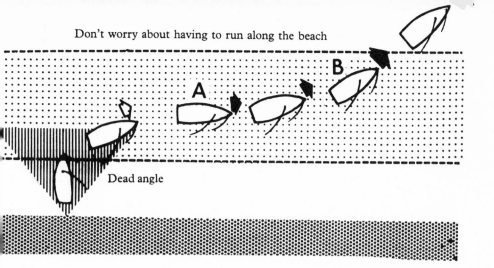

Don't worry about having to run along the beach

Dead angle

● the boat will generally tend to pay off, and you must sheet in the mainsail a bit. It will pay to start by running parallel to the beach while you pick up speed (A), being very careful not to sheet the sails more than necessary. You can then luff up gradually, dropping the centre-board as you do so, (B);

● but you must not come hard on the wind before the centre-board is right down. The thing to avoid doing is to point up too high too soon; the boat will drift away, and find itself at C before it has speed, when it will never come up to the wind. You can see beginners crabbing like this the whole length of a beach, and wondering why the rocks at the end have a fatal attraction for the boat.

The great thing is, first and foremost, to give the boat *all the speed you can*; you must let it run with sheets in as little as possible (but, of course, not lifting). Then you will get maximum drive and minimum drift component.

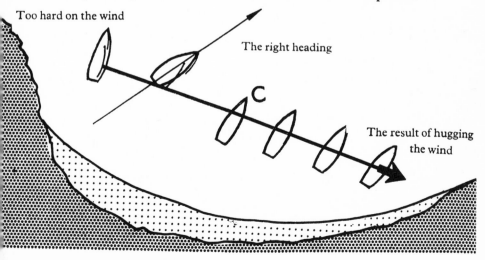

Too hard on the wind

The right heading

C

The result of hugging the wind

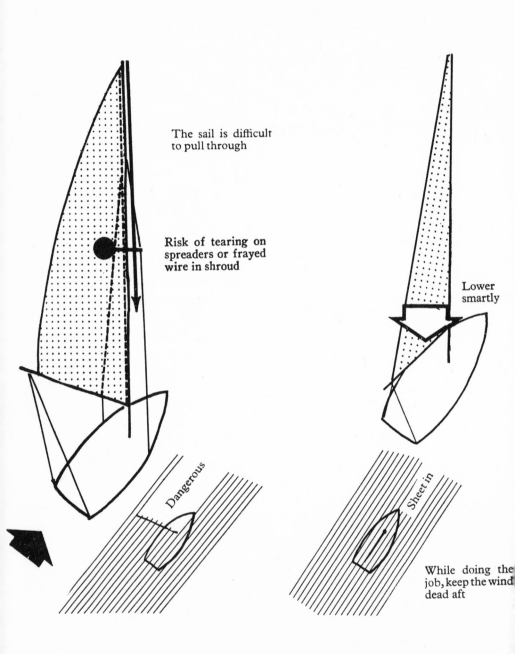

The sail is difficult
to pull through

Risk of tearing on
spreaders or frayed
wire in shroud

Dangerous

Lower
smartly

Sheet in

While doing the
job, keep the wind
dead aft

sailing with reduced canvas

We shall see that a boat returning to the beach may well do so under bare poles, or under jib alone.

Sail may have to be reduced in other circumstances; you may have to bring in the jib, and sail under *una-rig*, with mainsail only; or, on the other hand, you could *take down a reef* in the mainsail, or lower it altogether and sail under jib alone, and so on.

lowering the mainsail

We have seen that when ashore lowering or hoisting the mainsail is much easier to do when head to wind rather than with the wind aft; if the sail fills and the sheets are jammed, the boat might well capsize. Afloat, other factors arise; let us see why it is not advisable to lower the sail with a stern wind, and why it is better not to have the wind right ahead.

reasons for not lowering sail with a stern wind

For a start, it is a bad habit to get into; sooner or later on big boats it will be impossible. Then, the bolt-rope must slide easily in the groove on the mast; this is much easier when the sail is lifting, and that just does not happen when before the wind. Moreover, with a free wind the mainsail presses on the shroud and crosstrees. If the shroud is not in good shape, and has a strand of wire sticking out, that means a torn sail. If one of the crosstrees is not properly padded where it meets the shroud, that will lead to the same result.

Lastly, as we have seen, the boat is much too fast and uncontrollable with the wind abaft the beam.

If you can't avoid lowering your mainsail with the wind aft, this is what you have to do:

> sheet the sail flat;
>
> let it go on the run.

If the boat yaws the least bit, the wind will take the sail and slam it on one side or the other while you are trying to get it down. If there is not too much wind, you can lower the sail without bringing it right in, but mind it does not rub against the shroud.

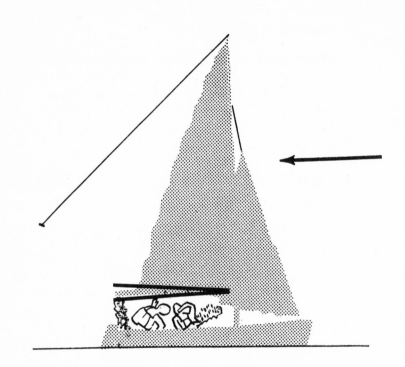

The sail, too, may obstinately refuse to come down, and here you are:

Current, say, three knots; the sail is half down, and stops you seeing to leeward; it is dragging in the water. You note this, and heave it aboard; the boom falls at your feet, but the top of the sail is still full of wind; you are busy trying to luff; your crew is trying to stop the sail ballooning out as it comes out of the groove; the boat heels, the crew realizes this too late, you can't let out the mainsail any more, and you may finish up with a capsize—not even a spectacular one!

So, it is primarily as a safety precaution that you don't lower the mainsail when stern to wind; you have no freedom to manoeuvre; the boat is very fast, goes off at a touch on the helm, and in these conditions a yaw is not easy to correct.

Unless in particularly atrocious weather, you must be able to choose your boat's course when at sea.

the drawbacks of lowering the mainsail head to wind

It is almost impossible to stay head to wind in a fresh breeze, because:

● the jib is flogging, both sheets are flying in the wind and lashing the crew, who will probably let go of the halyard in self-defence;

● the boom will thrash about wildly for a moment, and will make you both duck;

● the sail will be flapping, and will probably come down very fast, but not so fast that the boat will not have borne away till you have the wind abaft the beam;

the best way; lower the sail full-and-by

(more exactly, on the luff, coming up wind from a full-and-by).

● Start operations in an unoccupied stretch of water;

● choose your tack; starboard tack for choice, as the main halyard is fast on the starboard cleat;

● explain the sequence of operations to the crew, so that you will work as a team, sailing meanwhile full on a reach;

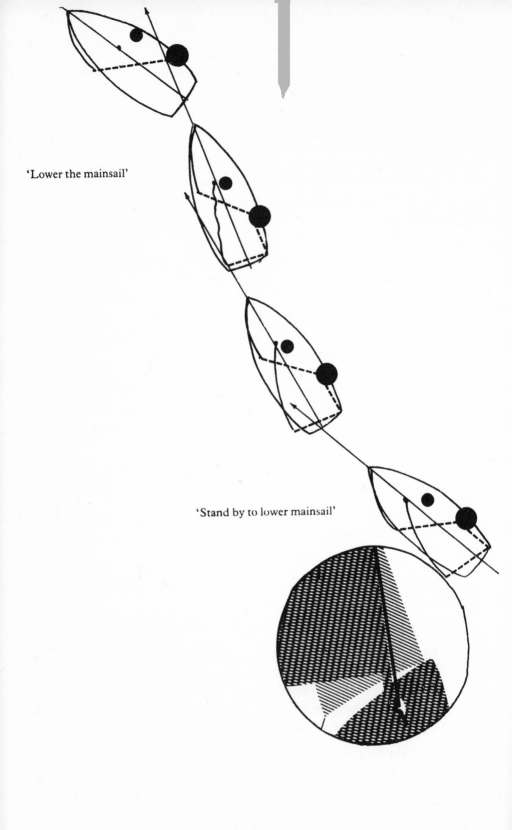

'Lower the mainsail'

'Stand by to lower mainsail'

- on the order: 'Stand-by to lower mainsail', the crew passes you the jib-sheet and throws off the turns of the halyard. Then you luff, sheeting in the jib for more speed;

- on the order: 'Lower the mainsail', the crew lets fly the halyard and hauls on the boltrope; it only takes a few seconds; don't let the sail lie about in the bottom of the boat; roll it up temporarily, with the battens along the boom, and push it on one side;

- pay off under the jib for continued speed;

- this method will keep you ready to manoeuvre and master of your boat; in this, as in everything else, hurry is dangerous. If your crew starts to lose his head, tell him to take his time.

sailing under jib alone

Valuable as a drill on a beginner's craft, and quite practicable on faster and more manoeuvrable ones. The one thing to realize is, that you can't sail close-hauled with jib alone, and that for several reasons:

- the boat carries lee helm, as the CE has moved to the centre of the jib, well ahead of the CLR; moreover, the speed has dropped, and, as we have said, a boat that has lost much of its speed carries more lee helm than one that has kept it;

- the sail area may have changed, but not the windage; in other words, the propulsive component has diminished more than the drift component.

If, then, you don't want to find yourself back on a reach under jib alone:

- sheet it in just enough to stop lifting along the length of the forestay. There is a tendency to sheet it in as you would when you had the mainsail;

- use your centre-board;

- heel the boat a bit to give it a tendency to gripe; you will end up by getting within 70° of the wind, which is not to be sneezed at.

CE

The boat carries lee helm

CLR

The jib flaps

Back the jib to help her round

Get up speed before you centre the helm

The speed drops; the boat is nearly into the wind

Sheet the jib flat

The crew heeling the boat

Move to leeward with the helm

going about under jib alone

This calls for a lot of skill.

● Start by getting all the speed you can off the wind;

● go round with the helm very gently, and move to leeward;

● follow the jib, sheeting in gradually; that is, as you shift from a good close reach, you will go through full-and-by to close-hauled. If you let fly the jib as soon as you start, you will have it flapping and making too much windage, braking the boat and paying off the bow. If you sheet it in in time with your luff, and neither ease it nor sheet it to windward till it starts to lift when sheeted flat, you are still diverting enough air to get drive out of it. So, during the luff, don't sheet in until you see the jib lift.

● As soon as you are head to wind, back the jib at once, grabbing it by the clew and holding it out to windward. This may not be necessary on a fast boat in smooth water, but with a beginner's craft, you must, especially at the start.

advantages and drawbacks

With a very fresh breeze, you won't point better than with wind abeam, but you can console yourself with the knowledge that, even with the mainsail, you would not manage to go about, or get up into the wind much better without an exaggerated heel.

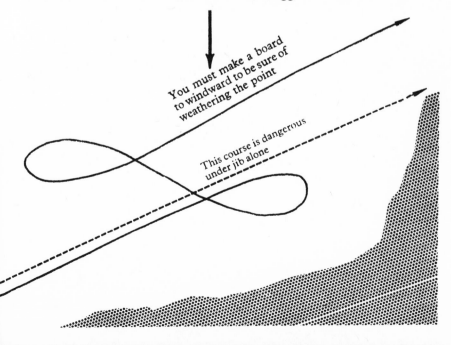

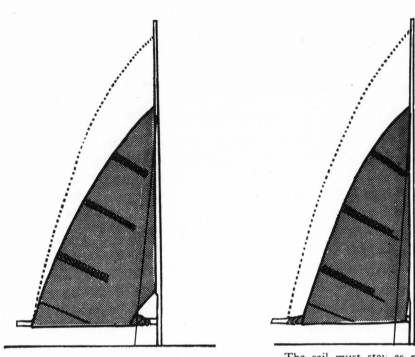

The sail must stay as near the mast as though a roll had not been taken

With a good wind, the value of sailing under jib alone is that you can gybe without the slightest risk.

It is well to know that you *can* make to windward without the mainsail, but the gain to windward will not amount to much, so don't try it in a crowded harbour, near the shore, in a narrow channel, in fact anywhere where a false step may have disastrous results. Failing to go about in open water does not matter in the least, but it is a much more serious matter to fail to get round when you have a rocky promontory, or a boat on moorings, ahead of you.

roller reefing

Before you try to roll down a reef afloat, you had better start by practising ashore (when you are rigging the boat), and then on moorings. We will look at rolling down a reef on a mooring, and then under way.

If you go aboard the boat on a mooring, you may be sure the boat will be lying head to wind if it is at all fresh, unless there is a fairly strong current, and, of course, if you don't put the centre-board down.

You can roll down either before or after you hoist the mainsail; if the latter, you must drop it enough to take the reef.

A reefed sail must be hardened down in just the same way as an unreefed one, both on boom and mast. On the mast, a swig on the halyard will do. On the boom, you must pull the leech aft, without pulling the bolt-rope of the luff along the boom, which would make frightful folds diagonally across the sail.

This is the process:

● the crew, sitting on his thwart (*pronounced, by the way, 'thought'*), slackens the halyard enough to bring the boom down on his knees. He makes the halyard fast for the time being;

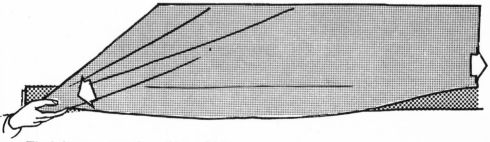

The helmsman starts by making a fold

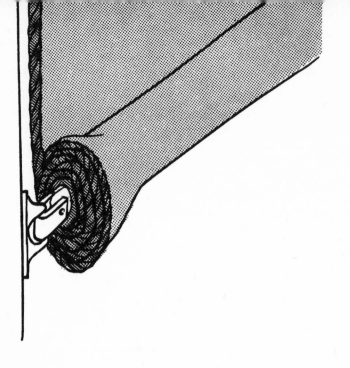

● helmsman and crew turn the boom, the one pulling the sail aft, the other making sure the bolt-rope rolls up properly without going beyond the forward end of the spar, and without spiralling toward the stern; a complete turn of the boom counts as a one-roll reef;

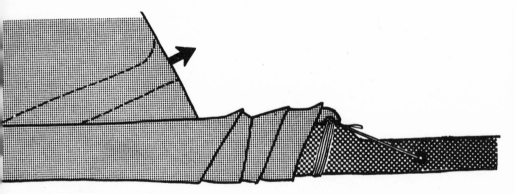

● then the crew, supposing he is sitting on the starboard side, holds the boom in the hollow of his left arm, puts the halyard in his right hand, and pays out halyard and rolls at the same time with his right hand;

● the helmsman helps turn, and stretches the sail after each turn;

● as soon as enough turns have been taken, the crew puts the boom back in its place on the gooseneck, so that it can't unroll (that is what the square piece or possibly spline, is for), and hoists hard up.

It is not hard to see that this very simple operation—on a mooring —may not be so easy under way. The crew cannot leave the jib-sheet, nor the helmsman the tiller.

Be that as it may, a trained crew can take four or five rolls in less than a minute from the time the halyard is taken off the cleat till it is on it again.

But, right from the beginning, if the weather is threatening and you know you will want some rolls down when at sea, take them down before you start—you can always let them out if you find you were too nervous about the wind.

By way of a drill, here is what you do when under way:

● start by getting full-and-by;

● cleat the jib-sheet, so as to have two hands free;

● helm a little to leeward, to make up for the paying-off tendency of the sheeted jib, and hold it with your knee;

● roll up the sail as best you can; you can adjust it when it is rolled.

That should at least let you ride out a squall which is not too severe, or get to shelter the shortest way.

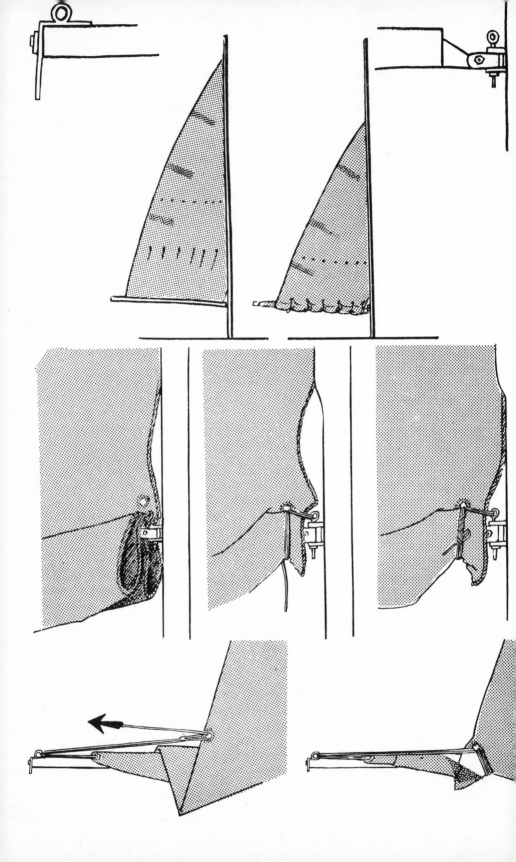

reef points

These are another, and older, method of reducing the surface of the mainsail. The process is more efficient than roller reefing. With the latter, it is not possible, when the sail has been rolled, to stretch it along the boom. It develops a bag in the centre and often sets very badly.

A reefing sail is arranged like this; two or three rows of eyelets run the whole length of the sail, parallel to the boom, from the luff to the leech. The rows are varying distances apart, round about a foot. Through these eyelets pass lengths of cordage which are called by names varying with their positions—*reef pendants* at the luff and leech bolt-ropes, *reef points* in between. There are metal fittings at the fore and aft ends of the boom to take the two pendants.

To take a reef:

● start by lowering the sail until the luff eyelet is on the boom;

● fold up the sail on either side of the boom equally;

● lash the sail, as close to mast and boom as it will go, with the forward reef pendant;

● lash down the clew with the other pendant, first of all heaving it aft (see the drawing opposite); then, using the rest of the pendant, lash down the new clew on the boom with two or three turns and a reef knot;

● you can then hoist the sail again, and tie up the reef points; the object of these is to tidy up the folds of canvas hanging under the boom, which would neither look pretty nor help the crew to go about their work; there is no need to heave these taut;

● don't get unduly worried if the sail shows a fold along the line of the boom; it is a little too much stretched;

● don't make unduly complicated knots, because you won't be able to undo them when wet; it is essential to be able to shake a reef out quickly.

You will get a lot of peace of mind when you have once mastered all this.

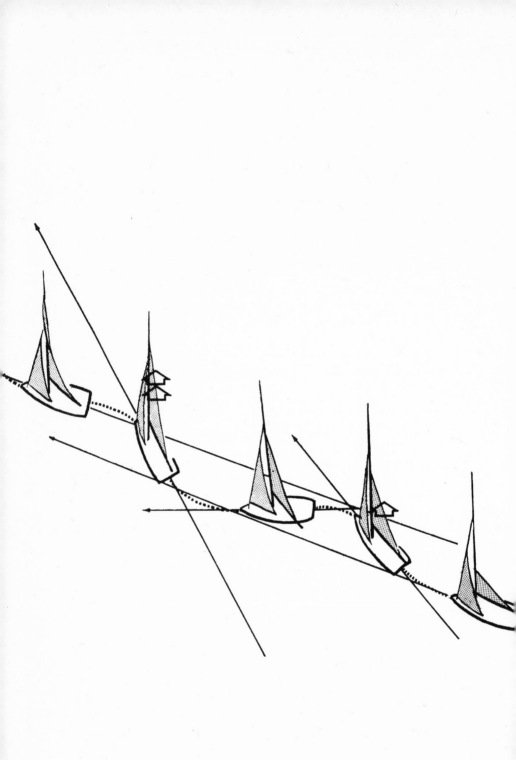

rehoisting the mainsail

There is no special difficulty about rehoisting the mainsail after having rolled or reefed it, or after sailing under jib alone:

- get preferably on the starboard tack;

- get some speed with a beam wind (the helmsman should take the jib-sheet while the crew is hoisting the sail);

- the crew pushes the boom on to the gooseneck, and then enters the bolt-rope in its groove;

- come up close-hauled; start hoisting; watch out that the battens don't get tangled up under a thwart or between your legs as you do it;

- as the boat will not sail close-hauled under jib alone, it will slow up, and then pay off;

- stop hoisting as soon as the sail fills and is bearing against crosstrees and shroud;

- pause a moment on the reach, to get enough speed to luff again and repeat the process;

- you gather speed and start again; when the need arises, the helmsman should take the weight of the boom, to help get the luff tight enough;

- continue the process till the sail is set.

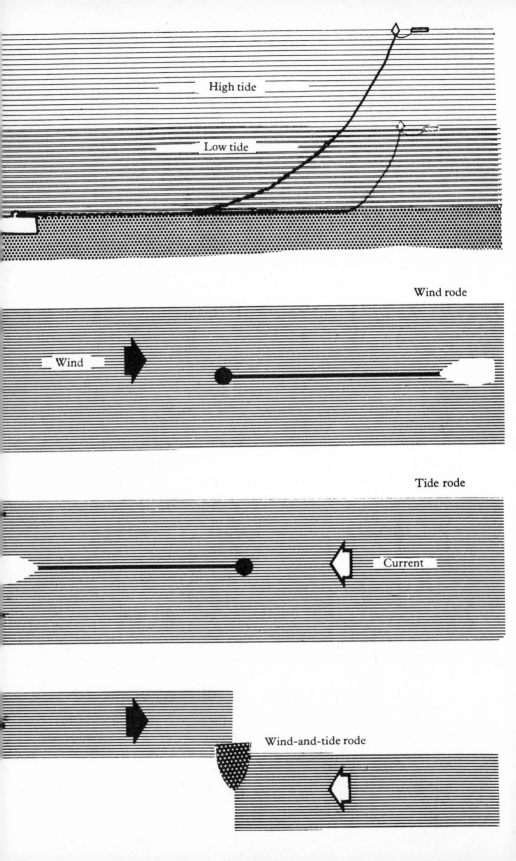

High tide

Low tide

Wind rode

Wind

Tide rode

Current

Wind-and-tide rode

mooring

Mooring a boat consists of making it remain stationary by means of either a permanent anchor or sinker.

You must have an anchor aboard, whether for river or sea sailing. It is essential that a boat should be capable of tying up at any time. But if the crew are to go ashore and leave the boat some time at moorings, for the night perhaps, it is better to use something safer than an anchor—a *permanent mooring*. This may be a very large anchor or some very heavy object (which you can't bring aboard a light craft, and which will withstand any strains imposed on it); it is connected to the surface by a chain and a buoy-rope with some form of float. The length of the chain and buoy-rope are such that the buoy will remain afloat in the fiercest tides and whatever the level of water.

The boat will behave similarly whether at anchor or on a mooring. It will swing about the mooring, heading into whichever is stronger, wind or current. Generally a boat is *wind-rode*, but if there is a current it may take up a position between wind and tide, or be completely *tide-rode*. When a boat lies head to wind it is because it is held by the bow, and the action of the wind on the upper works overcomes that of the current on the submerged surface.

We will go in turn into the operations of picking up a mooring, or tying up to a buoy, and then of anchoring.

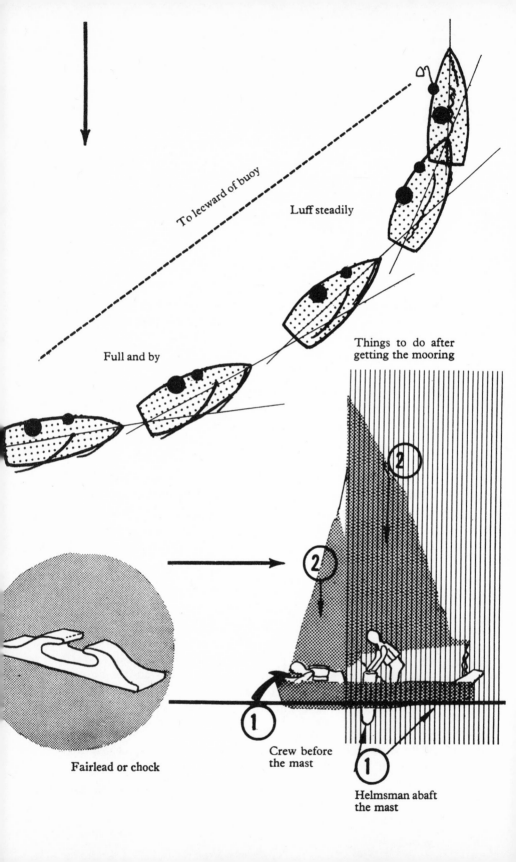

To leeward of buoy

Luff steadily

Full and by

Things to do after getting the mooring

Fairlead or chock

Crew before the mast

Helmsman abaft the mast

permanent moorings
picking up the mooring buoy head to wind

Picking up a mooring involves coming up to pick up the buoy without way on the boat; you must approach full-and-by, and come head to wind; you must, of course, know how much way your boat will carry.

Here is what to do:

1 ● come up to leeward of the buoy, full-and-by;
2 ● the crew passes you his jib-sheet; his job is to pick up the mooring, and, to this end, he places himself forward of the shroud;
3 ● luff up;
4 ● the crew picks up the buoy, and passes the buoy-rope through the *chock,* if the boat has one, otherwise between forestay and shroud, that is to say in the forward third of the boat's length; he takes a temporary turn round the mooring cleat or round the mast if necessary;
5 ● he lowers the jib,
6 ● then the mainsail,
7 ● secures the mooring properly,
8 ● and lastly, haul up the center-board, and unship the rudder.

note

● Never pick up a mooring except in the bow of the boat and when the latter is stationary; if you pick up the mooring over the side, the boat will pay off and sail round the mooring in circles; if you pick it up with way on the boat, you will be dragged astern, and again, forced to pay off.

● Prevent the boat from sheering about on the mooring:

by sheeting the sails right out, so that they do not draw;

by unshipping rudder and centre-board.

● Moor up properly before going ashore. The buoy-rope is provided only to lift the chain; if the buoy was attached to the chain, it would not be able to keep afloat, especially with a fast current. Pull in the chain, therefore, and make it fast to the cleat; but if you have to use the mast, take the end of the buoy-rope a couple of turns round it, between the step and the *partners* (the hole in the deck or thwart through which the mast goes), then two half-hitches. The buoy can be tucked into the bight *or hung in the rigging.*

If you are by yourself; come up so that the boat will be level with the buoy amidships; pick up the buoy and take it forward outside the shrouds. If you can't get hold of it till it is level with the stern, go round and try again.

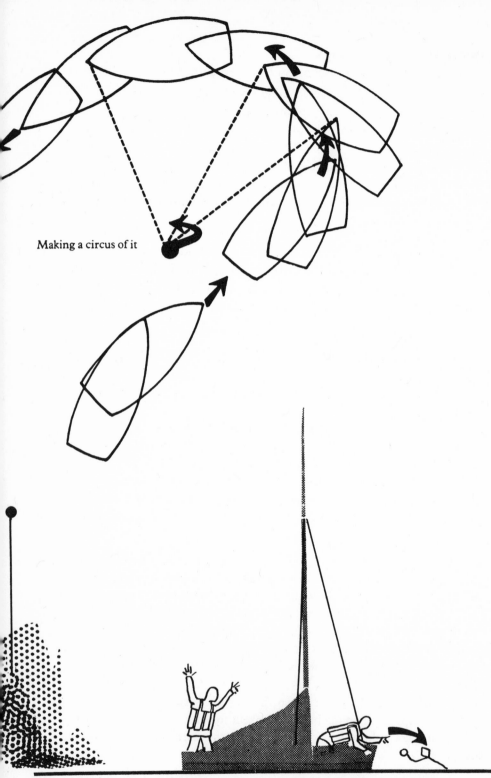

Making a circus of it

The over-enthusiastic beginner

The current may worry you when picking up the mooring; to detect its existence and direction, and to see how you will head, look at the other boats on moorings, with sails down—assuming they are of the same type. As for the strength of current, make a dummy run, coming head to wind on one side of the mooring, and seeing how fast you are coming towards it or moving away.

If the centre-board is down and sheets hardened in, the sail may fill, and the boat sail over the buoy; when it gets to the end of the buoy-rope, the boat will be stopped, but, as it has way on, the jerk will put it about, and it will career round the mooring like a circus horse in the ring. The only way to stop this performance is to unship the dagger-plate, or haul up the centre-board and let fly sheets. This is particularly likely to happen when wind is against the stream.

Don't lower mainsail before jib, and wait till you are made fast before doing either.

slipping the mooring

Thinking before hoisting sail and slipping the mooring will pay.

The effect of current may be much more powerful than that of the wind on rigging and upperworks. That does not matter if wind and current are in the same direction, but can be most annoying if wind is across current, and even more if they are opposed. In the latter case you cannot rig the boat, because you must come head to wind to hoist the mainsail.

Again, some overenthusiastic novice crews have only one idea in their heads from the moment they step aboard—to slip the mooring. So it is a good thing for the helmsman, who is directing the whole thing, to explain everything to the crew, and tell him exactly what to do on each order; these might be 'stand by to drop mooring' (the crew undoes the mooring chain and holds chain, buoy-rope and buoy in his hand): 'Slip!' (he throws the lot overboard).

We will consider two cases; wind and tide together, wind against tide. (Tide covers all sorts of current, including river current.)

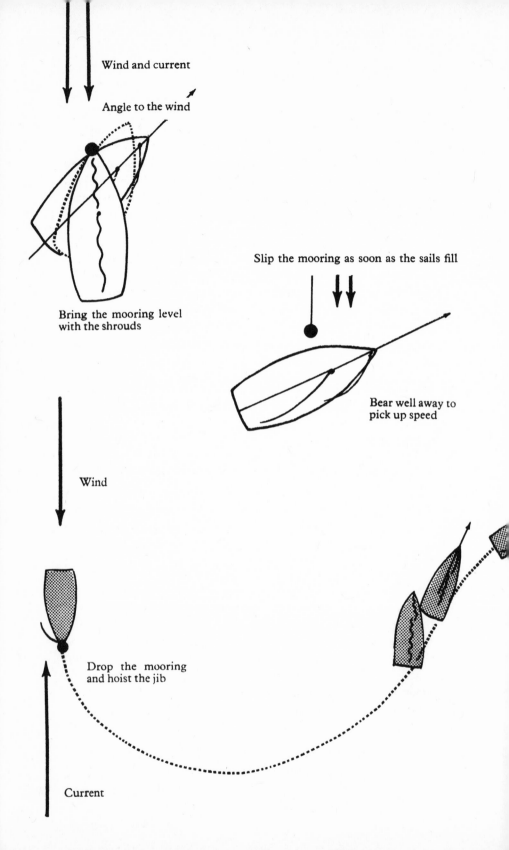

Wind and current

Angle to the wind

Bring the mooring level
with the shrouds

Slip the mooring as soon as the sails fill

Bear well away to
pick up speed

Wind

Drop the mooring
and hoist the jib

Current

wind and current together

Hoist sail first. You always, by the way, hoist the mainsail first—always the aftermost sails first when head to wind.

● When the rigging is completed, ship the rudder; if you do this earlier, it will just be wearing out its pintles, especially if there is any sea running.

● Untie the mooring on the order 'Stand by to slip mooring'; you can do one of two things then; either hold the buoy alone, or hold the chain and throw line and buoy over the side, forward of the stay. The latter is best.

● Now you must choose your tack, and you are ready to sail. You will go off on port or starboard tack, according to whether you hang on to the chain on the port or the starboard side of the boat; when you take the chain out of the fairlead, and carry it back to the level of the shrouds, you will be (stationary, of course) at the full-and-by angle to the wind; if you take it amidships, you will be at the reaching angle, and so forth.

● Now, and only now, drop the centre-board or ship the dagger-plate.

● Sheet in.

● Slip the mooring.

wind against tide

Quite a simple operation:

● Flake the sail along the boom, fit the battens and shackle on the halyard, in other words have the mainsail ready in all respects to hoist.

● Get the jib ready.

● Ship centre-board and rudder.

● Drop the mooring.

● Set the jib.

You then leave under jib alone, and hoist the mainsail under way.

note

You could move the mooring round aft, so as to lie head to wind.

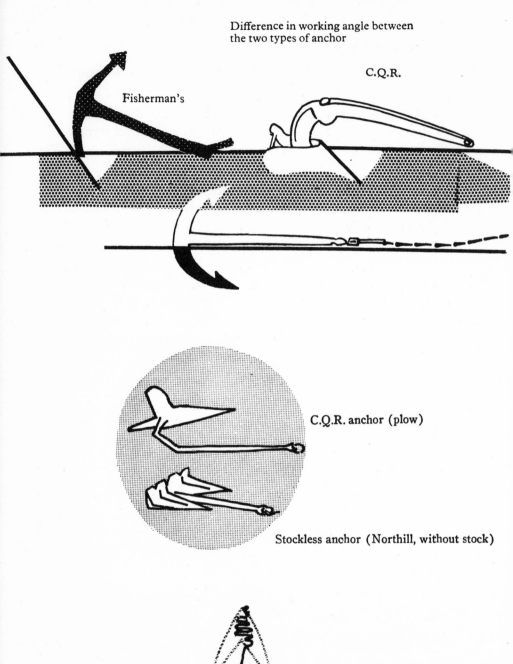

Difference in working angle between
the two types of anchor

C.Q.R.

Fisherman's

C.Q.R. anchor (plow)

Stockless anchor (Northill, without stock)

Make sure everything
is clear before you let
go the anchor

anchoring

The fact that you have a permanent mooring does not make an anchor unnecessary.

The conventional anchor, as seen in heraldry, is known as a *stocked*, or *fisherman's anchor*, but, even when to scale for a small boat, it is a clumsy thing, and more practical substitutes are the C.Q.R. or a stockless type. To give a horizontal pull on the anchor, and not a vertical one, you want a long enough scope of cable,[1] and a short length of chain should be shackled between the anchor and the rope cable. The chain will lie on the bottom by virtue of its weight, and will not wear through friction on a hard or rocky bottom.

Before using the anchor, make sure the cable is properly secured inboard. The connections between cable and chain, chain and anchor, are normally made by *shackles*, which are *locked* with a piece of wire; that is, you pass a bight of wire through the eye of the shackle pin and twist it round one arm of the shackle to keep the pin from unscrewing. An anchor for a light craft should weigh between five and ten pounds, so that you can just hold it at arm's length; you don't have to get up to handle it and throw it overside. Anchoring is generally done from the foredeck, but in a light boat the weight of the crew right forward impairs dangerously the stability, so all the anchor work is done from the mast thwart, sitting down. Be careful to pass anchor, chain and cable forward of the shrouds, and, if there is a fairlead, on the same side of the forestay as the fairlead.

The main thing about anchor work is the uncertainty as to whether the anchor is holding or not. It is therefore well to pay particular attention to this operation, and to be well up in the usual precautions.

---

[1] The correct length of cable is, for a fisherman's anchor, three times the depth of water, and four times for a C.Q.R. or stockless anchor. Seven or eight fathoms is plenty of cable for a light craft. Always remember the tide, and that the depth of water can increase quite a lot, and make the holding power doubtful. If the cable or chain does not lie on the bottom, the anchor will soon drag.

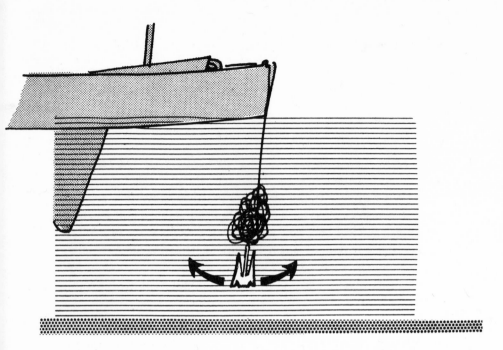

anchoring

The anchored boat lies head to wind dead to leeward of its anchor; the idea is therefore to come up head to wind and let the boat *gather sternway* before you let go.

● On the command 'Stand by to anchor!' the crew gets the anchor ready and checks that all is clear; don't fling over cable, chain and anchor done up in a parcel; you will find you have a sort of under-water pendulum.

● The crew answers 'Ready to anchor.'

● On the command 'Drop anchor!' the crewman drops it overboard. As the anchor bites, the cable will run out on its own.

note

If you have a bollard or a cleat on the foredeck and use chain cable rather than rope, don't take a half-hitch round it. It is practically impossible to undo in some kinds of weather. Three full turns are ample.

● Once the cable is out, you can drop the jib and raise the centre-board; but don't touch the main halyard yet; you *must* make sure your anchor is holding. Don't get into the habit of looking at the bottom; in fast-flowing water you will soon lose your sense of direction. Use *transits* on fixed points; you fix your position by lining up two seamarks or two stationary objects ashore against a shroud. If one moves in relation to the other, either the anchor is sliding on the bottom—the vessel is *dragging*—or the cable is stretching, or its elasticity is pulling you up to the anchor again. A transit bearing is the only certain way of making sure you are properly anchored.

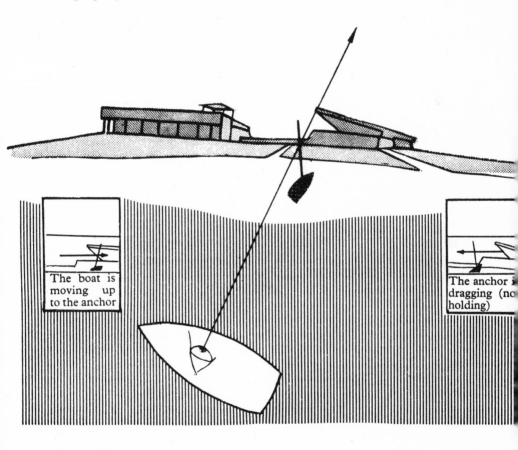

The boat is moving up to the anchor

The anchor i dragging (no holding)

● Once properly brought up, lower the mainsail and unship the rudder.

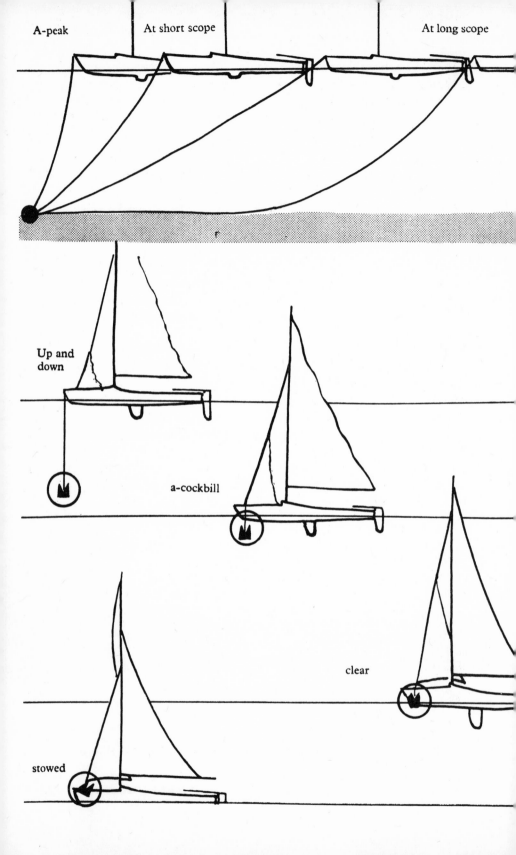

A-peak At short scope At long scope

r

Up and
down

a-cockbill

clear

stowed

weighing anchor

A very simple operation on a small boat; but you should now, more than ever, avoid getting between the mast and the bow.

There are several methods of weighing anchor:

A *An off-shore wind*

● Hoist the mainsail *and* the jib;

● ship the rudder;

● get ready to drop the centre-board; if it is a dagger-plate, enter it in the trunk; if a pivoting plate, take the securing pin out, or get ready to lower, according as to whether it is a metal or wood plate;

● the crew, sitting on his thwart, heaves up the cable gently till it is vertical in the water, or *a-peak*; it is still holding, but a touch will break it out;

● without letting go the cable, the crew takes the jib and backs it as indicated by the helmsman, at the same time *breaking out* the anchor;

● the boat will pay off; as soon as the anchor is broken out, he brings it aboard, drops the centre-board, and takes back his jib-sheet, which he will have passed to the helmsman whilst getting the anchor aboard.

note

The boat may gather sternway when it pays off; you are in the same position as when you miss stays in going about, and you have only to *reverse the helm*.

in a strong tide

If the tide is contrary to the wind and so strong that the boat lies head to or across the tide it is often better to weigh anchor or come to anchor under jib only, in a similar manner to leaving or picking up moorings under such conditions.

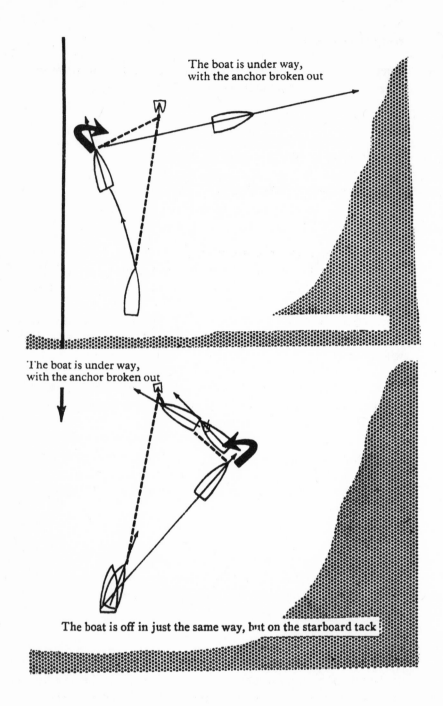

The boat is under way,
with the anchor broken out

The boat is under way,
with the anchor broken out

The boat is off in just the same way, but on the starboard tack

B *on a lee shore*

1 • As soon as sail is set, the rudder and centre-board shipped, sails are eased out, and the crew begins to get in the anchor rope.

2 • When the cable is up and down, back the jib lightly to bear away.

3 • If there is limited sea-room on one side or the other, it will pay you to make certain which tack you will go off on, in one of two ways:

4 • either weigh the anchor, not from the bow, but from one side, even with the shrouds—on the same side as the tack you want to go out on; when the anchor is a-peak, the boat is full-and-by on the right tack;

5 • or by using the speed imparted to the boat by heaving up to the anchor. In this case, you must act with care, having regard to the tack you want.

6 Suppose, for instance, you wanted to go off on the port tack, here is the process:

> a • the crew brings up the anchor from the bow;
>
> b • the boat gains speed; until now *no* rudder action;
>
> c • the helmsman puts the tiller to starboard; boat turns to port on starboard tack;
>
> d • the boat carries on, and in a few moments is checked by the anchor; this check will put it about, and as soon as the anchor is broken out, you will be under way on the port tack.

7 You'd do exactly the same to go off on the starboard tack, except that you would put the tiller *to port*.

towing

Towing is a complex matter, and does not really come within the scope of these practical notes. Still, on a calm day or following an accident, you may be led to take somebody's tow-rope—a motor-boat or sailing craft.

Towing under sail with a light craft is always difficult. This is briefly, what you have to do in either case.

A   you are offered a tow

• Start by dropping your sails, if you have not already done so.

• Raise the centre-board. Get the anchor and cable ready; they will act as the tow-rope if the motor-boat asks you for it.

● The towing craft ranges alongside you; he gives you his own tow-rope, or—preferably—takes your anchor and cable, which you will pass him, of course forward of the shrouds.

● Ask him not to start off with a jerk.

● Trim your boat down by the stern.

● During the tow, if the towing craft makes a sharp turn, don't turn at the same time as he does, but follow in his wake.

● If he is towing several boats besides you, you will have to take the anchor of the next astern. Come alongside him, near enough for him not to have to use his anchor like an old-time boarding grapnel. Make his cable fast inboard so that you can let it go in a hurry if necessary.

B   you have to take a boat in tow

● The crew of the boat to be towed makes sure his cable is clear, passes the anchor to you forward of the shrouds, and lets out the length of the cable (you will adjust the length of the tow as required).

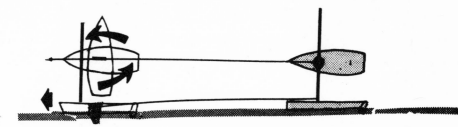

- You make the tow-rope fast inboard, not astern, but amidships, so that the pull does not prevent your stern from pivoting by counteracting the rudder action. You might take a turn round the centre-board trunk, but there would be some risk of interfering with the mainsheet. The best way is to jam the anchor of the towed craft under, say, a thwart. If you have a plain rope, with no anchor, take a turn and tie it round the thwart with a knot that can easily be undone. As you get under way, start slowly, thus easing the tension on the tow line.

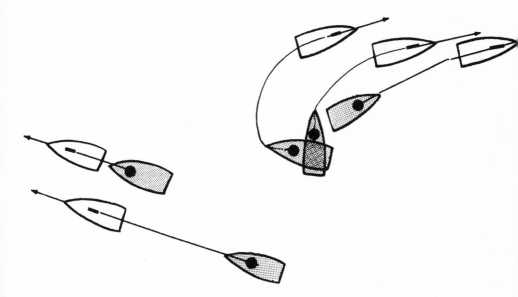

- To go about when towing another craft, you must get the weight of the tow off your boat during the evolution. Before you go about, pull inboard two or three fathoms of the tow-rope, get up full speed by paying off a bit, then go about and at the same time pay out the tow-rope; brake its last few feet with hand or foot, so as not to cause a nasty jolt when it takes the strain.

coming alongside

Coming alongside a boat is, on the face of it, a very simple matter—come near enough, hand a line to the crew of the other craft, and put yourself alongside.

It may in practice prove a little harder; there may be no one aboard to take your line, you may make a steering error, or have too much speed, or the wind may head you—and so on.

We will consider coming alongside a boat on a mooring, then a boat under sail, and lastly, a fixed pontoon.

coming alongside a moored craft

A boat at anchor or moored by a buoy, heads, as we said, according to which is the stronger influence; the wind or the tide. But if there is a choppy sea, or an unsteady wind, it may be constantly yawing about.

● Start by warning your crew. If there are only two of you, it will be up to him to hold the boat alongside, as he is farther forward than you.

● Come up full-and-by, and luff up so as to arrive alongside without forward speed—very much the same as picking up a mooring. (If, however, the tide is contrary to the wind it is better to run alongside under jib only, lowering the jib partly or fully to slow the boat as you get alongside.)

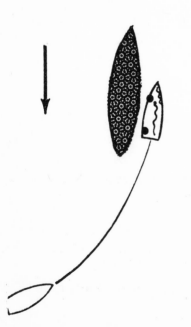

● Catch hold of his side with the flat of your hand, thumbs inside (if you put the thumbs outside, which you are tempted to do to stop your hands slipping, and the two boats came together with a bump, it might mean a broken thumb). Your arms will act as springs, and prevent the two hulls bumping together as far as possible.

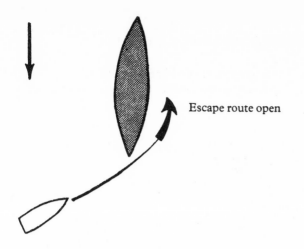

Escape route open

● You can come alongside the boat on either side. It is sometimes better to do so on the side which is not in view as you approach; you may be able, as the drawing above shows, to get away more easily by paying off if you fail to make it.

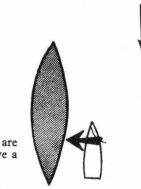

Be sure the jib sheets are free, or you will have a nasty bump

● If this is your chosen plan, you will pass under the stern of the boat, luff up and come alongside carrying your way. The crew will be careful to let fly the jib in good time, or you will meet the other boat with more violence than you expected.

● Come up slowly, or your crew will have too much to do in braking you, and you would risk dangerous contact between the two hulls or their spars.

note

If there is a sea running and the boat you are to come alongside is much bigger than your own, don't risk it unless absolutely essential; remember Aesop on the subject of the clay pot and the iron one.

coming alongside a boat under sail

The first thing to do is to have an understanding with the crew of the other craft, so that you will work together. Never come alongside a boat that is stern to wind:

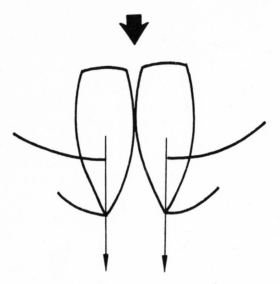

● with wind aft, imagine the consequences of a gybe;

● with a head wind, the two craft can pay off to one side or the other, together or in opposite ways.

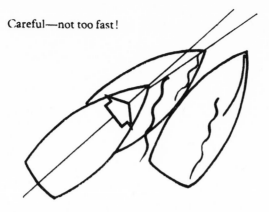

Careful—not too fast!

Both craft must be manoeuvreable for the operation to succeed; come up full-and-by, so that you have liberty to luff or bear away as needed. The craft you are coming alongside should be full-and-by, too, mainsail lifting and jib sheeted in, which is a good sail trim for slowing up, and he should maintain his course throughout.

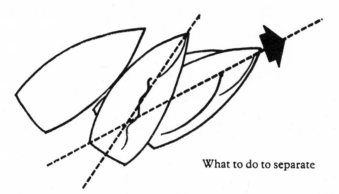

What to do to separate

● When two boats alongside of one another want to let go, the one who is to leeward should be the one to act; he goes off on his course.

● If you have to tranship anybody, take care the two masts don't come in contact during the process; they can do a lot of damage to one another.

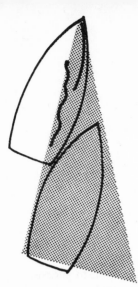

Look out for the wind shadow

• Don't try to come alongside a craft under sail from his lee side; blanketed by him, you would never get there—perhaps as well, because if you did you would be tangled up in his boom and rigging.

• Come on his windward side, then, so that at the end of the manoeuvre your bow is about level with his shrouds.

coming alongside a pontoon

A pontoon is nothing more than a floating quay, usually of no great height above the water, and solidly moored fore and aft; having mooring lines out in all directions, it will obviously not ride head to wind or to tide. When the wind is along the pontoon, proceed as though going alongside a craft, always remembering that if the wind is against the tide your boat might sheer off as it loses way. If the wind direction is at right-angles to the pontoon, it will do if you come up with a beam wind, letting your main sheet right off.

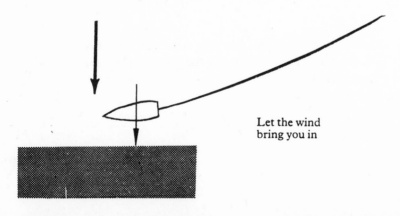

Let the wind
bring you in

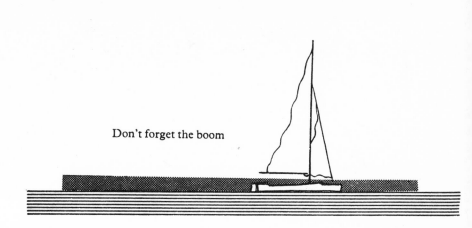

Don't forget the boom

But if the pontoon is high enough to stop your boom passing over it, you had better drop the mainsail first and come alongside under jib.

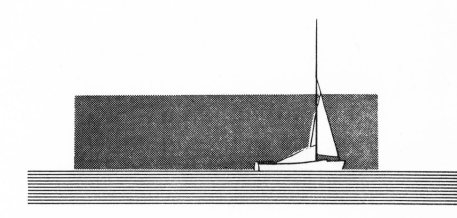

Such are the essentials of coming alongside. You must realize that while the hull of your boat is pretty fragile its stem is a particularly tough piece of wood and a menace to your neighbours; that spectators are readier to come to your help with tongue than with hand; and that it is a principle of nautical etiquette not to come alongside another craft without permission of its crew, if it can possibly be helped. Normally, permission is never refused.

Come up full and by

Luff, and come alongside
carrying your way

beaching

Beaching is generally easier than setting off from the beach. The procedure is different for a stern wind, beam or head winds, and for beaches with steeply shelving bottoms or the reverse.

Whatever the point of sailing, the object is to arrive with a minimum of speed on the boat at the moment when you are near enough to jump out.

Sometimes it pays to come in under full sail, sometimes under reduced sail.

under full sail

Beaching under full sail is called for when you have to be fully under control, generally when the wind is off shore.

The idea is to come up to the beach in a number of boards, and, when the water is too shallow for the centre-board, get up speed with a beam wind, luff and beach.

As the wind is rarely straight off the beach, you can usually come up to your chosen landing-point on one tack.

under reduced sail

The danger in beaching is to arrive too fast. That is usually the case with a stern wind. There are two ways of slowing up when coming in on this point of sailing:

- either come head to wind a few yards off and sail in astern, but if there is any surf this method soon becomes ticklish; besides, sailing the boat astern calls for a lot of skill;

- or, lower the mainsail and come in under jib alone—much the better way. Come in full-and-by, close-hauled a few yards off; lower your mainsail as we described above, under 'sailing with reduced sail', pay off and beach under jib; you can then unship rudder and centre-board, but not too soon; you want to keep steering as long as you can.

- If there is not much wind, come in under jib alone; it may seem unadventurous, but it is a good habit to get into for heavy weather days. Besides, putting a jib up or taking it down is so easy, and gives you such complete control of your speed.

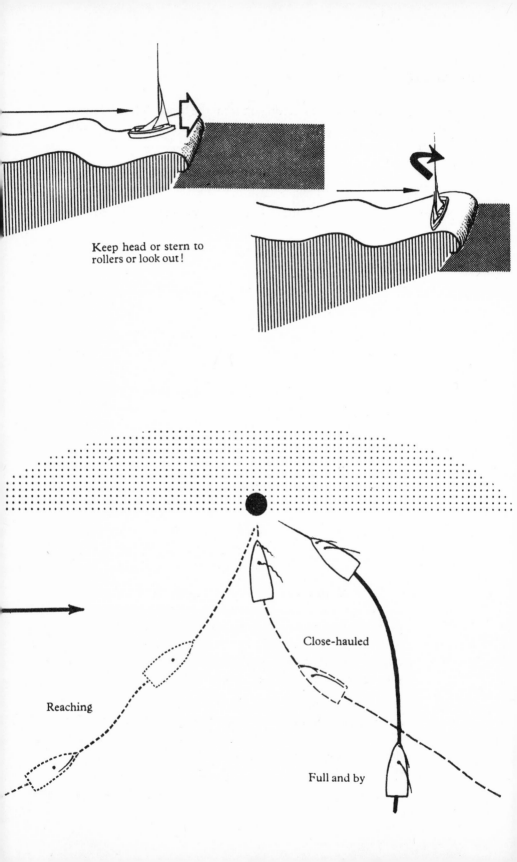

Keep head or stern to
rollers or look out!

Close-hauled

Reaching

Full and by

note

In a strong wind you may get rollers; coming in under jib alone, head them, and don't be stern heavy. If you come in three-quarters riding a roller to keep the wind aft, you stand a good chance of being turned over.

● Don't wait to jump out till the boat touches. The crew should jump out earlier; the boat will then be lighter and easier to stop, and if it strands at the same time no harm will be done.

● If you forgot to unship centre-board and rudder, your boat will take a nasty shock. Don't sit in the boat in a bemused state, asking yourselves what happened; jump out *at once* and unship rudder and centre-board from outside.

● Once the bow has grounded use the boat's impetus to draw it up several yards, out of reach of the waves.

If you are going off again soon, you don't need to bring the boat ashore; it will be enough to anchor it, bearing the tide in mind, so that it will not scrape on the bottom while you are gone. You can also moor, if you come in with a stern wind under jib only, a few yards off the beach, and let her come in astern; it will be much easier to get off, as you will only have to get in a fathom or so of cable and you will be in water deep enough for rudder and centre-board; you will then have to beat out, and you will avoid the difficulties of launching.

● If the wind blows along the beach, you can come in all standing or under jib alone, as you please:

> coming in on a reach to leeward of the chosen point, then luffing up, and coming full-and-by under all sail;

> or you can reach to windward of the point, and come in with wind abeam, under jib.

● Whatever point of sailing you come in on, you must control your speed, lowering sails, sheeting in, paying off, etc. Before you beach, a trial run is a good thing, especially if you don't know the beach.

● Remember, too, your boat is not an amphibian. You must at all costs avoid grounding on centre-board or rudder, but it is almost as dangerous to leave the boat half afloat, half ashore—the paint goes, the wood perishes, it is death for the boat. So, when you beach, jump out at once, either bring the boat up without delay, or keep it afloat, and don't let it scrape.

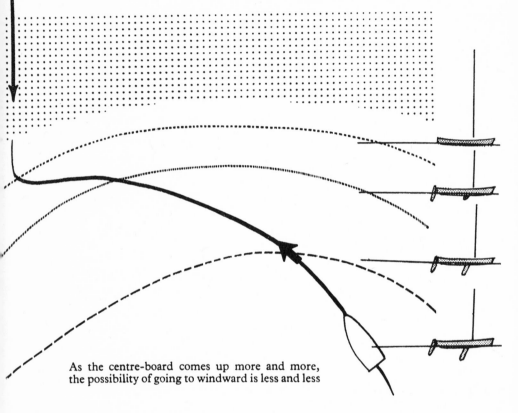

As the centre-board comes up more and more, the possibility of going to windward is less and less

conclusion

Before going in for any of these manoeuvres, it is a good thing to get some practice where there is plenty of sea-room—to get out to sea and learn how to sail without rudder, without mainsail, without jib and so on.

It is a good thing to practise on a wooden pontoon before you come alongside a concrete quay; don't wait for bad weather before you practise reefing and sailing with reefs down. This is true for beginners, but also for old hands going out for the first time in a new type of boat. Doing all these manoeuvres as a drill is the best way to find out your own capacity, that of your crew, and the possibilities of the boat; and whatever happens after that will never take you by surprise.

safety | 8

general

Like any other sport, sailing in small boats has risks, which must be taken with the eyes open; but this particular sport brings in two essential elements over which man has no influence whatever; wind and water. If, then, you are to avoid quite disastrous consequences, you must weigh up the risks you will take, and not underrate them.

Some of the varied risks run by the small boat are:

> capsizing,
>
> running aground,
>
> accidental damage of various kinds,
>
> being carried out to sea,

all caused by lack of technical knowledge, or by momentary forgetfulness, by negligence or error of judgment—such misfortunes are always the punishment of some mistake. The safety of a small boat will always depend on the alertness and competence of the crew

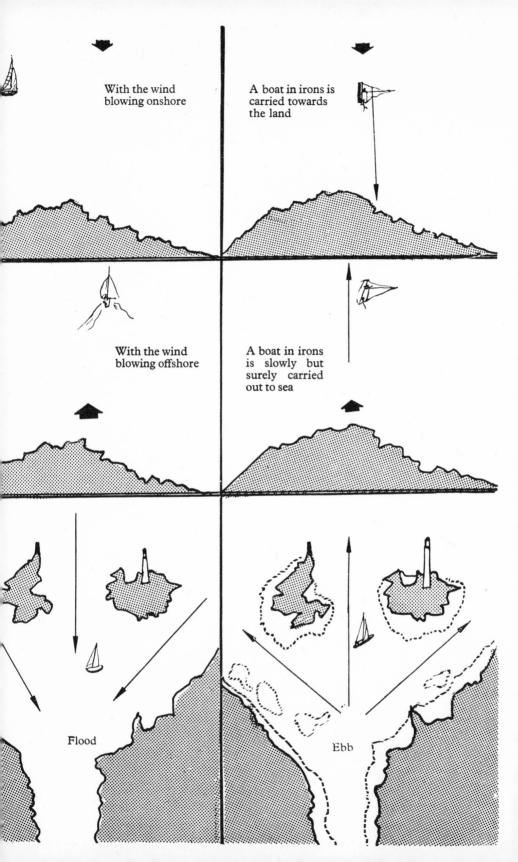

With the wind blowing onshore

A boat in irons is carried towards the land

With the wind blowing offshore

A boat in irons is slowly but surely carried out to sea

Flood

Ebb

rather than to material precautions. The risks taken and their relative importance can be classified under:

> the topography of the sailing area,
>
> the characteristics of the boat, and its condition, from the point of view of maintenance,
>
> the crew, its competence and its physical condition at the moment.

For instance:

The same stretch of water varies widely in the risks it offers, owing to differing force and direction of wind and tide, depth of water, temperatures, and so on; some or all of such conditions may rule at any given time.

But there are some risks that can be avoided:

> an unstable, overcanvassed craft will capsize;
>
> rigging will fail on a badly maintained boat;
>
> sails will blow out when a much stiffer seaboat carries too much;
>
> the most seaworthy of craft in the hands of an unskilled crew will upset and go ashore; and you may embroider on this theme to any extent your fancy leads you to.

strategy for safety

It is such a complicated question that it demands strategic thought in the first place. Strategy will determine your attitude to conditions on the spot; strategy will force you to *work to a programme.* You must bear every factor in mind; and from this go on to eliminating every foreseeable cause of accident, even though you have all known material means to lessen their effect—life-jackets, flotation gear, and the like.

It all comes down to seamanship, navigating with an eye to the weather, knowledge of the sailing area, correct choice of sail and of crew, and a readiness to modify sailing plans when necessary.

Additional material measures are called for, not to excuse mistakes, but to help remedy their consequences. They are bound up with the boat and its equipment, and we shall return to them, for they are all tied up together. But the *matériel* is not the root of the whole matter; there is a tendency to pay too much regard to it, neglecting the purely seamanlike aspect, the essential part of which is obviously the crew of the craft and its capacity for foresight.

Various layouts of buoyancy arrangements

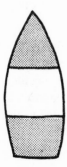  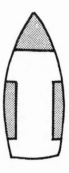

The projected cruise must take into account the experience of the crew, and the prevailing conditions: wind, tide, sea, shoals, visibility, possibilities of help from outside, and so on. For instance, it is not seamanlike to go sailing in an unstable craft in exposed and unwatched waters. It is always possible to detail a rescue crew and boat from among the numerous ones using a popular sailing centre, while the crew which sails unfrequented water must rely on its own resources to get out of every sort of trouble that may arise.

Don't go off on long sails without a companion who can be of real help in case of need; but companionship and buoyancy gear must not be an excuse for taking risks blindly; don't for instance, go fooling around among rocks in a fresh wind. One moment's loss of control, and your boat is lost, and you may suffer grave injury under the eyes of a companion quite unable to help.

Summer gales are not sailing weather even for the most experienced, except in sheltered waters or under the eye of a rescue organization. Then there are currents at sea; an inexperienced crew going out for a sail in the estuary, with no thought for the ebb tide, risks being carried out to sea—a very dangerous matter if he capsizes.

It is always a good thing to be up-wind of your port, and shelter; if you can't do that, don't go too far away, watch your navigation, and never hesitate to start for home in good time.

In an onshore wind, a jammed halyard or centre-board are minor mishaps, but can have the most serious consequences when the wind blows out to sea.

Don't try too much in the way of sailing. Come ashore when you are tired. It is an exacting sport and a crew which has been functioning perfectly over a period may tire and capsize, and righting a capsized craft is far too hard work for an exhausted crew.

Seamanship, we repeat, springs from foresight—from taking advantage of experience to look ahead and doing everything to reduce risks to man and boat.

The boat must be in proper order and water-tight; it should have flotation gear, enough to make it into a raft buoyant enough to support the crew. Excessive flotation gear may enable an experienced crew, if well trained and in good physical shape, to perform prodigies of spectacular righting in

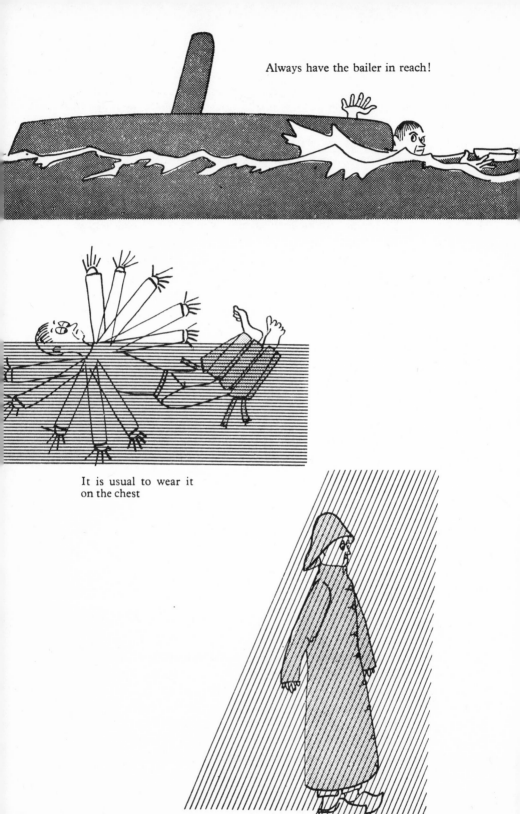

Always have the bailer in reach!

It is usual to wear it
on the chest

Cucullus facit monachum—The hood makes
the monk

favourable weather; but it can have the effect of allowing a capsized boat to blow down-wind faster than you can swim after it.

Equipment must always include sculls or paddle. They must be intelligently stowed where they will not be lost if the boat capsizes. Similarly, some means of mooring, a small grapnel or anchor at the end of a sound warp, must be properly stowed away; a bailer is essential, and it must be possible to reach it in a completely overturned boat. Making it fast on the end of a line makes it very awkward to use, and may very well cause a dangerous tangle. It is better jammed under a thwart, or in some other sensible place.

A few small items may well find their place in a pocket, or in a little bag carefully stowed away—sail thread, a length of marline, some copper wire, a nail, a claspknife, a pair of pliers, a spare shackle or two of different sizes, and so on.

There are one or two other items of personal gear: life-jackets, oilskins, warm clothing, and footwear.

Life-jackets should for preference be in bright colours, yellow, or, better still, orange. And the place for them is on the person, not neatly stowed away somewhere in the boat. Present-day ones are not a bit awkward to wear, so much so that it is not unknown for people to forget to take them off when the day's sail is over. It is a good idea to check on their condition and on the means of fastening them; a life-jacket with broken shoulder straps that slides down round the knees is a nuisance, and a potential danger when you end up in the water feet up and head down!

You cannot do without an oilskin for wet weather, on river or on sea. Its value is, of course, in keeping you dry, but it is also most useful in keeping the body heat in after an involuntary bathe.

In any case, it is neither seamanlike nor common sense to go off for a sail of some hours in a bathing costume. It is sound to have aboard a watertight kitbag in which you can slip a sweater and pair of trousers; the sun is not always shining, and you will welcome them at the first shiver. And the more clothes you have on the warmer you will be in the water, even if it is very cold; remember the shrimpers and shell-fish catchers who work often shoulder deep in water—smothered in sweaters and woollen pants.

And finally—something for the feet in case you go ashore on rocks, and to protect them against the toe straps when you are sitting well out.

It may well be asked, whether these precautions, the importance of which is so very much emphasized, do not themselves give a false sense of security, and are not likely to cause a dangerous neglect of common seamanship? Overdue trust in gadgets may well give a sense of false security. You see, for instance, crews in so-called 'self-righting' craft taking foolhardy risks of capsizing on the strength of the supposed righting capacity of their vessels. It is foolish; a capsize in bad conditions should never be deliberately accepted, for it can have the most irremediable of endings. You will not see a cruising yacht running its head into avoidable dangers because it has inflatable rafts, and in the same way you should take all seamanlike precautions to avoid getting into trouble, rather than to rely on being able to get out of it in a smart way.

accidents and what to do

There is never an accident which does not arise—perhaps indirectly—from a mistake by somebody. While the results may be serious, there is no point in overlooking that there is usually quite a lot that can be done to minimize them. It will always pay to think over in advance what you will do in the event of capsize, loss of rigging, spars or sails, carrying away your rudder, going ashore, being carried out to sea.

capsize

Capsizing is an unpleasant experience. It happens as the result of mistakes even in capable hands. It can happen through negligence or error of judgment.

It generally happens in a fresh breeze, and if it happens several times in the same outing, it indicates something wrong with the crew's technique.

Anyhow, in case of capsize *hang on to the boat* and don't abandon it at any price, even if the shore seems near. People who wait for help astride the keel of an upturned boat rarely suffer from anything more serious than a cold in the head, while unfortunately those who try to swim ashore stand every chance of being lost on the way or carried out to sea. A hundred yards in a swimming pool, in good shape physically and in bathing gear, is one thing; the same distance, fully dressed, tired, is quite a different matter.

Repeat to yourself—a boat is visible, when a swimmer is not. An upturned boat with two or three people on it can be distinguished from wave crests when white horses are running when a man's head cannot.

But never go to extremes; if a rescue boat comes out to you, don't hesitate to go aboard; and, if not too exhausted, don't sit and wait for rescue, but try to right your craft.

Righting a capsized boat is an operation which depends upon the state of the elements—wind and sea—the physical ability of the crew, 'know-how' and the disposition of the buoyancy reserves of the boat itself.

The term 'self-righting' is applied to certain boats, such as the 505, which have large reserves of buoyancy. They are easily righted in moderate winds if the crew is experienced: one of the crew jumps on the centre-board, while the other holds the boat head to wind. It is simple in good weather and a steady wind. In a fresh breeze it is more problematical, especially if the crew has had little practice previous to capsize. Ignorance of the difficulties and excessive confidence in the words 'self-righting' sometimes lead crews into taking dangerous risks. When you are tired and the boat drifts away you may not have the strength to regain and right it and to get aboard. Nevertheless, it is useful to learn the correct procedure of righting a dinghy under suitable conditions.

Of course, especially on this type of craft, you must avoid if possible a complete capsize to 180°, especially in deep water. For various reasons a

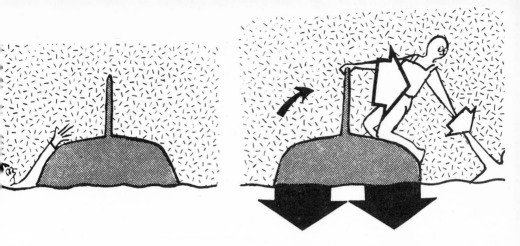

completely upside-down vessel has an astonishing stability inbuilt in it, and it is very difficult for a crew of ordinary height to reach the centre-board or centre-board trunk, the more so when too much buoyancy gear puts it farther out of the water.

Again, in this position there is a risk of the mast breaking off if the depth of water is not enough for the new—and very large—draught of the boat. A sailing craft generally capsizes to leeward, and the hull offers a large surface to the force of the wind, which helps to turn it right over.

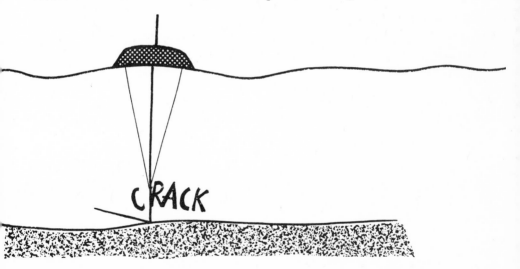

Another point—in shallow water with a muddy bottom, the mast sticks in the mud and tends to drive itself harder in through the force of the wind, till it is impossible to get it out without help, and hardly ever without breaking it. So, in these conditions, concentrate on lifting the mast, and on turning the hull so that the wind pressure will tend to right it rather than otherwise.

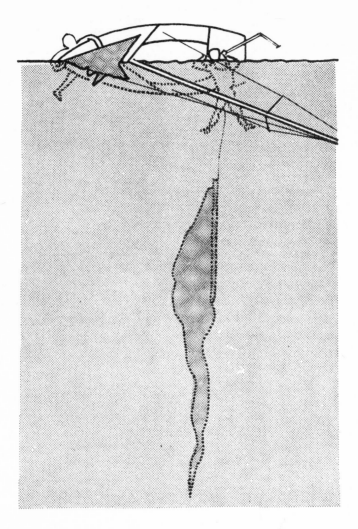

When you cannot get the boat up at once by the methods suggested, the usual way to prevent her capsizing again when she does come up is to get the sails off. This reduces tophamper, as the rigging will not hold water and will come up all the more easily, and, when up, the stability will be so much the better. You will, of course, make the halyards fast, and not let them go; you will need to use them when you want to get off again.

The next thing is to empty the boat. All sorts of tricks are worth trying; bearing down on one side, while the crew lifts the other sometimes works. You will always manage it with a bit of imagination, provided you are not too tired. If the buoyancy gear is right, it will bring the hull out of water enough for you to empty it. Use the bailer first from outside. When possible, one of you gets aboard and goes on bailing till the other can board without loss of stability. Once the boat is empty, all you have to do is to up sail and go.

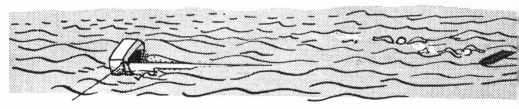

Unless you have shoals under your lee, it is not wise to anchor a capsized boat. The crew may try to rescue, for instance, some spar which is drifting away on the current, and may be carried away from the hull, which, being anchored, does not follow them.

running ashore

This is often the sequel to a bad take-off close-hauled from a beach, or to faulty seamanship when on a lee shore.

The first case is not too bad, as the crew are fresh. Remember that the weakest points of a boat are the rudder and centre-board fixings. The centre-board trunk is structurally weak, and the rudder pintles are particularly liable to get twisted. So, as soon as you see you are going ashore, jump overboard and unship the rudder, while the crew raises the centre-board and then follows you. Both hang on to the windward side of the boat, and try to push it round head to wind. You can then seize it by the forestay fitting, and, as soon as you are in your depth, tow it round to where you started, reflect on the cause of the trouble, and make a fresh start.

The second case may be a much more serious matter; the crew are tired without realizing it, and judgment of distances and reflexes are impaired. It may be the result of errors, pinching too close to the wind in the neighbourhood of rocks, dismasting, being taken aback, capsizing, and so forth.

It is generally too late to anchor, though smooth water may make this feasible.

If, on the other hand, there is surf and you are driven on to a reef of rocks, there is only one thing to be done: jump overboard, preferably to windward, and, if the bottom is flat, say stratified granite, try to hold the boat off. Unfortunately, the bottom rarely *is* flat on a rocky shore, but usually jagged, and all you will get out of trying to protect your boat will be a broken limb or worse.

on being carried out to sea

This is the most serious of accidents. It is easy enough to see how it could happen; an unexpectedly strong wind or current, or just lack of competent seamanship. If it is combined with a capsize, it is about the worst thing that can happen for a dinghy. Such a small bulk is hard to see from a distance, and, though anchoring might check the seaward drive, it is no good if the anchor does not hold, which is usually what happens, as small boats do not carry unlimited cable. In this case, more than ever, don't try to swim ashore. If your boat is seaworthy, you will certainly have an unpleasant time for a while, but you have a chance; fishing boats, friends who are worried about your non-return, yachts out for a sail, and so on. However that may be, from an aeroplane a boat may be seen, but not a swimmer.

If you carry away a shroud, try to go about and come back home on the other tack

Emergency repair to broken shroud. Easily done if you have gone about

To get home after this very unfortunate occurrence. Keep the board down, and stay at the tiller. Paddling should be done from the bow

In case of loss of tiller, you can as a fair weather makeshift, work the rudder by hand without it

carrying away a shroud

This generally happens when on the wind, when the rigging is under heavy strain. You often have time to come about if it is a shroud that carries away, or to bear away if it is the forestay. If you cannot get back home on this new point of sailing, an emergency repair is possible. If it is the forestay that has gone, you can often leave it to the luff wire of the jib to support the mast, and nurse the boat home. Taking a reef in the mainsail, or even lowering it altogether, will be a great help.

So far as shrouds go, you cannot do much about a broken chainplate in the absence of something to which you can secure a lanyard you have lashed to the shroud.

A broken fitting up the mast cannot be repaired at sea; you will have to lower all sail, unless you can get home on the tack which will not make any demand on the broken fitting.

If a turnbuckle breaks, you can easily reeve off a lashing on the lines of the lanyards that used to be found on old-time sailing craft.

The shroud itself will rarely part; it is the sort of thing that should never happen; the trouble is usually the result of a drawn eyesplice or sleeve. Periodical inspection should have prevented this, but if it happens just the same, at the bottom of the shroud, you can use a *stopper-knot*.

More common is the loss of a shackle, either on the chain-plate or the eyesplice; this is a simple matter if you have a spare by you. It should have had its pin locked.

broken spars

A broken stay can involve a broken mast. This often follows a weak piece of rigging, bad adjustment or a capsize. The remedy is to bring the mass of wreckage into some semblance of order, pack up the pieces, and paddle or scull home. This is possible in quite a fresh wind, as the windage of the mast no longer hinders the boat. You will practically never break your boom on a small boat. If you do, you can easily take the sail off the boom, and use it loose-footed, if you cannot get home under the jib.

Losing part of your steering gear is not very serious if you have learnt to handle your boat without it.

If it is the tiller, you can work the rudder by hand while manoeuvring to pick up the tiller, or to come home. If it is the rudder itself, you will steer by sheet adjustment and putting your weights in the right places. This will let you get the rudder back, or get home.

This picture is not necessarily funny . . . Put yourself in their place. . . .

Whatever accident you may have met with, it is easy to think it might have been worse, and you will readily admit you might have avoided it by proper seamanship. But now is not the time to regret carelessness; what you have to think of is getting outside help. Anything abnormal serves to attract attention and, maybe, bring help; shouts, gestures, clothes hoisted up the mast, a dishcloth flown as a flag, are some of the things to use . . .

If you see a craft in difficulties, your only thought must be to go to the rescue; but don't plunge in with your eyes shut, unthinkingly.

If the boat in trouble is on a lee shore, dismasted, you could take it in tow if you were quite sure of yourself, and if there were plenty of water between it and the shore; but don't try to sail too close, and remember it will be hard work coming about. And take the tow on the right tack.

If you feel it won't come off, don't waste time; satisfy yourself with taking the crew off.

In the same way, if you see a boat of your own type capsized, the best thing is to take the crew off, but if you realize you are not up to it, tell them you are off to port to get help.

Act with common sense and think; think first of the people, and only then of the boat, which is only an inanimate object, a means to enjoyment rather than an end.

And finally, for your own safety, see that your boat cannot be faulted, that you are physically in good shape, that the visibility is good enough, that the wind is not over the force at which you will find beating difficult (Force 5–6), that there is not an undue sea running, and that someone ashore knows where you are going and when you hope to be back.

Don't let some innocent go out in an unseaworthy boat; it is a matter of life or death for him. Never be afraid to call off a sail; don't go out because you decided last night that you would, or because you have guests, but because circumstances are favourable now.

Don't be afraid of being laughed at; experienced people may go out of their way to tell you why you ought to have gone out, but they won't laugh at you. And, for the last time, having made your decision, make sure that someone who is staying ashore knows what you are going to do.

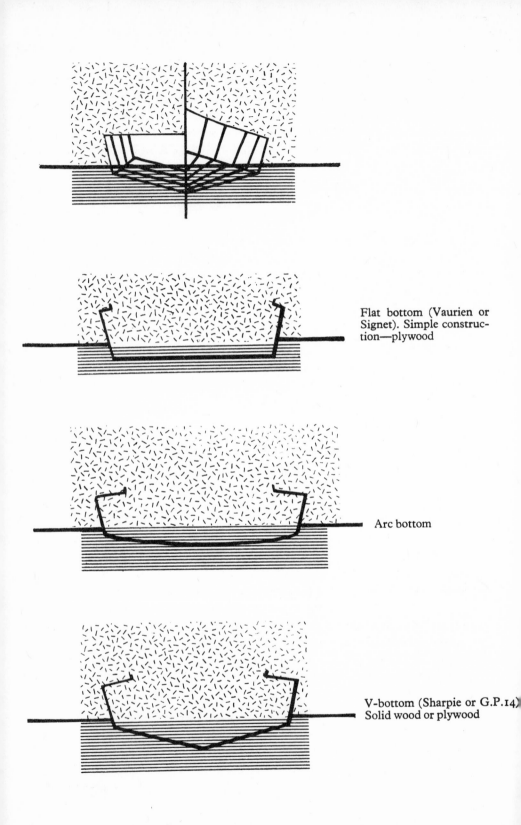

Flat bottom (Vaurien or Signet). Simple construction—plywood

Arc bottom

V-bottom (Sharpie or G.P.14) Solid wood or plywood

practical hints
on the hull

9

Hulls of all lengths between 9 and 18 ft have usually a certain minimum of fittings. There may be a deck forward or shelter round the cockpit, possibly thwarts and no deck, possibly side decks of more or less width. They must combine:

- rigidity;

- robustness;

- lightness;

- cheapness.

There must be a certain rigidity in the hull of a small craft. It is not advisable to let flexibility allow the waterlines to distort beyond very narrow limits. It may well be noted that in large craft too much rigidity is a fault; beyond a certain weight and, more important, beyond a certain length the different parts of a boat are acted on in contradictory ways by the sea, and the hull would be put out of shape if some flexibility were not built in.

Robustness can never come amiss in a boat. But security questions do not impose such a high standard on the small-boat scale as for sea-going craft.

Strength is therefore often neglected in the interests of lightness, especially if the material or processes used make this desirable.

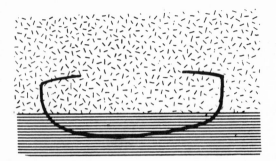

Round bilged
Conventional construction,
laminated wood or plastic

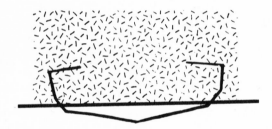

Double-chine construction

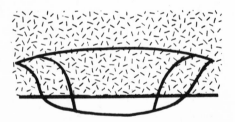

Moulded boats may have
flared sections

Lightness is essential for a small fast boat that is to plane; this conflicts with all the other essentials—rigidity, robustness and cheapness. More, lightness may very well mean loss of power in a seaway (less inertia), and reduced performance to windward when the sea is choppy. But the power of a small boat must be *dynamic*, that is, power brought about by *speed* (kinetic energy), which you get through lightness and freeing off the wind a bit. The big boat, on the other hand, owes its power to its mass rather (inertia), and is therefore built solid and flexible at the same time, to withstand the sea. The small craft, on the other hand, gives way to the seas and eases itself over the waves. Its lightness makes for quick acceleration, which is at the root of its excellent performance. And, of course, without lightness—no planing.

Cheapness is less vital for competition craft, but it is very much sought for in these days of sailing as a popular sport. It comes from mass production, which involves sections and materials involving minimum man-hours.

We will not speak here of qualities due to design of hulls, as this is more a question of planning than of construction.

Beside these common elements, light craft can be classified under several categories, which merge into one another.

They may be round-bilged, or hard-chined; they may have a centre-board, pivoting or dagger-plate type, or a ballasted keel, keel and centre-board, or plain keel. In the latter case, it will generally be a fin-keel, as small craft practically never have a turned-in garboard and moulded keel, as the Dragon has, for instance.

methods of construction

Any of these types of craft seem pretty much alike in their conception, and seem to show little difference in dimensions or lines, but one must remember they are built in widely different ways. The same type of boat may be built in two different materials— say in moulded wood or in plastic. We are going to take a quick look at the different methods of building.

conventional construction

The conventional way of building small boats is simply a scaling down of big-ship methods.

Conventional construction over mo

Carvel building,
glued and nailed

Clinker building

Here, we will only give just a glance at the application of conventional shipbuilding methods to the building of small boats.

construction over moulds

The skeleton of the boat is made up of *frames* or *moulds,* either profiled, or sawn out to shape, or steamed, connected lengthwise by the keel, *keelson* and the *stringers* (*shelves* and *chines*). This framework is covered by *planking,* which forms the skin of the boat. The planking is fastened to the stem, the frame timbers and the transom. The rigidity of the whole is reinforced by *floors* (extra strong frames which do not come up as high as the deck each side) and by *deck beams* (thwartship beams that support the deck).

The simplest way of planking the boat consists of laying the strakes at right-angles to the frames. These strakes, which are sawn to shape before fitting, are *rabbeted* into the stem. The first strake on each side, along the keel, the *garboard strake,* is rabbeted in the same way into the keel. The edges are fastened in place, and water-tightness ensured by caulking with oakum and white lead.

The immense amount of work necessary is obvious; it calls for a great deal of skilled man's time, and is very expensive, especially when you consider the amount of good-quality wood used.

clinker building

Clinker construction used to be the most common way of planking boats and dinghies, and is still found on some types of light craft. The sides are covered in the same manner as shingles cover a roof.

This type of planking makes a strong boat, and enables the frames to be lighter. The longitudinal rigidity is greatly improved. The building is still a skilled operation, and when the strakes begin to work loose the boat is difficult to repair.

strip-carvel building—strakes glued and nailed

This construction uses narrow strakes, which are more easily fitted (a few strokes of the plane thin them off fore and aft). This process originated in the building of model boats; its fairly recent invention coincided with the appearance of modern adhesives.

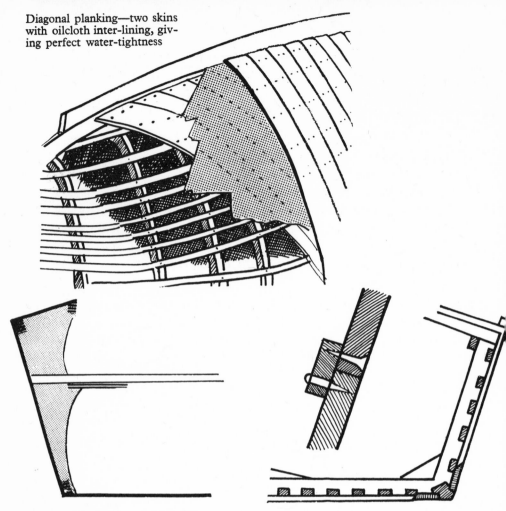

Diagonal planking—two skins
with oilcloth inter-lining, giving perfect water-tightness

Hard-chine construction

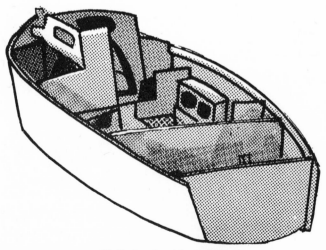

Hull fitted with bulkheads,
showing the cellular structure
which gives great rigidity

There is no caulking, and strength and water-tightness are improved. You get a light boat, and a comparatively cheap one. The strakes do not slide over one another, as they are nailed down, and the side is very rigid.

Finally, one other process, *diagonal planking*, consists of using two thicknesses of wood at 45° to one another, separated by a glued sheet of oiled cloth and riveted to each other. This construction is used for life-boats, and gives a very seaworthy craft, which is, however, rather sensitive to knocks.

It should be noted that none of these forms of construction are employed now (except for clinker building) on small craft.

hard chine construction

This produces a boat with lines less easy on the eye, and also theoretically of poorer performance. Also, the structure is no lighter. But there are certain advantages:

- the frame timbers are cheaper to produce;
- the side panels, too, are very wide and easier to fit. The only thing calling for fine workmanship is the fitting of the chine. The building therefore is much simpler, and is within the powers of a good amateur;
- the sharp angle in the hull gives great rigidity, which gives it the property that it will break rather than twist (just as you can break but not bend a cigar-box); this, as we have said, is a desirable property in *small* craft.

This construction is strong, cheap and rigid, which explains why many small craft were built on this system, many of them still in use. The great drawbacks are the weight, which remains high, the difficulty of getting a water-tight chine, and difficulties of maintenance.

modern processes

New materials and new techniques go to make up modern boat-building. They have been worked out for small craft, so are well adapted for that purpose. It is no longer a matter of scaling down the shipbuilder's work. In point of fact, the reverse is seen; modern methods, first used on small craft, tend to be used for much larger ones—large cruisers in plastics, for instance.

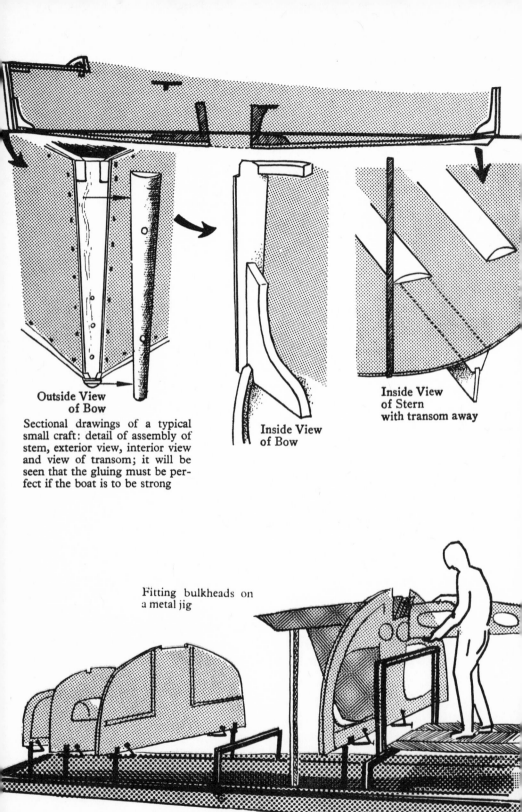

Outside View of Bow

Sectional drawings of a typical small craft: detail of assembly of stem, exterior view, interior view and view of transom; it will be seen that the gluing must be perfect if the boat is to be strong

Inside View of Bow

Inside View of Stern with transom away

Fitting bulkheads on a metal jig

frameless plywood construction

In this case the material, marine plywood, has governed constructional methods. The standard-sized sheet of plywood is light, robust and flexible. When it is bent it becomes rigid; the bending stress is transformed into tension and compression forces. The value of plywood planking is obvious; it is light, rigid (in one direction), and does not warp severely, as is possible with conventional planking. There is one drawback, but it is a serious one; you can only bend plywood in one direction at a time. It can only therefore be used on conic curves, although some tolerance is possible—round the stern, for example.

Hard chine construction is therefore necessary. But hard chines improve still more the rigidity of the whole, so much so that a plywood boat needs no frames; thwarts or bulkheads are enough to keep the sides apart, strengthened as they are by the curves imparted to them; the bottom is reinforced by floorboards to distribute the weights of the crew.

This type of boat is *glued*, which increases the rigidity and strength of the assembly; if it is properly done, it completely solves the problem of water-tightness, especially at the chine, where an extra boning-piece can be fitted.

Mass production is feasible; the different parts are produced *en masse* and assembled on a mould. All dimensions are adapted to the standard sheet size of marine plywood, to reduce off-cuts. The necessary rigidity, robust-ness, lightness and economy are therefore provided to a certain degree by the frameless plywood craft. The only drawbacks are: first, the hard chined hull is less refined in shape than a round-bilged hull, and, second, the difficulty of tracing from the plans to get the required lines.

Calling as it does for a mould, and for extremely accurate fitting work, this system of building does not lend itself to amateur work.

Boats of this type have become extremely popular, thanks to very low selling prices, as compared with any other boat of similar performance and dimensions, but built to a different system. The process has reduced the price of a small cruising yacht to that of a popular car. A double chine appears in some larger craft.

moulded wood

This entirely new process came in with modern resin adhesives. The great feature is that a boat is built with its sides in a material similar to

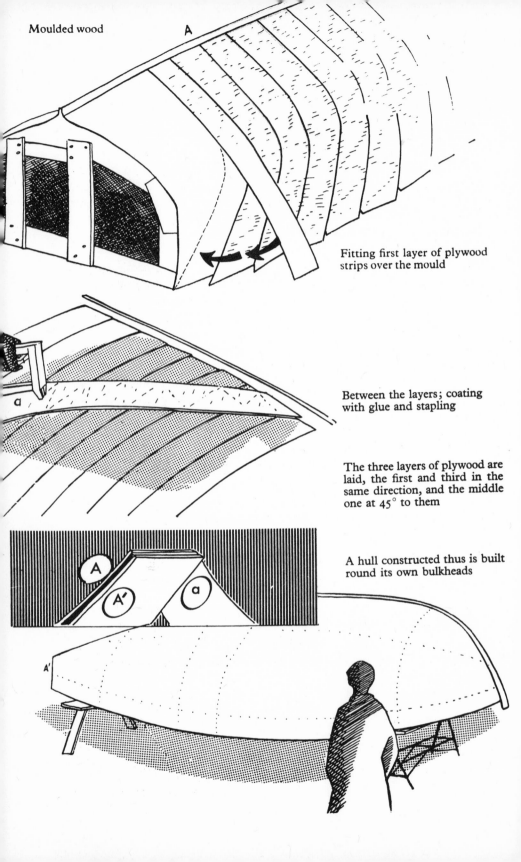

Moulded wood

Fitting first layer of plywood
strips over the mould

Between the layers; coating
with glue and stapling

The three layers of plywood are
laid, the first and third in the
same direction, and the middle
one at 45° to them

A hull constructed thus is built
round its own bulkheads

plywood in all its properties, but able to be moulded on a form. As a result, instead of using ready-made sheets of plywood of standard size, the skin is made in the required shape, by gluing three veneers of wood, about 0.1 in thick, one above the other and laying the grain of the wood in three different directions. In practice, this can only be done by means of a mould, on which the plies of wood are tacked in the form of strips.

The *ribands*, the stringers or length-wise members, can be put in place either before or after the skin is made, according to the mould; some types have none—the Finn does not.

But the moulded hull calls for some tacking of the strips, as in conventional construction, which takes time and care. The fitting is nevertheless much easier than for conventional planking, which might be as much as an inch thick. The first layer of strips is laid on the mould; the second is glued to the first, and similarly with the second, each with the grain in a different direction. During the gluing, the strips are held temporarily by staples, put in with a stapling machine.

When the hull comes off the mould there is some rather skilled fitting involved in the decking, and the interior reinforcements—bulkheads, floorboards, buoyancy tanks.

You get a very light and rigid boat, and of any shape wanted. Unfortunately it costs a lot of money, for there are many man-hours of work involved. If an amateur could hire the mould and specialized tools, he would find no difficulty in making a good job of a moulded wood hull.

Most boats for international and other important competitions are of this construction.

mixed construction: *unframed plywood and moulded wood*

Attempts have been made to combine the cheapness of the first of these processes with the excellent shape given by the second. Bottom and sides are ordinary plywood, chines of rounded shape, moulded.

The parts can be prefabricated, and the assembly is well adapted for mass production. The moulded wood part is made of short enough pieces to avoid fastenings. These parts are made by mass production and assembled on the mould. You get a shaped, rigid boat, a little heavier

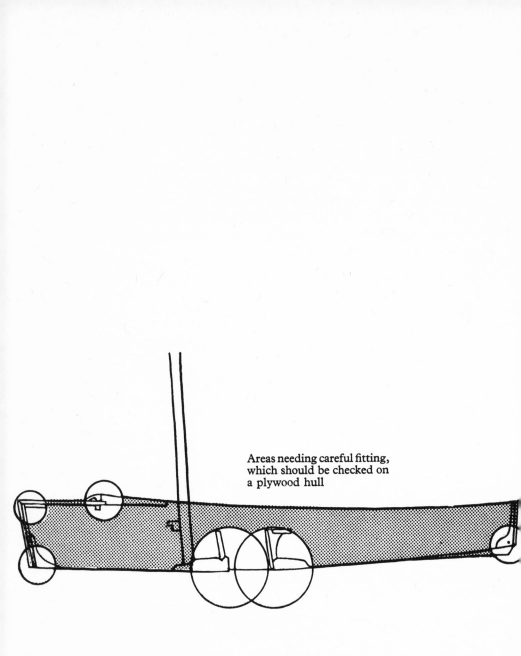

Areas needing careful fitting,
which should be checked on
a plywood hull

than a moulded wood one, but much cheaper. Boats of mixed construction have a good performance and plane easily.

This construction, too, has been used for much larger craft.

reinforced plastic construction

The sides of a small boat must resist forces of tension and compression. Certain materials, such as glass fibre and paper, have excellent resistance to tension forces; others, the synthetic resins, resist compression. The combination of such materials gives a sort of 'reinforced concrete', which can be used to build boat hulls. The boat is built on a mould, by the super-imposition of several layers of glass fibre (or paper) and of resins (hence the name of reinforced plastic).

Hulls so built are very resistant to knocks, and proof against the atmosphere and animal pests. They are rigid, very light, but are liable to bad distortion, incurable and unforeseeable, if removed from the moulds too soon. These materials are essential wherever wood will not stand the climate, in the tropics, where it lasts better at least than wood. Now that the technique has been perfected, warping, at least in small hulls, is less and less common. There are a number of different classes built of these materials.

defects of construction

After this review of the different types, it may be useful, especially as regards wooden boats, to look at some of the main defects of construction. Broadly speaking, they fall into four categories:

- faulty fitting and joinery;
- faulty scantlings;
- faults in quality and type of materials;
- gluing defects.

A badly put together boat will lack strength and leak. The important points for the buyer to check are:

> the fitting of the strakes to the rabbets in the stem, and of the garboard strake to the keel rabbets;
>
> in the case of a hard chine boat, the joints between chine and planking of side and bottom;
>
> fitting of deck, and of sides, around the gunwale and rubbing bands;
>
> fitting of planking to transom:
>
> finally, if there is a centre-board, the fitting of its trunk.

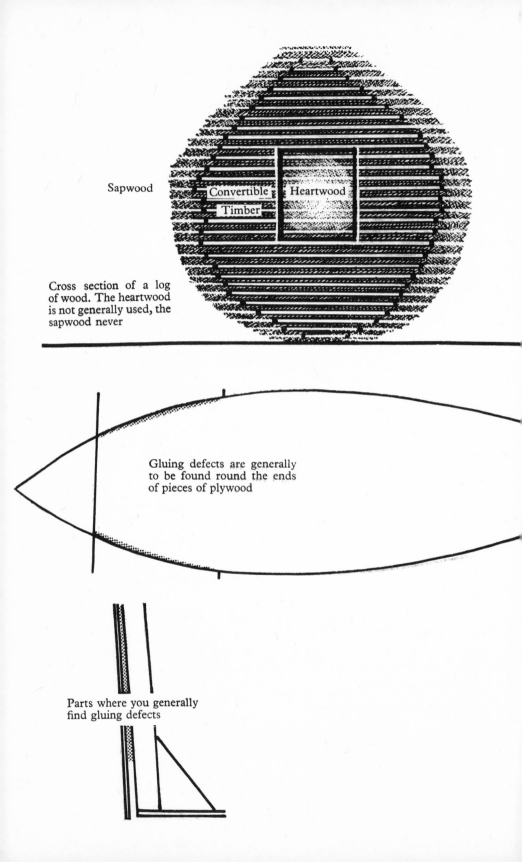

Sapwood

Convertible Timber Heartwood

Cross section of a log of wood. The heartwood is not generally used, the sapwood never

Gluing defects are generally to be found round the ends of pieces of plywood

Parts where you generally find gluing defects

These points are often hard to check; a defect in workmanship is often covered up with cement and a coat of paint which will disappear the first time the boat is sailed. The best way to avoid bad workmanship is to go to a good builder, and to remember it is better to pay a fair price for a properly built boat than to get some old tore-out, leaking like a sieve, as a 'bargain'.

Faulty scantlings, too, are a danger. It is a badly built boat which has the various structural members unmatched as regards strength. Every part should be related to the work it has to do; a sturdy, staunch boat with faulty rudder pintles is just as much of a danger as a boat that leaks badly. Just the same applies to a boat with solid planking and a weak deck. This is one thing you avoid with mass-produced craft, except on the early models which act as the prototypes.

Choice of materials is of importance because:

- bad quality wood will very soon give every appearance of extreme old age;

- quickly deteriorating fastenings and fittings are incurable weaknesses.

The materials used must be homogeneous.

- Electrolytic action attacks different metals when they are used close to one another in water;

- it is not a bit of good putting copper fastenings into a boat built of old packing-cases.

Materials must be properly *protected*. When the boat is being built, the parts must be painted *before* assembly, otherwise damp will get into the seams, and then into the wood, which will rot.

Lastly, *gluing defects* are a very serious trouble on modern boats. Apart from defects caused by bad workmanship, you get troubles from wrong mixing of the adhesive, from the temperature and humidity at the time they were applied, and from the operation being done too quickly or too slowly; they may all be disastrous. Another equally serious gluing trouble arises from using wood that has not been properly dried out, which the best of gluing will not hold. A builder's reputation rests very largely on his gluing.

wear and tear

The causes of wear and tear of a boat are still many. Frequent removal from its natural element, hard knocks and general bad treatment all play havoc with a small boat.

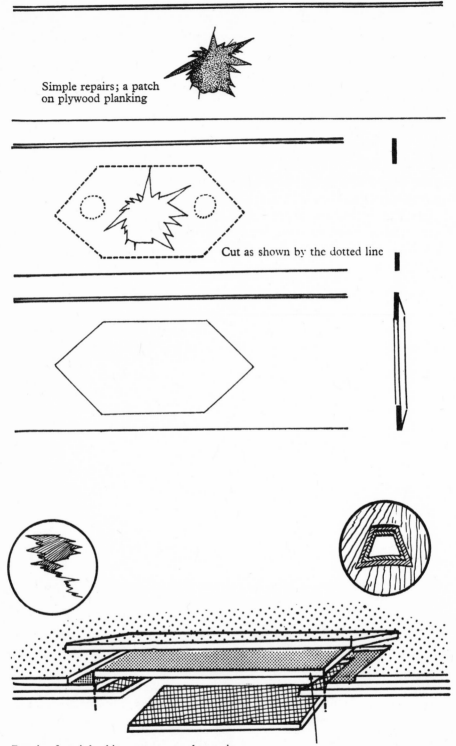

Simple repairs; a patch
on plywood planking

Cut as shown by the dotted line

Repair of a triple skin; not so easy, but quite
feasible if care is used and the hole is not too
big. The piece of the centre layer is the one
to glue first.

collisions and accidental damage

Errors of judgment often lead to collisions and very hard knocks, which put an unfair strain on all parts of the boat; stems and planking suffer in collisions, centre-boards, centre-board trunks, rudders, even planking and chines in stranding.

Even if no damage is at once apparent after a knock, except perhaps for scratched paint or a jammed centre-board, it is not wise to come to the hasty conclusion that all is well. The hole in the side, the leaking chine or centre-board trunk, the twisted rudder pintles—such things often come to light as the result of an accumulation of minor knocks the boat has had when sailing or being handled ashore. You will get the bill—and a pretty big bill—one day for all the petty damages you overlook as not worth attending to at the time.

Minor repairs are within everybody's powers; you don't need a perfect tool-kit or special knowledge. The great thing is to act in time. Everybody knows how to tighten a nut, but it is not everyone who can deal with the results when it falls off through lack of this simple attention.

The repair of more serious damages, leaks, holes, and so on, is more or less difficult according to what part of the boat they are found in. Replacing planking on a conventionally built boat is a job for a professional, or a very good amateur. The repair of a hole in a moulded wood or plastic hull is strictly a job for the professional.

On the other hand, it is fairly simple to mend a splintered hole in plywood. You cut out a square or rectangle big enough to take in all the damaged or cracked surface, and fit a similar-shaped piece of wood of the same dimensions in the hole you have made. This piece you glue to another, a bit larger, inside, taking care to put on a good coating of special cement, or, even simpler, a thick coat of paint.

Any large repair calls for time, the proper tools and a modicum of skill. The great thing is to attend to the small items of damage before they start bigger troubles.

causes of wear and tear

Heat, damp, and, most of all, alternate heating and chilling, wetting and drying, are the lot of most small boats, and the biggest causes of damage. Such alternations make the wood swell and contract in turn, which it cannot endure for ever. It is a living substance, and is subject to old age.

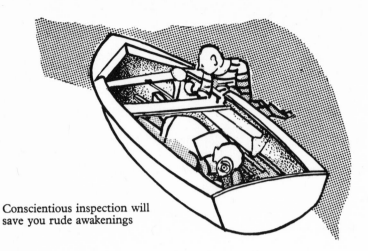

Conscientious inspection will
save you rude awakenings

Weather plays havoc with the boat's assembly, and may, particularly in the case of a conventional hull, start leaks through opening up of seams, and warping which makes fastenings work and weakens the whole craft. The boat perishes rapidly if it is kept in a warm, damp atmosphere and does not get plenty of ventilation. This is *wet rot* caused by sundry micro-organisms. There is also a form of decomposition known as *dry rot*, also caused by micro-organisms, and occurring in a dry, non-ventilated atmosphere. This kind of thing is common in boats which spend a lot of time in unaired boat-houses, and generally starts in the bilges.

No amount of paint or varnish will keep a boat from rapid deterioration in some tropical climates. Whatever precautions you take will only retard the work of the elements, and of animal pests; hence the value of plastics in such latitudes. In Europe, careful maintenance, painting, providing a ventilated boatshed, and so on, will protect wood efficiently.

note

We are not talking now about the damage caused by larger forms of animal life, ship worms, teredo and the like, which we don't get in these parts except in craft which have been almost abandoned.

The *fastenings and fittings*, if metal, are often attacked severely, especially in boats used at sea. It should be noted that the corrosive action of sea water is not too serious except when two different metals are used close to one another, setting up electrolytic action. The lower base metal is attacked by electrolysis and rapidly eaten away. A galvanized iron fastening may be excellent and last a long time if there are no copper bolts or rivets in the hull. And duralumin will do very well in the absence of stainless steel or bronze. You choose one metal, for its mechanical properties . . . and by the length of your purse . . . and stick to it.

maintenance

Remember, a boat should have attention every time it goes out, and any small faults should then be put right, e.g. a loose chain-plate, which may well come adrift and bring the mast down; a rudder hinge which may well when loose jam the rudder and lose a race or cause a collision. A small leak may indicate serious damage, especially in chines, bows, transom or centre-board trunk. A boat is liable to wear and tear like everything else. Daily maintenance is essential, otherwise your boat will soon become dangerous and useless.

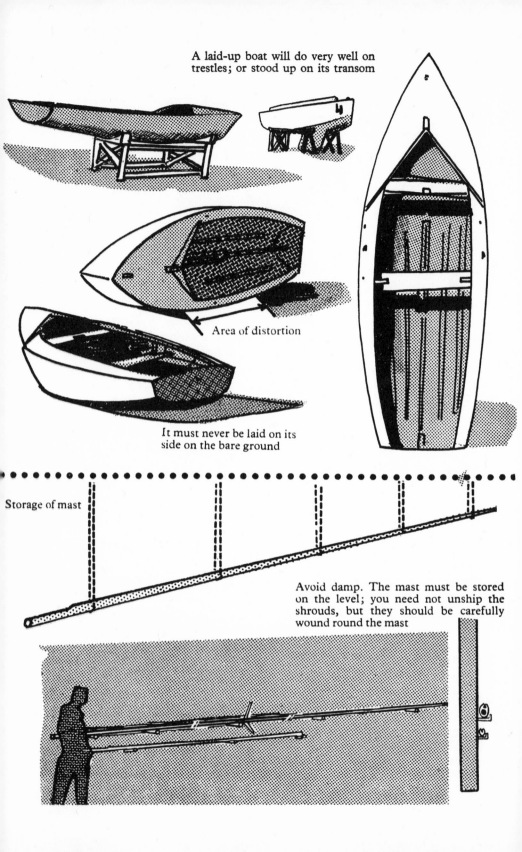

A laid-up boat will do very well on trestles; or stood up on its transom

Area of distortion

It must never be laid on its side on the bare ground

Storage of mast

Avoid damp. The mast must be stored on the level; you need not unship the shrouds, but they should be carefully wound round the mast

the boathouse

It is probable that a small boat will only be put in the water when it is going to be used, though it may be left afloat on a mooring. At any rate, for the seasons when it is not in use it will be laid up and stored in the dry, in a boatshed.

A laid-up boat should be unrigged, the hull stripped of everything that might trap damp—rags, sponge, mud and assorted filth. There must be ventilation. The boat should be put on a cradle or on trestles to avoid distortion. It can well be stored upright, sitting on the transom with blocks underneath to stop it resting on the rudder pintles. This method of storing is particularly useful for clubs, which have storage of ample height but limited floor space; you can get a lot of boats in like this. The inside of the hull must get as much air as possible; if there are water-tight buoyancy tanks, their plugs must be out; any locker doors should be left open. The surroundings should not be too dry, nor too damp, and the air should be kept moving. Needless to say, the boat should be thoroughly washed before laying up, preferably in fresh water.

When you put a conventionally built boat in the water, leave it for the seams to take up before you go far in it.

The boat may be put away in a boatshed every day when in use. If the store is high enough for the boat not to have to be unrigged each time, so much the better. You can put a cover over the boat, in which case, there must be air circulation under the cover. Never leave a boat, except for a very short time, lying on the ground, or on grass; the wood will perish rapidly.

Lastly, a boat lying on moorings will want its bottom cleaned frequently. Weed grows very fast under the hull and forms a big drag on its speed.

what to avoid

There is, broadly speaking, nothing in daily maintenance that your ideas of cleanliness and common sense would not suggest. We have already suggested the value of repairing all minor damage as soon as possible. But there are two or three things that you should avoid:

● Don't let sand gather in the bottom of the boat. When the boat is out of the water seams open up a little, a grain or two of sand gets in, and when the boat gets back in the water these grains stop the seams from closing again;

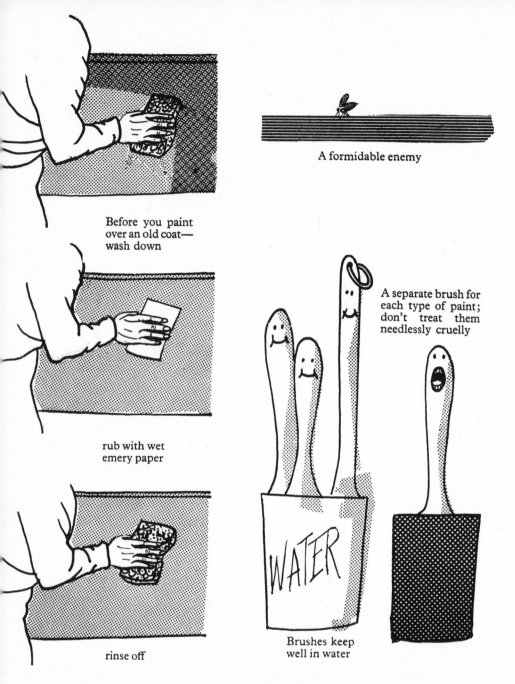

Before you paint
over an old coat—
wash down

A formidable enemy

rub with wet
emery paper

A separate brush for
each type of paint;
don't treat them
needlessly cruelly

WATER

rinse off

Brushes keep
well in water

Only use good paint-brushes. Good brushes are not necessarily new ones; they must be looked after; clean them in turpentine or in the solvent recommended, after each period of use, or even hourly when in use. They must be kept in water. Finally, brushes must be kept for one kind of paint, and never used for any other (oil paint, plastic paints, bitumous paints, varnish).

- never let water stand in the bilges or in water-tight compartments;

- never drag the boat along the ground, particularly over sand; the paint will rub off, and you will be down to the bare wood. Once more, you carry a boat when it is on land. For the same reason, when you are beaching, jump out before the boat touches the sand;

- never lay a boat on its side for any length of time, for storage, for instance, in a low shed; it is ten times better to unrig it, or leave it outside.

painting

We will confine ourselves to one or two essentials on the subject of painting. If a coat of paint is to stay on, the surface below must be properly prepared. It must be rubbed down and sanded with great care, with progressively finer grade glasspaper. The surface must be thoroughly dry, and the air free of excess humidity.

When you are painting on bare wood, prime first, then put one or more undercoats, then stop holes and cracks with filler or plastic wood. When painting over old paint, it must be washed off to remove grease, smoothed down with emery paper and rinsed off. Painting which has crazed, cracked or starred is paint which has been badly put on, or, which comes to the same thing, put on a badly prepared surface. This coat must be taken right off before repainting. Coats must be *thin*, and if the paint does not spread well, you must put on more coats.

Before putting on a coat of paint, make sure the layer below and the one you are going to put on 'mix' in a chemical sense. For instance, if you have a coat of bituminous paint, you can't put plastic paint on top of it. If they are not compatible, you must put on a coat of the appropriate under-coating—in this particular case an aluminium undercoat.

Never forget that a well-painted boat is not only a pleasure to look at, but it goes faster with a nice smooth hull (less surface resistance); and, finally, the wood is protected by the paint, which minimizes ageing and distortion.

A boat must be painted whenever the paint shows signs of wear, through rubbing or knocks, perhaps once a year, sometimes more if the boat is hard worked, sometimes less if it is not. An occasional touching up is a good thing, both for appearance's sake and for protection of the hull.

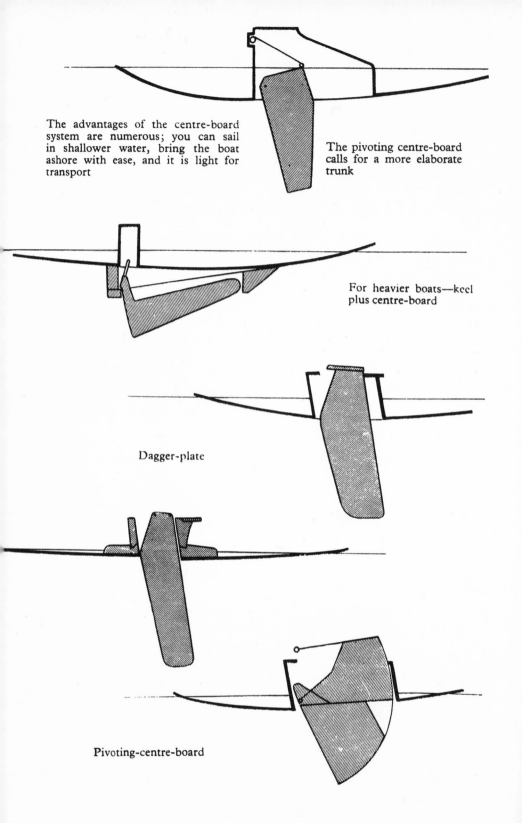

The advantages of the centre-board system are numerous; you can sail in shallower water, bring the boat ashore with ease, and it is light for transport

The pivoting centre-board calls for a more elaborate trunk

For heavier boats—keel plus centre-board

Dagger-plate

Pivoting-centre-board

centre-board, rudder, buoyancy tanks

We have already explained how stability is a factor of speed and safety. This stability may come about through the lines of the boat, by means of ballast, or by a combination of the two.

Ballast may be inside or outside the boat. But a sailing craft, while it must have stability, must be able to go to windward without undue leeway. Exterior ballast, sticking out more or less under the hull, lowers the centre of gravity of the boat, and lessens drifting, or leeway. For small craft which use sheltered waters, stability can be had without fixed ballast; it is provided by the lines of the boat and the weight of the crew. But such craft must go to windward as well as bigger ones; to this end, they are fitted with a fin protruding through the bottom of the boat, called a *centre-board*, or *centre-plate*. The advantages of the system are many; shallow draft, easy beaching, lightness for transportation, etc.

It would be useless to lessen the draft amidships if you could not do so aft; so the rudder assembly is made to unship, and often, to come up without unshipping.

We are going now to look at centre-boards, rudders, and—since an un-ballasted boat is always liable to turn over, the various means of making it unsinkable.

centre-board and centre-board well, or trunk

Opening up a hull to the sea below the waterline poses problems of water-tightness to the builder. The conventional centre-board (we will not touch on lee-boards) runs along the centre line of the boat; the slit to accommodate it weakens the keel. Besides, to avoid shipping water through the slit, it has to have a raised partition round it. There is therefore a sort of raised well in the boat, called the *centre-board trunk*. See cross-section of centre-board well on next page.

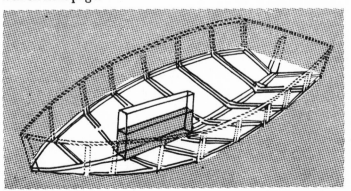

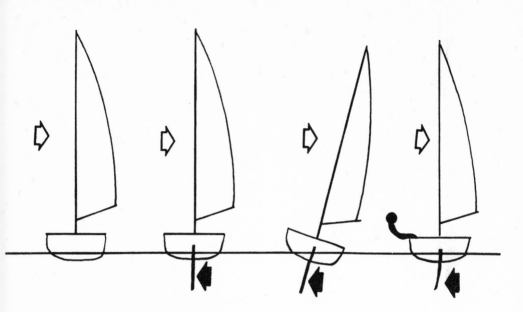

how the centre-board works

The wind, as we know, exerts a certain lateral pressure on the sail of a boat sailing, for instance, with the wind on the beam. If it is sailing with the centre-board up, it will go crab-wise; put down the board and it will sail in a straight line; a force of water pressure acts on the centre-board, opposite to the lateral wind pressure; a couple is caused, and the boat tends to heel. The crew will sit out and stop this heel, but the pressure on the centre-board will remain, and tend to flex it. Hence the value of stout anchorages for the top of the centre-board.

Moreover, if the boat accidentally grounds with the centre-board down, it is essential the board should not split. Various inside and outside reinforcements have been designed to give it the necessary strength. Some are shown in the drawing.

the two types of centre-board

A drawback to the centre-board is that it is very much in the way in the boat. Some craft have what is known as a *dagger-plate*, which slides into place in the well like a dagger being slipped into its sheath. Wells for dagger plates are comparatively narrow in profile, and there is a much shorter slit weakening the keel.

Owing, though, to the length of the dagger-plate, it is an awkward thing to handle, and interferes with the boom, and with the boom downhaul if fitted. And the dagger-plate gives very little control of the position of the CLR in relation to the CE.

Some craft have pivoting *centre-boards*, which tuck away inside the well, rather like the blade of a pocket-knife.

The drawback to this system, which gives very useful control over the CLR, and makes manoeuvring much simpler, is that the keel is weakened over a much greater length, and inspections of the centre-board are not easy to make.

the make-up of a centre-board

We have just said that a centre-board is liable to forces tending to bend it—flexion.

What would happen if one *did* bend the board would be that the material on the convex side would be lengthened and that on the concave side shortened. In the centre the material would not be affected in either of these ways.

So if you want to save weight you can take a good deal of material out of the interior of a piece of wood, practically without effect on the rigidity of the whole—in the case of a centre-board you reinforce the outside. With this in view, you use plywood, with the outside plies very much the stronger.

If the outside plies have the grain vertical, gashes in plies 'a a' would have the effect of weakening the centre-board considerably, for it would be the plies 'c c' that would be doing the work.

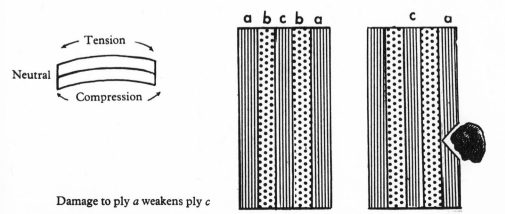

Damage to ply *a* weakens ply *c*

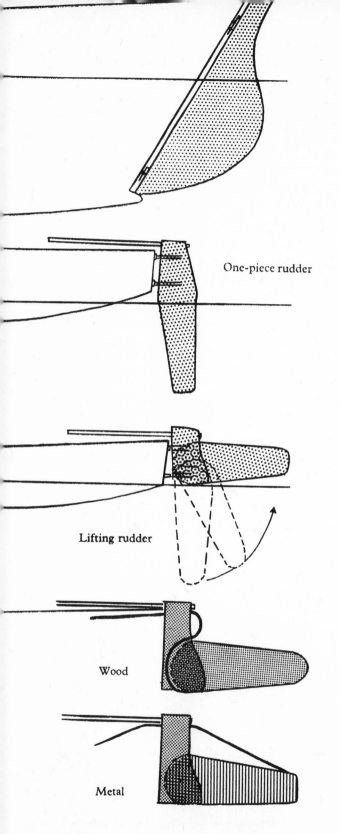

All types of boat have
a removable rudder

One-piece rudder

Lifting rudder

Wood

Metal

rudders

On all boats carrying a visible stern rudder, the rudder can be unshipped more or less easily according to its weight and the system of hanging it, which must be simple but robust.

There are two types of rudder: the conventional one-piece one (see drawing), and the *lifting* rudder, with controllable draught, which is coming into use more and more. This is the one we are going to describe.

It is in two parts: the tiller mounts on the part above water, and to the rudder are fitted the *pintles* for fixing it to the hull; the below-water part pivots on it. The system lets the rudder remain shipped in shallow water. The rudder is lifted as follows: the upper part is shaped top and bottom, at the top to take the tiller, below to take the pivoting blade.

The fittings are mounted on the upper half of the rudder and on the transom, being fixed by bolts or rivets (the latter making repairs more difficult); they take a lot of strain. For this reason, don't put on too much helm when the rudder is only half down.

control over rudder depth and centre-board immersion

The moving part of the rudder and the centre-board may be wooden or metal; in the latter case, the centre-board when down provides a certain amount of ballast.

A line is used to lower or raise the centre-board, depending on whether it is wood or metal; the same applies to the rudder.

This line must be watched; a centre-board which cannot be dropped, or which will not come up, especially the first, can be a considerable nuisance.

maintenance of centre-board and rudder

Centre-boards can be made of solid wood, of plywood, or metal.

● A solid wood board will warp if it is left in the sun or on damp ground. You can try to put things right by leaving it in the opposite condition for some hours; but the warping is often incurable.

● A plywood centre-board as we saw, does most of its work on the outside faces; you must be careful not to jam pebbles between the centre-board and the walls of the trunk, a thing that often does happen in a popple, especially at the edge of some beaches. These pebbles may score the outside

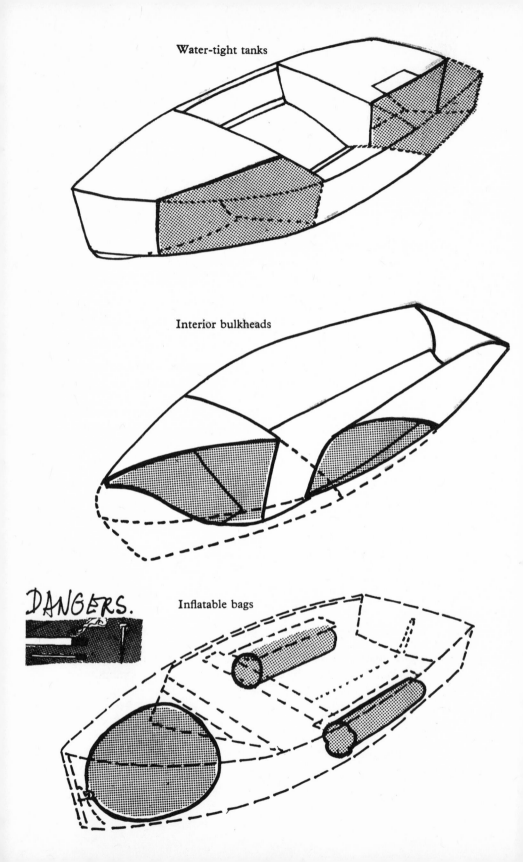

Water-tight tanks

Interior bulkheads

DANGERS.

Inflatable bags

plies, and thus weaken the whole set-up of the centre-board; if the centre-board sticks, don't force it, but try to get rid of the object which is jamming it.

● Lastly, if you have a metal centre-plate, you must see it does not rust.

All we have said about the centre-board applies equally to the rudder. In addition, see that the joint for the tiller does not wear too loose.

buoyancy equipment

The object of this is to keep the boat above water, no matter what happens; it comes in three different types.

Built-in tanks formed by hull, deck and a bulkhead, fore and aft or thwartships, built into the hull and sharing its rigidity.

In one type the fore-and-aft transverse bulkheads do no structural work; there is an inspection cover on deck, which also gives ventilation.

In the second type the bulkheads run fore and aft, but perform a much more positive rôle; they may affect the stiffness of the hull; but this last system has the advantage that the effects of bilge water are largely counteracted.

Expanded plastic substance:

> ● Polyurethane foam, which can be blown up *in situ*; that is to say, you mix two liquids in the place where you want the foam, and it is produced there.
>
> ● Polyvinyl foam, which is rather expensive.
>
> ● Polystyrene foam, fairly cheap.

Inflatable bags:

Bags of reinforced plastic, very tough, but always at the mercy of a cigarette-end, or of a knife point or blade.

When you are dealing with either plastic foam or bags they must be well fastened down; their buoyancy is such that they can burst out of a boat filled with water.

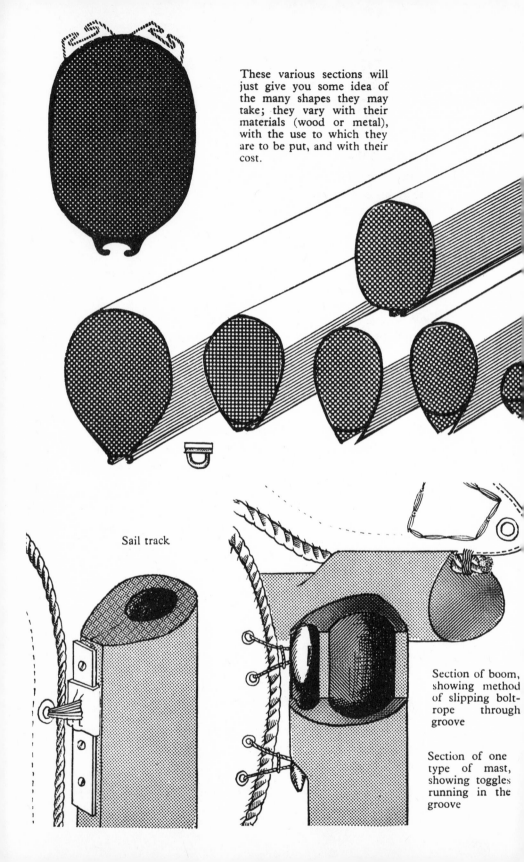

These various sections will just give you some idea of the many shapes they may take; they vary with their materials (wood or metal), with the use to which they are to be put, and with their cost.

Sail track

Section of boom, showing method of slipping bolt-rope through groove

Section of one type of mast, showing toggles running in the groove

practical hints
on spars, sail and rigging | 10

mast and boom

description

Modern sailing sloops are practically universally rigged as Bermudian *sloops* or *una-rig*. Their only spars are a mast and boom.

These spars are nearly always fitted with a groove to take the bolt-rope of the sail. There are other ways of holding the sails to the mast—trackways, mast-hoops, wire spans and piston hanks; but the most generally used method is the groove worked in the mast and taking the bolt-rope itself or slides or toggles attached to it. It provides aerodynamic continuity between mast and sail, is simple and very strong.

Masts are often rectangular or oval in section, to increase their longitudinal strength; the greatest strain is imposed on the mast, except with a stern wind, in the direction where the staying is least effective.

Small boat spars, at least on small, cheap and mass-produced ones, are usually made of wood, although light alloy masts are becoming increasingly popular as aluminium techniques improve. Wooden spars may be solid or hollow. So far as concerns mechanical strength, hollow ones are to be preferred. They are, weight for weight, stronger than solid spars, and, in particular, less susceptible to bending under compression strains; as the halyards may go through the inside of the mast, windage is reduced. Solid spars, however, have the advantage of being much cheaper, as they do

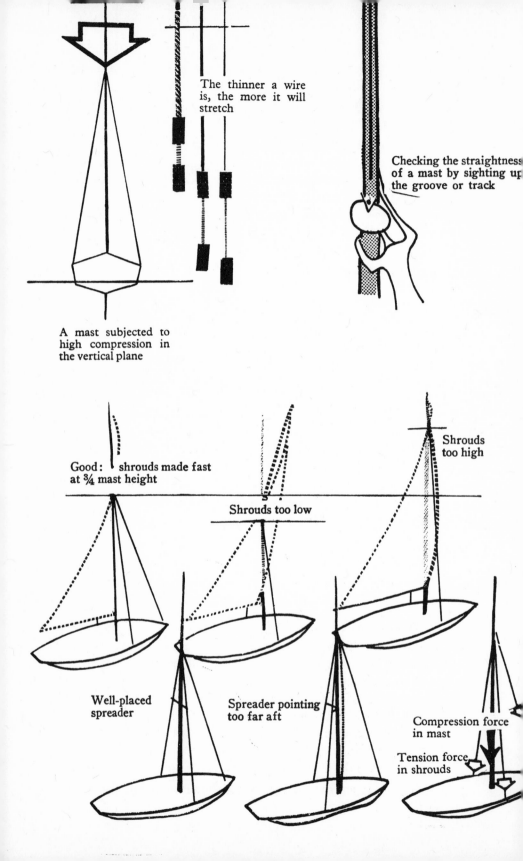

The thinner a wire is, the more it will stretch

Checking the straightness of a mast by sighting up the groove or track

A mast subjected to high compression in the vertical plane

Good: shrouds made fast at ¾ mast height

Shrouds too low

Shrouds too high

Well-placed spreader

Spreader pointing too far aft

Compression force in mast

Tension force in shrouds

not have to be hollowed out, and, moreover, can be made of ordinary wood; hollow masts call for special skill, and very special wood, straight grained and free of knots.

Care should be given to the maintenance of spars. They should be revarnished whenever the wood is likely to absorb damp. When the spars are laid up, after the boat has been unrigged, they should be kept flat (on the groove for preference, that being the straight edge of the mast), on plenty of chocks, in a sheltered but well-ventilated spot. The spars should be stripped of stays and cordage. Fittings which cannot be removed should be greased to avoid corrosion.

how a mast works

A good mast must be of low weight, in order to keep the CG of the boat as low as possible. Its function is, obviously, to hold up the sails, and to transmit the forces set up by them.

Unless you have particularly strong masts, with no weak points and an even bending effect, such as the Finn's masts, hollow and unstayed, (and these are obviously going to be uncommonly expensive if light enough), you must have a system of stays, and accept the resulting windage.

From the mechanical point of view, the object of the shrouds is to convert thwartship and fore-and-aft flexion forces into vertical compression ones.

It is unusual for a mast of adequate section to break as the result of compression in the vertical plane; usually, a mast breaks because the stay system is badly positioned; this produces bending, and then collapse.

simple staying

The simplest system of staying consists of a *shroud* each side, leading a little aft from the mast, and a forestay, which often has the jib's luff clipped to it. These three stays are made fast about three-quarters up the mast.

How does such a rig resist the strains? First, we must assume the mast is rigid enough for the forces exerted by the sails at given points to be converted into a single force, acting at the level of the hounds, and perpendicular thereto. Given this, all forces imposed here are theoretically resolved into:

- a compression force in the mast,

- tension forces in the stays.

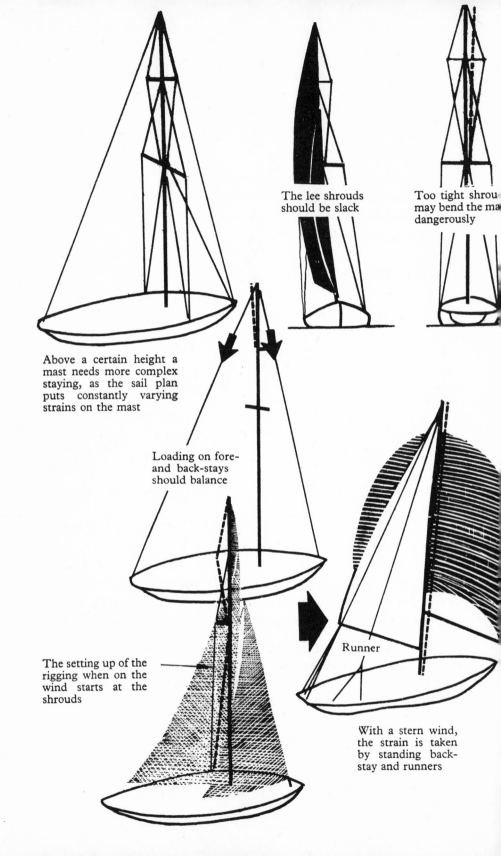

The lee shrouds should be slack

Too tight shrou[ds]
may bend the ma[st]
dangerously

Above a certain height a mast needs more complex staying, as the sail plan puts constantly varying strains on the mast

Loading on fore- and back-stays should balance

The setting up of the rigging when on the wind starts at the shrouds

Runner

With a stern wind, the strain is taken by standing back-stay and runners

The forces, quite powerful when on the wind, set up by the jib through luff and halyard, are transformed in the same way (see lower right hand sketch p. 418). A mast, in fact, especially in a small boat, does as much of its work in flexing as any other way.

more complex stay systems

When the mast is fairly thin, as it is on a solid mast for a small boat, *spreaders* are effective in counteracting bending strains on the mast at the point where they are fitted.

When the mast is higher you will find crosstrees and *lower shrouds*. The use of the crosstrees is to open up the angle at which the shrouds exert their pull, while the lower shrouds balance the force exerted by the crosstrees, which would otherwise leave too much of the mast unsupported.

To stay the mast with the wind aft, if the two sets of shrouds are not enough, *standing backstays* or *runners* are often fitted, the latter if the boom is too long to allow a standing backstay, or if it is desired to stay the mast at points other than the one where the backstay is attached. Runners are movable backstays, tensioned by a tackle or lever. The windward runner is set up, the leeward one slacked off, so that you have to change them whenever you tack. Runners and backstays are also useful when on the wind, as they give a powerful pull on the luff of the jib, which is essential for going to windward; but you will not often see them on small boats, which rarely boast a mast over 30 ft high.

There are other even more complicated staying systems, but you will not find them on present-day small boats.

adjustments

Whatever system of staying is used, it will be effective only if kept in proper adjustment. Normally, the test of properly adjusted rigging is that the mast is straight when you are on the wind.

Adjustments depend on the type of rigging. Some boats want the shrouds very taut; on other, more complex, rigs, you must tension the lower shrouds very moderately, for if they are too tight they will cancel out, and even reverse, the action of the topmast shrouds and bring about a collapse of the mast.

On a complex rig, you generally go about adjustment as follows; harden down the topmast shrouds and forestay, leaving the others fairly slack. *When on the wind*, in a light breeze to start with, tension the other shrouds till you get a straight mast.

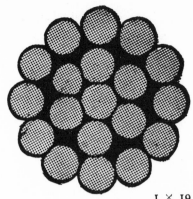

1 × 19
Non-flexible
(for shrouds)

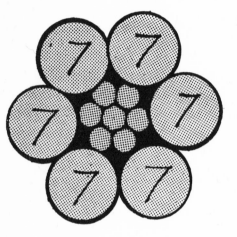

7 × 7
Non-flexible

7 × 19
Flexible

6 × 19
Hempen heart
(very flexible)

rigging

shrouds

The shrouds and stays, which constitute the *standing rigging* (that is to say, fixed, whatever happens to the boat), are of wire rope of section proportional to the work they are to do. The allowable load is shown on the rigging plan of the individual yacht. The *allowable load* increases with the square of the diameter, or the area of the section. There are two principal types of wire rope—flexible and non-flexible. They may be made of ordinary or stainless steel.

Flexible rope is dearer, not very durable if galvanized, and is used for running rigging, not for standing gear.

Ordinary non-flexible wire is made up of several metal strands (usually six) laid up round a metal heart. It has high strength in tension, but breaks easily if passed round too small a radius, for instance round the sheave of a pully. It does not stand up well to corrosion, and must be protected; either grease it regularly (a messy practice, though an effective one) or use a protective paint—lead paint, for instance. A coat of paint flakes off easily when the shroud is distorted.

In winter, after laying up, it will pay to coil up the shrouds, being careful not to kink them, and put them to soak in oil.

Rustless non-flexible wire rope may be made up normally in strands and a heart, or just with strands of stainless steel with no heart. The latter is now most common, and so cheaper. Its main inconvenience is that you can't splice it. The upkeep of stainless wire is obviously simple, but it is not cheap to buy. Nevertheless, the advantages of freedom from rust are such that almost all small boats have their rigging of stainless steel.

The shrouds are very simply made; you cut off a piece of wire of the right length, and work an *eye splice* and *thimble* into each end. The eyes will be made fast to the fittings with shackles, rivets, bolts or turnbuckles. The thimble is to avoid wear on the splice.

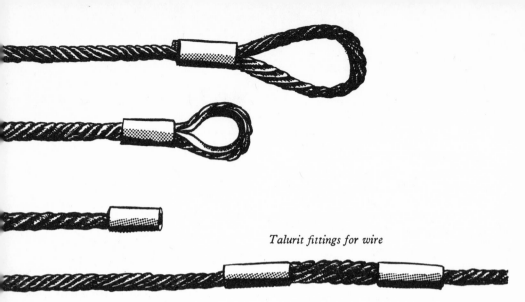

Talurit fittings for wire

Size varies with the material

Strands made up of rope-yarn

The rope is right-hand-laid

Strands are laid up to the left

Yarns right-hand-laid

Materials used—hemp, sisal, manilla, cotton, nylon, terylene

Splicing wire rope is a difficult job and takes time. It must be served to avoid cut ends of wire sticking out. All splicing can be avoided by using Talurit metal sleeves, which are put on by a special tool. The process is rapid, so cheaper than splicing, and needs no serving. But as the sleeves are of alloy, you may run the risk of electrolytic action; it would be well to check the sleeves, and varnish them carefully. Talurit is the only way of working an eye into 1 × 19 stainless steel wire, barring screw-down clamps, which are heavy, unreliable and an eyesore.

If properly maintained, shrouds should last a long time, especially if they are made of stainless steel. But rust is not the only danger. Friction against a fitting, or an accidental kink when fitting out, or other accidental causes, may break one or more of the strands.

This weakness will increase progressively, and all the strands will break one after the other. It is necessary, therefore, to handle stays with care, coil them without forcing them, and check them often. The broken strand which often appears and buries itself in your finger is not only dangerous (it leads to whitlows) but a certain symptom of a stay nearing the end of its life. When more start to appear it is time for a new stay.

Rust, too, shows by broken strands appearing. You can tell the age of a strand by gently bending it; if it doesn't go back to its original shape, and if several grains of rust appear, the strand is perished. Rust attacks the inside strands more quickly than the outside ones (damp gathers at the centre).

running rigging

Running rigging comprises all ropes used to work the boat, that is to say, to hoist sails (halyards), to control their trim (sheets), to raise or lower the centre-board, and so on. These ropes run round blocks, or sheaves, for the most part, hence the name.

On a light craft running rigging is almost all vegetable or synthetic rope. Flexible steel wire (stainless or ordinary) is used very little, except for halyards and the centre-board purchase. It is generally coiled up on a small winch.

The value of winches on small craft is doubtful. There is not all that much hard work to be done. On high-performance racing boats they are of value, as they are very compact. Their use calls for a lot of maintenance, as they are very liable to seize up.

Braided cotton or terylene recommended for main sheet; does not tie itself in knots

Four strands laid up round a heart

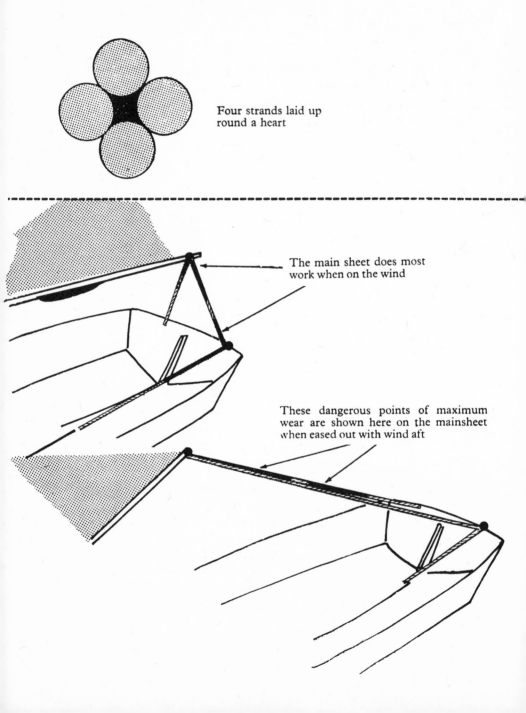

The main sheet does most work when on the wind

These dangerous points of maximum wear are shown here on the mainsheet when eased out with wind aft

There are several sorts of natural vegetable fibres:

- *Hemp*, strong, fairly flexible, fairly cheap, very much used, especially for warps.
- *Cotton*, very flexible, rather dear, vulnerable to friction, mostly used for sheets, as it is very easy on the hands.
- *Sisal*, very flexible, very cheap, but rough and not very strong.

synthetic ropes

Size for size, nylon is stronger than vegetable fibres, is more elastic and weathers better. Above all it does not shrink when wet. However, it is liable to heavy wear under friction and is expensive. It is used a lot on small craft, especially for anchor cables, but is often regarded as too slippery and elastic for sheets.

A recent type of nylon rope on the market is claimed to be less elastic than formerly. Terylene stretches less and is widely used for running rigging, especially in yachts as in its thicker sizes there is little 'give', so that it is ideal for halyards.

It should be noted that, as far as ropes go, economy is not a big consideration on a small boat; the number and length of ropes are very limited. Besides, a rope that is dear to buy will prove the cheaper in use if it has a good long life.

maintenance

Running rigging should be changed as soon as signs of wear appear; if you cut them long enough in the first place, you can cut off worn ends to change the points of friction. Don't forget—you just cannot change a main or jib halyard at sea in a small boat if it does break.

You must therefore anticipate an incident which may have serious results. Wear always appears in the same way, whatever kind of rope it may be; the yarns break, especially at friction points, which gives the strands a characteristic 'hairy' look.

Besides, a vegetable fibre perishes. Perishing is encouraged by humidity, and by salt air. When you lay up, you must wash out all rope in fresh water, and hang it up in proper coils in an airy spot. An old strand will uncoil easily—the fibres separate when you twist a yard. It is a certain sign of age. Again—on an old rope, the strands are no longer round, but flattened or square.

normal types of running rigging

There are plenty of styles in running rigging. Everyone has his own fancies and his own little tricks.

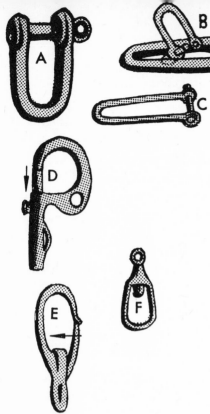

A 'D' shackle

B Shackle spanner

C Long 'D' shackle

D Snap shackle for jib

E Snap hook with concealed spring

F Swivel

G Blocks

H Jamming cleat

I Sheet fairlead

J Turnbuckle, or
Bottle screw

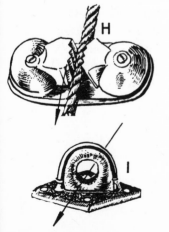

The various fittings
shown are all in
current use in small
craft; there are many
other types

fittings and chandlery

No doubt it is in this field that you have the widest choice—just look at the yacht chandlers' catalogues. It is quite impossible to describe all the kinds of fittings, winches, cleats, jamming and otherwise, sliding fairleads, and the like. We will confine ourselves to giving some general ideas which may lead you to make your choice, and some ideas on maintenance.

Mast fittings, and generally all deck gear on a boat should be as light as possible. But it is no good letting a passion for lightness blind you on questions of strength and resistance to corrosion. In the world of gadgets the main factor in your choice must be the price you are prepared to pay. Don't forget the question of electrolytic action. And appearance counts for much here. A stainless-steel fitting will not be much stronger than a galvanized-iron one, but it will be much nicer to look at, and easier to keep up. It will also be a great deal more expensive.

As regards maintenance, protection against rust is the great worry in dealing with anything made of metal and exposed to damp. A most effective way is to grease everything made of metal, especially working parts (threads of bolts, turnbuckles, shackles, and so on). When you lay up you might well take all fixed fittings to pieces and soak them in hot grease; they will be cocooned in grease, which will protect them.

Blocks are an important part of your deck gear. They must be light and strong, must not seize up, and not wear the rope that goes through their sheaves. The best type of block is undoubtedly the Tufnol, laminated plastic or nylon kind; it is pretty expensive, and doesn't look as nice as a bronze one, for instance; but it is far the best kind. The conventional block with cast-iron sheave and wooden cheeks is not for small boats; it is too heavy and needs too much upkeep.

Whenever you ship any sort of fitting you must consider if it is man enough for the job it is to do. You must get away from the idea of monster articles which are too strong to let you down, just as you must avoid putting a dolls' house shackle, say, on the tack of the jib. Moderation in all things!

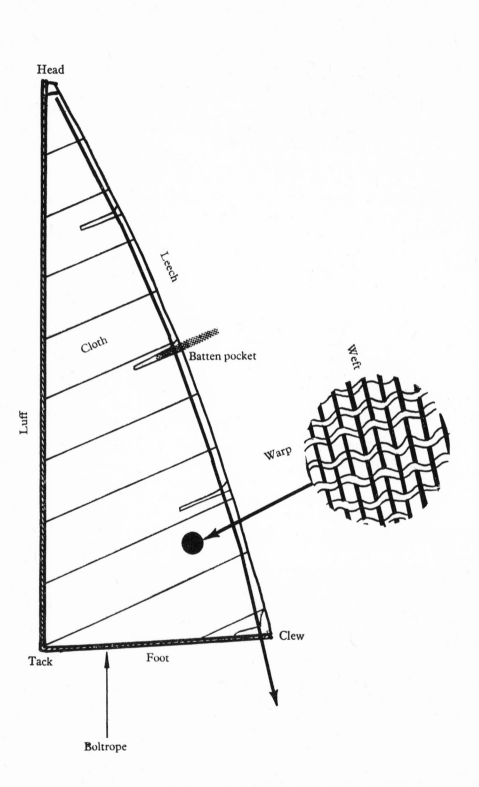

sails

The way the sails work, and the way to control them—all that we have already spoken of. We will again explain how they are cut and made up, the damage they may suffer and how to look after them. Small craft are generally rigged as Bermudian sloops or Una rigs. We shall therefore only deal here with Bermudian mainsails and jibs. Here are some general remarks on the cloths used in sailmaking.

The Bermudian mainsail

Remember the vertical side of the sail running up and down the mast is called the *luff*, the horizontal side along the boom, the *foot*, and the hypotenuse the *leech*. The round of the leech is kept flat by *battens*, inserted in *pockets*.

The luff and foot are reinforced by *bolt-ropes*, which are ropes to which the canvas of the sail is sewn. They are used to hold the sail on to the spars in the grooves provided for that purpose, and especially to limit stretch along mast and boom, in which areas the material is working on the bias. The most important tension on the sail is along the length of the leech, and, broadly speaking, parallel to it. The sail is trimmed through the sheet, which has strong purchases by means of its tackle and pulls strongly on the leech. In this direction parallel to the leech the material should have as little stretch as possible, if the sail is to keep its shape.

Woven cloth is composed of two rows of interwoven threads; a longitudinal one called the warp and a transverse one called the weft, put together by the shuttle. The weft is much more stretched than the warp (see sketch); so the fabric is more elastic in the direction of the warp than in that of the weft. The sail is therefore cut with the cloths (widths of fabric) so placed that the weft is parallel to the leech of the sail. The cloths are at right-angles to the leech.

To reinforce the foot and the luff, bolt-ropes are sewn on. The whole art of sailmaking lies in the sewing of the bolt-ropes. You must either sew the canvas on to the bolt-rope, giving more length of canvas than length of rope, or vice versa. Why? A fabric is very elastic in the direction of the diagonal (try it on your handkerchief!). The places where the threads cross may be regarded as so many little hinges. The angle, originally 90°, between warp and weft, can be considerably distorted. Now on the luff and foot we saw that the cloth is exactly on the diagonal, so that the warp is at right-angles to the leech. If you stretch the bolt-rope, the latter,

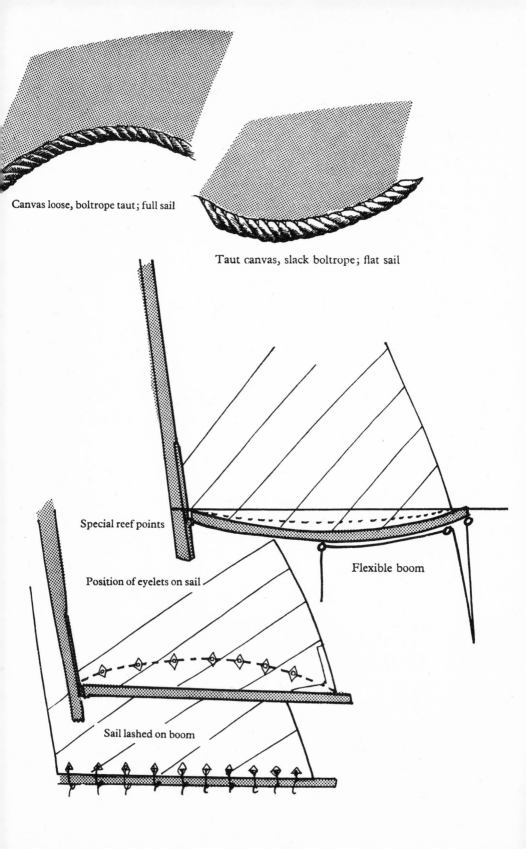

Canvas loose, boltrope taut; full sail

Taut canvas, slack boltrope; flat sail

Special reef points

Flexible boom

Position of eyelets on sail

Sail lashed on boom

being moderately elastic, will elongate, the angle will open out, while the threads keep their respective lengths. A crease will then appear along the length of the spars.

The wind pressure will tend to make the crease disappear. The luff crease tends to bring the flow of the sail forward, which is aerodynamically desirable (Manfred Curry: maximum belly at one-third forward; Ted Wells: maximum belly at the centre). If there is no wrinkle at the luff at rest, the flow will be too far aft when the wind blows. The sailmaker therefore sews the luff to the bolt-rope in order that this crease appears at a normal degree of hardening down, otherwise he would have made it too flat, that is sewn too much canvas on to a given length of bolt-rope.

The luff bolt-rope regulates the position of the flow, the foot bolt-rope regulates its dimensions. The less hardening is done, or the flatter the sail is, the less marked is the crease at the foot—and less wind will be needed to take it out altogether; the flow will be great. On the contrary, the more you harden down the tack, the more wind it will take to remove the crease, the flatter the sail is. Harden down less in light winds, and more in heavy ones. Similarly, a light-weather sail will be cut very full, a heavy-weather sail sewn flat. All this shows the importance of bolt-rope tension and cut in controlling the shape of a sail. There are also other ways of regulating the flow:

● A 'roach reef' along the foot;

● bending the spars, as, for example, on a Star or Finn.

A new sail stretches under initial wind pressure and is therefore cut with what appears to be too much flow. But take care, and don't expect a new sail to set properly at once. It has to be broken in gently; it must be hardened down progressively, but not to an exaggerated degree. This would overstretch the weft, and the sail would be distorted and prematurely flattened. The stretching of the bolt-rope in relation to the sail must be gradual. On an old sail it will not do to stretch the bolt-ropes too much. One can revive it by soaking it in water.

At the head the sail is narrow and the fabric takes a higher strain than elsewhere; the same at the tack. The bolt-rope must be sewn very stretched, that is with little flattening of the sail, so that the cloth is not pulled away from the leech. The fabric must be able to stretch uniformly; this is the origin of the wrinkles that come at head and tack of new sails. They vanish quickly.

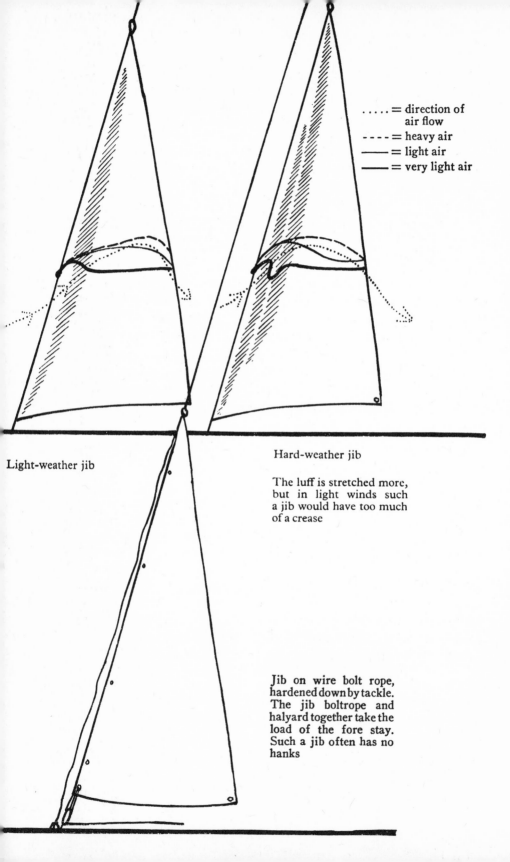

..... = direction of air flow

- - - = heavy air

—— = light air

———— = very light air

Light-weather jib

Hard-weather jib

The luff is stretched more, but in light winds such a jib would have too much of a crease

Jib on wire bolt rope, hardened down by tackle. The jib boltrope and halyard together take the load of the fore stay. Such a jib often has no hanks

the jib

Jibs are made quite differently from mainsails. A jib has no boom and it undergoes several kinds of force:

- one, the length of, and parallel to, the luff;

- one, in prolongation of the sheet, following roughly the bisector of the clew angle.

Most small-boat jibs used to have bolt-ropes of wire, practically inelastic within the limits of the forces imposed on them. (Modern jibs with Terylene bolt-ropes are quite common, see below.) The wire luff-rope permits very great tension, so that it does not sag, (fore-stay not curved much). Such curvature or sag is very harmful when sailing close-hauled. Stretch in the luff bolt rope and in the halyard are cumulative, and hence doubly harmful.

As the luff wire is not elastic, it is not possible, as with the mainsail, to alter the flow by varying the tension. Jibs are made flatter or not according as to whether they are light-weather or heavy-weather sails. A light-weather jib will be full. There is generally a choice of jibs; if not, you choose a medium one which will crease in light weather and have a little too much flow in heavy winds.

The control of the flow is got through the tension on the sheet; in light weather the sheet will be eased (maximum flow); in heavy weather the sheet will be heaved well in. The control is also got by moving the fairleads. Movable fairleads pay, as does studying their position in various strengths of wind; it is all a matter of experience. Jibs are cut in two main styles:

- cloths at right-angles to the leech;

- cloths at right-angles to leech and foot, the seam following the bisector of the clew.

Stretch is of less importance than on the mainsail. You can, in fact, always sheet a jib well home, but it is not easy to distort a boom or a mast. And only one side has a bolt-rope. Stretch, apart from the wrinkle the length of the luff, is distributed evenly.

Permanent distortions (shrinkage, etc.) are, on the other hand, much more serious. They deform the sail, incurably and inevitably. We will go into them more.

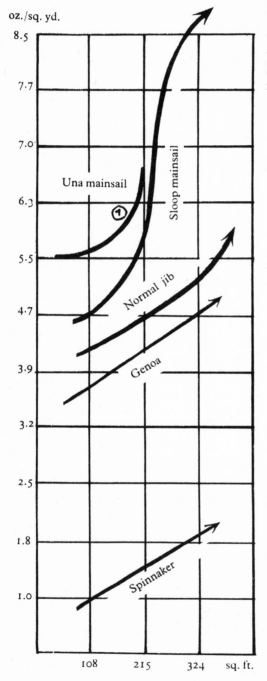

oz./sq. yd.

The table indicates the average weight of cotton sail cloth used in various types and sizes of sail for light craft

Over about 215 sq. ft., Una rig disappears.

materials used

There are two main classes of sails:

- conventional sails of cotton;

- modern sails in synthetic fibres.

Conventional sails use cotton of various qualities. The best are obviously those which are strongest in proportion to their weight, but also those which are most *stable*, that is which shrink least.

Cotton sails have hemp bolt-ropes; a very tough hemp is used, which is not very sensitive to humidity, and which does not stretch too much as it grows old.

Modern sails make use of various synthetic fibres. *Nylon* is too elastic, and is used practically only for spinakers. Terylene is used more and more. It is strong, non-elastic, insensitive to damp, and does not shrink. Weights in Terylene tend to be the same as for cotton for the same sail. We might add that the new methods of treating Terylene (calendering, glazing, etc.) end up by practically doing away with the differences in length between warp and weft, so that the sail stretches much more evenly.

Bolt-ropes are of synthetic fibres. They show the same characteristics as the material of which the sail is made, so that they do not stretch unevenly. It is possible to use a Terylene bolt-rope, which solves the flattening problem, as the rope is of the same elasticity as the fabric, but is stronger. This procedure is so economical of man-hours that it is coming into general use. Sails of light craft are more and more being made of Terylene. They call for higher skill from the sailmaker, as the tolerances are low. A Terylene sail is also harder to set correctly, although not deformed by damp, and it will often be necessary to adjust the halyard tension several times during a race, especially with the wind aft.

pests and maintenance

A sail can come to grief in several ways:

- it may be permanently distorted;

- it may get mildewed;

- the fabric may wear or get torn; the sewing may chafe through.

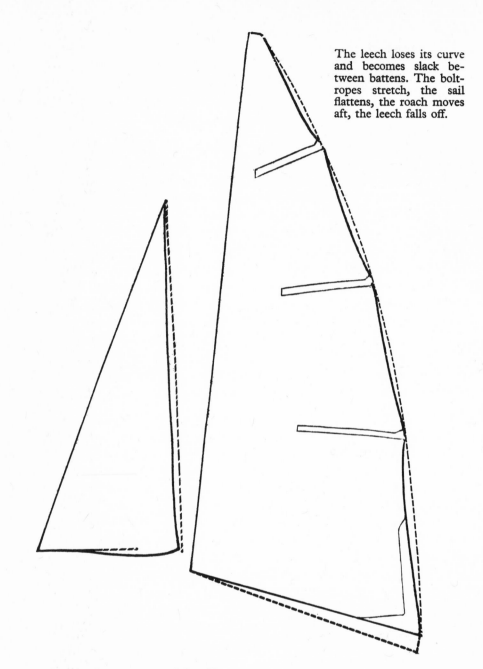

The leech loses its curve and becomes slack between battens. The bolt-ropes stretch, the sail flattens, the roach moves aft, the leech falls off.

distortion on an old sail

Natural cotton is not a stable material. It contracts as it grows older. This shrinkage represents 0.5 to 1 % of the length along the weft and 2 to 5 % along the warp. A bolt-rope of natural fibres also ages. But it stretches instead of shrinking. All natural fibres have a certain elasticity, which means that they can lose shape temporarily when subjected to a steady tension, and will gradually regain shape afterwards. But there is a degree of hysteresis; the bolt-rope does not go back exactly to its old shape, but remains very slightly stretched; this hysteresis ends up by lengthening the bolt-rope.

note

We should note that the elasticity has a long period; it takes a long time for the bolt-rope to resume its shape (several hours) after having been stretched. This explains why a sail that has been hardened down too much for, say, an hour, will not set properly, although the tack is slacked off, until some time after. This must be remembered when you adjust the tension.

The shrinking of the sailcloth and the lengthening of the bolt-ropes have the effect of reducing the slackness. An old mainsail, even if it has always been used properly, will get flatter and flatter, and its flow will move towards the after end. This is taken account of in the making; curve is exaggerated, the cloths are widened a little towards the leech, to avoid the sail forming a pocket (flow moving aft), and in order that it may stretch a little in the leech, which is a good thing.

There is not much to be done about shrinking. Generally a sail will only really get too flat when it is already very worn. It is no good renewing the bolt-rope if that is so. But it can be done, giving more flow if the fabric is worth it.

For jibs, shrinking is a serious matter:

● Along the length of the luff, it first irons out the fullness, then the fabric continues to shrink, so much that it is not possible to stretch the bolt-rope when you set the jib. The more you heave on the halyard, the more you stretch the fabric without stretching the luff wire. The tack wrinkles, and the setting is deplorable. The only remedy is to renew the luff wire.

● Another consequence will be that the clew position will be moved. On jibs of the first cut (cloths parallel to the leech), it does not matter very much; it is enough to move the fairlead aft. On the other type of jib (seam following the bisector) there will be two pockets formed. The transverse seam will be much stretched. The jib will have to be recut, or this should be allowed for in the making.

The inconveniences of shrinking are avoided by using synthetic textiles which have great elasticity, much less hysteresis, and which go back to shape at once after stretching. Moreover fabric and bolt-rope are made of the same material, which avoids distortion caused by incompatible materials.

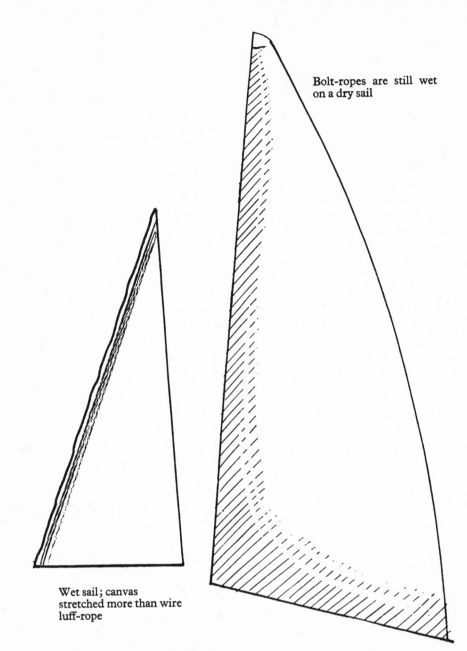

Bolt-ropes are still wet
on a dry sail

Wet sail; canvas
stretched more than wire
luff-rope

distortion due to damp

Wet materials and fibres swell, while their length decreases. So that a
completely wet sail would be smaller than a dry one. But, even supposing
the canvas and the bolt-rope shrank equally, which is wishful thinking
and rarely happens (especially when the bolt-rope is wire!), a wet sail
will not dry uniformly; the bolt-rope, protected by the tabling and thicker,

will still be soaking wet long after the canvas, in the wind, is dry. Result: the sail is too flat; it is no good hardening it down, it already shows wrinkles through insufficient hardening. You must wait for the bolt-rope to dry; if you sail with a wet sail which is in course of drying, you must take up the tension at head and tack from time to time (every quarter-hour or half-hour).

A sail which is wet at certain points only will only shrink at those points: wrinkles will form which will not always go when the sail is dry. Wetting a sail without wetting the bolt-ropes risks irremediable stretching of the fabric, as the local degree of tension become much too much. Therefore, if there has been spray, showers or fog, or even just at nightfall (that is, whenever humidity increases), you must gradually slacken off halyard and foot. If you neglect this precaution, the bolt-rope may break, or the sail may become permanently out of shape.

Don't forget, if you go to sea, that sea water is salt. A sail wetted in salt water retains the salt in the fibres of the cloth and in the bolt-ropes after the water has dried out. At the least change of humidity the salt attracts the dampness of the air, the sail gets damp again, and loses shape. Soaking in fresh water has often restored to youth sails which before treatment looked shocking and quite impossible to set (particularly jibs with wire bolt-ropes).

note

It should be remembered that synthetic sails are not sensitive to damp. It is just as well, though, to rinse them in fresh water now and again. Do not expose them to the sun.

mildew in sails

There often appears on sails a sort of little grey or greenish stain; the sail is said to 'spot'. This mildew is nothing but a mould caused by micro-organisms whose activity is encouraged by damp and especially by lack of ventilation.

If you fold up a sail when it is still a little damp, and stow it carefully away in a locker, it is certain to get mildew. The real way to deal with a sail is to hang it up somewhere dry and airy. Such a place is sometimes hard to find. The best thing then is to hand sails over to a sailmaker for the off season. In season, if the club has not room to spread them, sails must be laid out in as airy a place as possible, loosely bundled, and not folded; the air circulates better thus. They must, of course, never be left on board bent on, or bundled up, even though they were intended to be used. (We are

Wear through friction

Mainsail:

Head
Tack
Batten pockets
Shroud and cross-tree marks

Jib:

Clew (against mast)
Cross-trees and hounds

talking of dinghies; on a cruiser you can't very well do otherwise.) The chance should never be missed to rinse them and dry them completely.

All these precautions matter less for synthetic fibre sails, which do not rot, although they can become spotted with mildew.

There are treatments for cotton canvas which make the sails less sensitive to damp. The best known is tanning. But it is not usual to tan small boats' sails; on cruising boats, on the other hand, it is almost essential. There are also anti-mildew and colour treatments available.

wear

A sail always wears however carefully it is used, and however well things are padded. Friction is the great enemy. The principal friction points are:

- along the bolt-ropes; rubbing of the grooves along the length of the sail; sand in the groove;

- at the batten pockets; never use battens too long and force them in—the battens should be free to move a little lengthwise;

- on the shrouds and cross-trees when running; they can be padded, and that increases the windage; or you can double the material at the friction points.

A very important source of wear is slatting sails. It is essential not to let a sail slat in a strong wind. Always lower the sail if you are staying (on a mooring, at a wharf, on a beach) or at least sheet in hard to avoid slatting. Don't forget that when working normally a torn sail is rare. On the other hand, it is not uncommon to see a slatting sail tear. You must watch the wear on sails. You must repair seams that give way as necessary. You can easily darn small holes. But for any important damage, don't hesitate to send the sail to the sailmaker. An annual overhaul by the sailmaker is always a good precaution to take. You must always use a *fine* needle, and cotton, nylon, or Terylene sail thread, whichever is appropriate.

One of the main inconveniences of Terylene sails (even for a small boat) is that the thread used for seaming does not really bed down into the synthetic material, in view of the hardness of the latter and therefore stands out and is easily broken by friction. The seams wear much more rapidly. The only remedy so far found is to double, and even treble sew the seams.

index